INSIDE
MONTANA
POLITICS

A Reporter's View from the Trenches

MIKE DENNISON

THE
History
PRESS

Published by The History Press
Charleston, SC
www.historypress.com

First published 2019

Manufactured in the United States

ISBN 9781467142755

Library of Congress Control Number: 2019936989

Notice: The information in this book is true and complete to the best of our knowledge. It is offered without guarantee on the part of the author or The History Press. The author and The History Press disclaim all liability in connection with the use of this book.

To Jack & Bev —

I couldn't leave written this and pulled it off w/o your lovely daughter

love, Mike

To all my colleagues in journalism, in Montana and everywhere.

CONTENTS

PREFACE

This book is not a memoir. It's about being a political reporter in Montana and the people and events that I've covered, with an emphasis on the latter. It's also a history book, focusing primarily on major political figures who helped shape Montana for most of the past four decades. I chose to write about three governors (Marc Racicot, Judy Martz and Brian Schweitzer), three U.S. senators (Max Baucus, Conrad Burns and Jon Tester), one company and its CEO (Montana Power Company) and one person who is neither famous nor influential, simply because his story is one of the most compelling and ultimately rewarding stories I ever covered.

I also chose these subjects because, with each one of them, I had unique interactions that went beyond the mundane interview. Marc Racicot, for example, wrote several multipage, single-spaced letters to my editor and publisher after a critical story, castigating me as an inaccurate and unprofessional reporter. Brian Schweitzer tried to kick me off his campaign car after he had agreed I would spend the entire day with him. And Max Baucus intervened to get me a press seat at the U.S. Supreme Court, covering one of the biggest hearings of the decade, after the court initially said I couldn't be there. But I've said too much already. I don't want to give away any more of the stories!

Reporters cover events, issues or beats. It's how we order our day, our week, our next story. But the most compelling element of any story is not the what, when or where—it's the who, the person, the character that drives it. That's why I organized this book around a few intriguing people who stood out in my career and Montana history as central characters who drove the story.

Each chapter, or story, is drawn largely from my own reporting at the Associated Press, *Great Falls Tribune*, Lee Newspapers State Bureau and the Montana Television Network (MTN)—as well as some original reporting, solely for this book. Almost all the quotes are direct and verbatim, from news stories already published or my own interviews. A very few of them are reconstructed from memory, based on my personal conversations with people. These quotes are as close to the exact words as I can recall; the nut of these conversations is dead-on accurate. I've also interwoven the reporting of others, from Montana journalists to the *New York Times*, and cited their work, but the narrative is entirely my own.

ACKNOWLEDGEMENTS

Putting out a news story involves a whole host of people, from the writer to sources to editors to production staff. The same goes for a book—perhaps even more so.

I did the bulk of the research and all the writing for this work, but many indispensable people helped me along the way, both in assembling the final product and in my career, which is reflected in this book.

My first thanks go to The History Press and John Kuglin, my former boss at the Associated Press in Helena, Montana. John got me in touch with The History Press and senior acquisitions editor Artie Crisp, who's been encouraging and helpful from the beginning.

Another big thank-you is owed to the *Great Falls Tribune* and, in particular, former editor Jo Dee Black, who allowed me to use and helped me accumulate many photographs taken by the talented staff at the *Tribune*. The National Farm Broadcasters Association also kindly allowed me to use several shots it had of former U.S. Senator Conrad Burns, who was inducted into NFBA's Hall of Fame.

Two other *Tribune* hands also get special mention here: former managing editor Gary Moseman and former city editor Dan Hollow. Before the closure of the Great Falls Tribune Capitol Bureau's physical office in downtown Helena, they rescued several file cabinets full of *Tribune* clippings that go back decades and transported them to the Cascade County Historical Society. Without access to those files (after I left the *Tribune*), I doubt I could have even attempted this book.

Many of my colleagues in Montana journalism also have been a great source of assistance, encouragement and inspiration. I wouldn't be here today without the counsel and support of some great editors and bosses—in particular, Steve Prosinksi, Tom Kotynski, Jim Strauss, Dan Hollow, Mike McInally, Sherry Devlin, Linda Caricaburu and John Kuglin, as well as the late Bert Gaskill and the late Terry Dwyer.

I also couldn't have written these accounts without drawing from the work and camaraderie of some of the best journalists in Montana, including Chuck Johnson, Bob Anez (who gave me great feedback on some chapters), Kathy McLaughlin, Erin Billings, Jennifer McKee, Ed Kemmick, Sanjay Talwani, David Fenner, Jacquie Burchard, Jackie Yamanaka, Peter Johnson, Gail Schontzler, Jim Gransbery, Tom Lutey, Gwen Florio and John Adams.

And while I've had several employers in this business, one stands above all others: the Montana Television Network. In 2015, when I thought my career might be over, MTN not only hired me but also embraced me and my work, allowing me to keep doing what I've loved and been doing for almost forty years. I owe a great debt of gratitude to everyone at MTN, but especially to Jon Saunders, Heath Heggem and Joel Lundstad for taking a chance and hiring me; to the late Dennis Carlson, Sanjay Talwani and Melissa Jensen, who showed me the TV ropes at the beginning; to Jay Kohn, Paul Humphrey, John Riley and Eric Jochim, who gave and continue to give me invaluable advice on how to do the job; and to David Parker, who's been a great partner in many political and professional endeavors. But really, I could mention everyone at MTN, which has been welcoming from top to bottom.

I also must thank Jerry Holloron, the toughest and best journalism professor I had at the University of Montana, who read some chapters and had good advice and encouragement. Lastly, but of course not least, my wife, Sue O'Connell, remains one of the best journalists/editors/writers/ researchers in Montana. She not only read my drafts and gave me the unvarnished advice that no one else gave me but also had to listen to me talk about this project for years on end.

Finally, I must say thank you to all the sources who talked to me for all these years—including the subjects of this book. They let me invade their lives and careers, sometimes in a very unpleasant way, and almost always treated me with professionalism.

Chapter 1

BOB GANNON AND THE FALL
OF MONTANA POWER COMPANY

Y ou want me to take a picture of Bob Gannon's *house?* From the *lake?* But I'd need a boat!"

That was me, in August 2003, talking to my boss, *Great Falls Tribune* city editor Dan Hollow. I sat alone at my desk in the Tribune Capitol Bureau's office on Jackson Street in downtown Helena, talking to Dan by telephone as he sat at his desk ninety miles away in Great Falls.

"You can rent one," he said. "Hey, somebody else did it. I'm looking at a picture of Gannon's house right now, in the *Whitefish Pilot*, taken from Flathead Lake. You ought to see this house. It's like a palace."

"Yeah, well what's the story?" I asked, rather petulantly.

I was grumpy, as any reporter gets when an editor suggests something not the reporter's idea. I'd already written hundreds of stories about utility executive Bob Gannon and his then former employer, the Montana Power Company, as they had launched what became one of the biggest corporate meltdowns in Montana history. Another installment on this tortured tale didn't appeal to me that particular day, especially not a manufactured one focusing on Bob Gannon's luxurious house on the shore of northwest Montana's Flathead Lake.

"What's the story?" Dan said. "We can tell what happened! The whole mess! And who it affected and how, and what happens now. And we can tell it all with a great picture of Gannon's house, sitting right there on Flathead Lake, looking excessive as hell."

Montana Power Company CEO and President Bob Gannon, 2001. *Wayne Arnst*, Great Falls Tribune.

"And I have to rent a boat, to get out there on Flathead Lake, to take a picture."

"*You* don't have to take the picture. We'll hire a photo stringer. But you'd have to go with him."

"Well…." Well, all right, it wasn't a bad idea. Maybe even a good one. I started thinking about the story, the whole incredible, greed-soaked, wrong-headed, heartbreaking story of how one of Montana's most venerable companies, the Montana Power Company, had gone from staid, money-making utility to Wall Street star to bankruptcy and ruin, all in less than a decade. How one of the state's most potent economic and political powers had convinced policymakers to embark on the colossal blunder of Montana's 1997 utility deregulation and throw consumers into a soon-to-be-manipulated open market. And how this streaking comet of a business gamble had made millions for a few and drained untold millions from the rest of the state, from the destroyed pension funds of those whose MPC stock became worthless to the businesses and consumers who paid obscene prices for electricity on a deregulated market gone mad.

Yes, it would be—was—a hell of a story, which I'd been covering almost from the beginning. That beginning for me started almost by accident, like many stories do, when a near-random occurrence gets you paying closer attention to a news subject, just as that subject is about to launch a historical arc of events.

But in the eyes of many Montanans, it started with Bob Gannon, the president and chief executive officer of Montana Power Company. Although he had plenty of help, from his fellow executives to New York bankers to some of Montana's leading politicians, it is Gannon who came to be identified as the company's architect of its demise.

Gannon was the hometown boy made good. He grew up in Butte, the headquarters of Montana Power and the home of the once powerful Anaconda Copper Company. He was schooled at Notre Dame, the University of Montana and Harvard and joined the company as an attorney in 1974, rising to become its CEO in late 1996.

In late 1995, Gannon and company officials started talking about something guaranteed to put the average newspaper reader to sleep but which became the germ of the beginning of the end: "Restructuring."

"It's not going to happen overnight, but we think it's only a matter of time before…all [power] customers will be able to choose who they buy their electricity from," Montana Power vice-president Jack Haffey told me in December 1995.[1]

"Restructuring" was utility-speak for deregulation of wholesale and, by extension, retail power markets. In other words, instead of the vertically integrated utility that produced, delivered and sold the electricity to consumers at a regulated price and profit, the utility would be "restructured" so it could sell its power at whatever the market would bear—and consumers would, theoretically, be able to shop the market and buy power from whoever could sell it to them the cheapest.

It was the sort of argument that had instant appeal to any good capitalist, which certainly included the executives of Montana Power, large companies in Montana and most Republican and a few Democratic politicians. Hey, we can buy our power from anyone and shop around, just like we shop for stuff at the grocery store, and choose the cheapest option! Who could be against that?

When Gannon rose to the position of president in early 1996, company officials said the restructuring of Montana Power would now get "some high-level, full-time, excellent attention."[2]

Thus, the wheels of change were set in motion. For all of 1996, whenever they had a chance, Montana Power executives would talk up the magic of "restructuring" and the theory that this golden goose of capitalism would free the company and its consumers from the chains of regulation, allowing them to plumb the hallowed market for new and unbridled profits and deals.

ALTHOUGH I WAS THE *Great Falls Tribune*'s chief reporter on politics, this story initially didn't grab my attention. What reporter in their right mind would want to delve into something as inherently dense and boring as "utility restructuring"? No thanks. But then came that random moment, when you should reject something as not significant or worth your time, but for some reason, you don't.

It came as a phone call from a Helena attorney in the fall of 1996. His name was Mike Uda, and he had clients who owned natural gas fields in north-central Montana. He maintained that his clients could sell natural gas from their wells to Montana Power for as little at one dollar per thousand cubic feet (mcf), but Montana Power instead bought gas only from its own wells at four or five times the price and then passed on that cost to consumers.

I'd never before scrutinized the arcane and complex details of utility regulation, but I sensed it was an important story. Uda's main client, an oil and gas producer in northern Montana named Charles Jansky, said that Montana Power gas consumers had been overcharged to the tune of $100 million over ten years. He and others had brought the case to the state Public Service Commission, which would decide whether ratepayers should pay the company for its costs of investing in the expensive gas wells. It was a tough story to tell, and I struggled with it, ultimately failing to convey it with the clarity it deserved. But it gave me two things that proved invaluable in the months and years to come, as I covered the unfolding story of utility deregulation and all that came with it: the help and trust of a knowledgeable source—Mike Uda, a smart, tenacious lawyer when it came to utility issues—and a healthy mistrust and skepticism toward those who ran Montana Power.

Until then, when it came to covering Montana Power, I'd been like most reporters in Montana: show up at its news conferences, read its press releases, explain why it wanted a rate increase and call it a day. A utility just didn't seem like a very interesting story, and its rates were regulated, so why worry about it?

As the Jansky/natural gas story heated up in early December 1996, I had a telephone interview with Montana Power vice-president Perry Cole, set up by the company's spokesman, Cort Freeman. They knew the angle I was pursuing, so the critical slant of my questions wasn't a surprise. But as we got into the latter part of the interview, where the questions get a little pointed, Cole suddenly blurted out, "That's a biased question! You're a biased reporter!"

"Well, that's funny," I said. "Because I was just talking to Charles Jansky about ten minutes ago, and he told me what a shitty job I was doing telling his side of the story." (A true story—Jansky had just spoken with me and castigated me for not telling things like he thought they should be told.)

Cole laughed, and I did too. Freeman assured me that Cole didn't really mean it when he said I was a biased reporter, and I told him not to sweat it, that I hear that sort of thing all the time and it didn't bother me. We finished up the interview and I wrote the story that week.

Yet I remember thinking as I hung up the phone that day: This is a company used to getting its way, with regulators, politicians and probably most reporters, and had been doing so for many, many years. It had convinced itself and policymakers from both political parties that what was good for Montana Power was good for Montana—and now Montana Power was preparing to make perhaps its biggest business gamble ever. But the play couldn't be made without the help of the Montana legislature, which convened in a matter of weeks, in January 1997.

Gannon and Montana Power had geared up to roll their "restructuring" bills through the legislature, with the company's usual full stable of lobbyists. As a reporter, I was ready too. Uda and other sources had told me that this fight would be a big one, with millions of dollars at stake—and that few lawmakers or policymakers came close to comprehending its potential impacts. My lead story the first week of the session said that utility restructuring would be the "sleeper issue of the 1997 Legislature," calling it "a complex, multimillion-dollar behemoth that affects everyone in Montana, but which almost no one fully understands."[3]

Not everyone was on board. Montana's rural electric cooperatives, which provided electricity to almost half the consumers in the state, counseled caution. They wanted to create a committee to study the issue for two years and come back to the 1999 legislature with recommendations.

And State Representative David Ewer, a Helena Democrat who became one of the most prominent skeptics of restructuring, said that rushing into this complex issue was crazy. "I say, if even [the utilities] aren't sure, then why should we change the status quo?" he said in a January 13, 1997 story. "We have to remember what the status quo is: We pay some of the cheapest rates for electricity there is in America.... Everybody keeps talking about consumer choice. Well, maybe that 'choice' is a choice of paying higher rates."

A response by Perry Cole—he of the "biased reporter" comment—brushed off Ewer's concerns. "We think it's better to learn by doing than by studying," he told me. "We've already been through the study process."[4]

I would learn much later that leaders of the Republican majority in the legislature had decided this thing was a go—that the utility deregulation bills were greased and it was only a matter of working out the specific details and throwing a few bones to "consumer protection." All of Montana's big industrial consumers—mines, refineries, manufacturing plants—supported the idea, thinking they could buy electricity at reduced prices on the open market. The electric co-ops and Montana's other private utility, Montana-Dakota Utilities, also stepped aside as possible opponents once Montana Power agreed to exempt them from any "restructuring" edicts. Even the Montana Public Service Commission, which regulated utilities and was composed of five elected Democrats, voted 3 to 2 to support Montana Power's bills.

Two months into the legislature, after the bills to allow Montana Power to unwind its regulated electricity and natural gas businesses had been introduced and had a hearing or two, I was attending my older son's Boy Scouts troop meeting in Helena. One of the other "Scout fathers," a local attorney and a former Democratic state representative, often spent the meetings in the back of the room with me, jawing about politics. That night, I wondered out loud whether the restructuring bills would pass.

The former lawmaker arched an eyebrow at me, looking almost incredulous at my comment. "Mike, of course they're going to pass," he said, as though talking to a child.

"They are?" I said, trying to sound more resigned than surprised, a weak attempt to hide my naïvete.

"They have no institutional opposition. If there's no institutional opposition and the [legislative] leadership is on board, a bill is going to pass. There's nothing to stop it."

But what about the environmental groups, I said, and some of the consumer people. "That's nothing," he said. "And what 'consumer people'? The environmental groups are not consumer people."

I'd been reintroduced to a fundamental law of politics in Montana or perhaps everywhere: If the big industrial and business powers or "institutions" are for something and nothing substantial stands in their way, you can bet on its passage—regardless of whether it may be good or bad for the public at large. The converse is also true: If these same political powers oppose something as a group, it's usually dead. Utilities, in particular, are especially powerful.

Our conversation that night prompted me to write a story that ran on March 21, 1997, asking the question: Who *was* representing the consumer in this critical debate before the legislature?

The answer I got from legislators was that the Montana Consumer Counsel—an office that legally represented consumers in utility rate cases before the PSC—should be and is the entity that's speaking for consumers at this critical legislature. In reality, however, the Consumer Counsel and a few other consumer advocates made some suggestions, but if the company didn't like those ideas, they were ditched. The real consumer stance would have been not to pass anything.

The Consumer Counsel, a five-person office headed by an attorney, was controlled by a committee of legislators. The committee's three current members included a Republican who said maintaining a strong utility was in the best interest of consumers, a Democrat from Butte (headquarters of Montana Power) whose glass company sometimes did business with the company and Republican Senate Majority Leader John Harp, whose family-owned construction industry, Harp Line Constructors of Kalispell, Montana, did $7 million per year in business with Montana Power. Harp's firm installed power lines and other lines for the company and its subsidiaries.[5]

Harp, who flirted with the idea of running for governor in 2000, eventually sold his construction companies to Montana-Dakota Utilities (which, at its request, had been exempted from the restructuring bill) for an undisclosed amount.

But when it came to the architects and supporters of utility deregulation in Montana, Harp did one thing that many politicians did not: he apologized for his role, many years later, saying he and others had been "hoodwinked" by the utilities—namely, Montana Power.

At the 1997 legislature, a few raised their voices in opposition to the main restructuring bill, but as my fellow Scouting father predicted, it passed with ease: 78 to 22 in the Montana House and 36 to 14 in the Senate. Governor Marc Racicot signed it into law in April.

The bill, written primarily by Montana Power's attorneys and other officials, required Montana Power to submit to the Public Service Commission its plan for separating its production and sales functions—"restructuring."

The company did so, but buried in this arcane, five-hundred-page plan was an economic and political bombshell: Montana Power proposed to charge customers for its "stranded costs."

A "stranded cost" is the portion of a utility asset, like a power plant or energy-supply contract, that would become worthless in the newly deregulated market. For example, if Montana Power had a coal-fired power plant whose cost of production was two cents per kilowatt hour (kWh) and, in the new market, consumers could buy that power for one cent per kilowatt hour, MPC would have a stranded cost of one cent per kWh—times the millions and millions of kWh that plant could produce. Put another way, Montana Power had invested a lot of money into that coal-fired plant and had been charging its regulated, captured consumers for the cost of that investment (plus a profit). Now, if those customers could shop and buy their power elsewhere, MPC would no longer be recovering the cost of that investment it had made to supply power for its customers. It would be left holding the bag for that investment.

The bill took care of this financial inconvenience in a very straightforward way: it said consumers must pay those stranded costs.

In its plan filed in July 1997, Montana Power said the stranded costs were $800 million, to be paid for by its 270,000 electric customers. For the average homeowner, the bill was $127 per year, spread over fifteen to twenty-five years.[6]

Coal-fired power plants at Colstrip. MPC sold its share of plants as part of 1998 divestment of its power plants. *Montana Television Network (MTN).*

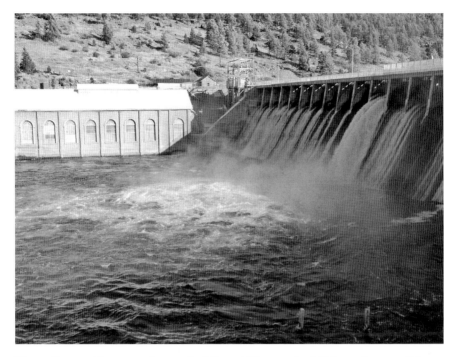

Hauser Dam and its power plant on the Missouri River north of Helena, also part of the MPC sale. *Mike Dennison.*

Montana Power and its officers apparently assumed that getting the commission to approve the stranded costs would be much like getting approval from the legislature: throw out some numbers, make a few plausible-sounding arguments and watch the votes fall their way.

But unlike the legislature, the commission is a quasi-judicial body, where the company must prove its case with hard evidence. Other parties, like the Consumer Counsel and big industrial consumers, also become parties in the case and can scrutinize the proposal and submit their own evidence that may contradict Montana Power's case. In mid-November, a source told me that I should take a look at this countervailing evidence.

I did, and it led to a front-page story on the November 30, 1997 *Great Falls Tribune*, with this opening paragraph:

> *Energy experts are blasting Montana Power Co.'s plan to deregulate its electricity business, saying the MPC plan will make it next to impossible for its Montana customers to reap any benefits from competition in the coming deregulated market.*

Experts hired by the Consumer Counsel, the industrial customers and other groups shredded Montana Power's plan, taking special aim at the stranded costs. "MPC's plan…aims at maximizing the interests of Montana Power Co.," wrote Larry Nordell, an economist for the Consumer Counsel. "It proposes to retain significant advantages for MPC's unregulated activities at the expense of competition."[7]

I reported that the experts said the stranded costs were "grossly overstated by hundreds of millions of dollars." One even suggested that Montana Power might have *no* stranded costs at all and might even have to *pay consumers back* for consumers' investment in the plants through rates.

This wall of vociferous, well-informed opposition probably caught Montana Power off-guard. The company's response, however, did more than catch people off-guard.

ON DECEMBER 9, 1997, Montana Power's board of directors met in Butte and made a dramatic decision: The company would sell every electric power plant it owned in Montana—twelve hydroelectric plants and a storage dam along the Missouri, Clark Fork and Madison Rivers, including some that had been in the company since the turn of the century, as well as its shares of four coal-fired power plants in southeastern Montana, valued at $600 million or more. The sale also included more than a dozen power-supply contracts with independent power plants—electricity used to supply MPC's 270,000 customers in the state.

The decision produced screaming headlines in every daily paper in Montana the next day. Critics of the company barely knew what to say that Tuesday afternoon—although one of them, Pat Judge, an energy expert for the Montana Environmental Information Center in Helena, hit the nail on the head. "We're basically losing control of Montana's cheap power," he told the *Great Falls Tribune*. "That's a big concern for consumers."[8]

Gannon and other company officials, however, quickly fanned out across the state, speaking to Rotary clubs and other civic organizations, assuring them that all would be well. If the new buyer paid more than the $600 million book value of the plants, some of that profit could go to the consumers, Gannon told the Great Falls Rotary Club in January 1998. And Montana Power planned to take its profits and sink them into its power-marketing arm in the new deregulated wholesale market and its growing subsidiary, Touch America, which was building a huge, underground fiber-optic network.

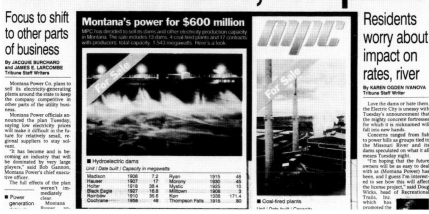

MPC to sell dams, coal plants

Focus to shift to other parts of business

By JACQUIE BURCHARD and JAMES E. LARCOMBE
Tribune Staff Writers

Montana Power Co. plans to sell its electricity-generating plants around the state to keep the company competitive in other parts of the utility business.

Montana Power officials announced the plan Tuesday, saying low electricity prices will make it difficult in the future for relatively small, regional suppliers to stay solvent.

"It has become and is becoming an industry that will be dominated by very large players," said Bob Gannon, Montana Power's chief executive officer.

The full effects of the plan weren't immediately clear.

■ Power generation Montana Power an...

Montana's power for $600 million

MPC has decided to sell its dams and other electricity production capacity in Montana. The sale includes 13 dams, 4 coal-fired plants and 17 contracts with producers; total capacity: 1,543 megawatts. Here's a look:

■ Hydroelectric dams
Unit / Date built / Capacity in megawatts

Madison	1906	7.2	Ryan	1915	48
Hauser	1907	17	Morony	1930	45
Holter	1918	38.4	Mystic	1925	10
Black Eagle	1927	16.8	Milltown	1908	3
Rainbow	1910	35.6	Kerr	1938	171.4
Cochrane	1958	48	Thompson Falls	1915	80

■ Coal-fired plants
Unit / Date built / Capacity...

Residents worry about impact on rates, river

By KAREN OGDEN IVANOVA
Tribune Staff Writer

Love the dams or hate them, the Electric City is uneasy with Tuesday's announcement that the mighty concrete fortresses for which it is nicknamed will fall into new hands.

Concerns ranged from fish to power bills as groups tied to the Missouri River and its dams speculated on what it all means Tuesday night.

"I'm hoping that the future owners will be as easy to deal with as (Montana Power) has been, and I guess I'm interested to see how this will affect the license project," said Doug Wicks, head of Recreational Trails, Inc. which has promoted the

The 1998 sale announcement made headlines in newspapers across the state. *From the* Great Falls Tribune.

At the company's annual shareholder meeting several months later, Gannon gave the eight-hundred-plus people gathered at the Mother Lode Theater in uptown Butte a hint of where he thought the company ultimately should go: telecommunications.

He said that no decision had been made on how to "redeploy" the $600 million the company expected from selling its power plants. But he talked glowingly about the expansion of Touch America, a subsidiary since 1983 that had been quietly building an extensive, underground fiber-optic network for transmitting telecom signals.

Before the main meeting began, company executives and one of their consultants, G. Bennett Stewart III, met with reporters over lunch in a small room just off the theater lobby. Stewart, a senior partner in a New York consulting firm, came to brag about something he helped develop called EVA, which stood for "economic value added." EVA principles required a business to subtract its cost of capital from profits, he said, to show if it was earning more than its cost of capital and thus adding "real value" to the company. He said it forced managers to "use assets more intelligently and allow them to build competitive advantage." Gannon chimed in to tell us that Montana Power had been integrating EVA principles into its business for about a year and was "really excited about it."[9] Bennett called it "the most socialistic form of capitalism going."

At week's end, I wrote a column for the *Great Falls Tribune* on our conversation with Mr. Stewart:

> *It was asked* [at the luncheon] *what social benefits or value have been accruing to the people of Montana. The answer? According to Stewart and MPC executives, our social benefit is the increase in Montana Power's stock value.*
>
> *"Creating shareholder wealth is the engine of all societies' benefits," Stewart said....*
>
> *In other words, what's good for Montana Power Co. is good for Montana. The corporate interest is the public interest.*
>
> *Increase the wealth of the big and the powerful, and it trickles down to the rest of us.*

The same column ended with my recounting of executives' claims that by selling its power plants and looking to a new future that included telecom, the company would stand a better chance to remain independent and remain "in the driver's seat, rather than being the passengers."

"So, Montana," I wrote, "hop on board. It looks like we're all along for the ride, whether we like it or not."[10]

While my gut told me it all sounded too good to be true, it was hard to argue with the initial success Montana Power and its high-flying executives had engineered.

Company stock hit eighty-five dollars per share in April 1999, nearly quadruple its value from just two years earlier, when the deregulation bill passed. Stock analysts said the power plant sale and Montana Power's new emphasis on its telecom subsidiary, Touch America, had fueled the boom.

In May 1999, I wrote a piece on the progress of Touch America, which had laid thousands of miles of fiber-optic cable in the West and was reaping the rewards of the explosion of the Internet and its appetite for networks that could transmit data at high speeds. "Anyone you can name in the telephone industry buys space from us," said Mike Meldahl, the head of Touch America. "We have the largest network in the Northwest, of anyone."[11]

Touch America also had some partners in its line construction, including a company called Enron Corporation. The future looked bright. Money was rolling in. Montana Power's stock was a hot commodity. What could go wrong?

AS THE STATE DIGESTED the news that Montana Power planned to sell off its power plants, talk surfaced about what else it might sell. MPC, however, denied any such intentions. Gannon answered the rumors with a series of columns that ran as paid advertisements in the state's major newspapers, including one column in March 1998 headlined "Montana Power: We're Staying in Montana."

"YES," Gannon wrote, "Montana Power Is STAYING IN MONTANA!," using all the punctuation and capitalization power he could muster. "My vision is to be a Montana-based company that is successful in marketing and delivering energy and telecommunications products across Montana and throughout the western United States." The rest of the column, without a trace of irony, went on to explain why Montana Power was forced to sell its power plants because of political forces beyond its control.

In October of that year, I reported that three firms were on the short list to buy the power plants: TransAlta, a Canadian firm headquartered in Calgary, Alberta; AES Corporation of Alexandria, Virginia, a power wholesaler that already owned some ninety power plants around the country; and finally, from Allentown, Pennsylvania, PP&L Resources, the parent firm of Pennsylvania Power & Light.

Montana Power executives and officials would tell me nothing about who planned to buy the plants, but word had leaked to investment analysts and others close to the company, and on November 1, 1998, we reported that Montana Power was in final negotiations with PP&L Global, a subsidy of PP&L Resources, to sell all seventeen plants for as much as $1.2 billion. The editor of the *Tribune*, Jim Strauss, sounded nervous when he OK'd the story based on unnamed sources—but we had it right. PP&L turned out to be the buyer.

MPC 1998 ad in which Gannon declared the company would remain in Montana. It had sold nearly all of its properties within three years. *From the Great Falls Tribune.*

No one at Montana Power ever said a word to me about getting the scoop. Yet the spokesman for PPL in Allentown, Dan McCarthy—a former reporter—congratulated me and tried to get me to tell him my sources, knowing full well I wouldn't. The difference in the reaction was striking. In the worldview of Montana Power, I had a classic case of bad manners, shoving my way into the party early and drinking from the punch bowl. In PPL's view, I had simply done my job.

Then the other shoes started to drop. Gannon confirmed in 1999 that more parts of Montana Power could be up for sale, including its coal mines, oil and gas wells and perhaps Touch America, the telecom subsidiary. The company eventually brought in New York financial firm Goldman Sachs to help it decide what to do.

In March 2000, there was another bombshell announcement. Touch America would become a separate company, which we expected. But then came the kicker: Montana Power would sell off the entire remainder of the company's holdings—coal mines, gas wells, oil wells, power contracts and its thousands of miles of pipelines and power lines—and cease to exist.

Gannon told Bob Anez of the Associated Press that Montana Power was "basically reinventing a corporation" and becoming Touch America. Its headquarters would remain in Butte, and Montana Power shareholders would see their shares converted to Touch America. Consultants called it a "bold stroke," and Gannon shrugged off the doubters who wondered whether it was a good idea to abruptly turn away from a utility business that had prospered for eighty-nine years. "The future is what we need to focus on," he said. "I haven't seen too many people focus on the past."[12]

The public also soon got an unvarnished look at where some of the benefits would flow—or not. In interviews with financial writers in New York and Washington, D.C., Gannon said the company had no intention of sharing any of its profits from the sell-off of Montana Power utility properties with its rate-paying customers.

And on April 13, I reported that Gannon and other company executives had "golden parachutes" worth nearly $1 million each—or more if they lost those jobs in a company takeover, a keen possibility in the rapidly evolving world of telecom in 2000. Gannon and other executives, in addition to their salaries and bonuses, also had substantial stock options that had become quite valuable in recent years. Gannon and Jerrold Pederson, the company's chief financial officer, had options worth about $2.7 million each when I wrote the story, on top of their 1999 salaries of $991,000 and $838,000, respectively.

But as Montana Power prepared to leap off the telecom cliff, those stock options began to look a little less valuable. The stock price peaked at sixty-five dollars per share when the announcement of the sell-off was made—a whopping *six times* its value in mid-1997. But in five short weeks, Montana Power's stock plummeted by more than one-third, down to about forty-two dollars per share.

Gannon said that negative press about the company's proposed sale of its assets had played a role, but he also reasoned that technology stocks, which had been on a screaming bull run for many months, were cooling off. On that point he was right, but it was just the tip of the iceberg of the tech-stock and overall market meltdown of 2000 and beyond.

Stock price worries or not, Montana Power quickly forged ahead with it plans to unload all but its Touch America business. It sold its oil and gas wells and coal mining unit that summer and then, in October, announced the biggest piece of the sell-off: the transfer of its entire distribution system—gas pipelines, electric power lines and the local distribution system to bring gas and electricity to its now 300,000-plus customers—to a little-known utility based in Sioux Falls, South Dakota, called NorthWestern Corporation, for $1.1 billion.

We knew next to nothing about NorthWestern, and its name hadn't been mentioned to me by insiders speculating on who the buyer would be. The company had relatively small utility operations in South Dakota and Nebraska but had been expanding in recent years, buying up a string of telecom, propane, plumbing-and-heating and computer consulting businesses and interests. Little did we know then that financial storm clouds had started to form over NorthWestern, in large part due to its aggressive push into non-utility businesses (like Montana Power) and some creative accounting practices. The tanking of its non-utility investments would eventually lead the company into bankruptcy reorganization in 2003.

In three short years, Montana Power had arranged the sale of $2.5 billion in assets—its power plants, oil and gas wells, coal mines and utility operations. All that remained was Touch America, the new telecom golden boy, over which stock analysts and investors salivated about its prospects.

The day of the NorthWestern sale announcement, Gannon told me and other reporters that Touch America would be "our future and our focus." "We're extremely pleased with the results, not only of this transaction, but with all of the transactions," he added.[13]

It might have been one of the last times Gannon was "extremely pleased" with anything that was about to happen to his company.

As GANNON AND COMPANY began to wring their hands over their stock value, the shine also started to fade from their initial bright idea: deregulation and the "free market" of electricity prices.

Montana Power's residential and small-business customers remained under a price freeze until mid-2002, as part of the 1997 deregulation law. But many of Montana Power's large industrial customers had jumped into the open market at the advent of deregulation and "restructuring" in 1998, ditching Montana Power as their electricity supplier and buying at whatever price they could get from whatever supplier they could find. This flexibility had been sold as the beauty of the free market, and initially it looked pretty good, for wholesale prices were at historic lows in the Pacific Northwest. Industrial plants snagged electric power for rock-bottom prices of just over twenty dollars per megawatt hour. Industrial users consumed thousands and thousands of megawatt hours.

Things began to unravel, however, in the first half of 2000, fueled by the deregulation debacle unfolding in California. It had been the only other state in the West to drink the deregulation Kool-Aid, and in 1996, a year earlier than Montana. It made sense for Californians to chase the deregulation genie, for they were paying some of the highest power prices in the region, about double the cost of power in Montana and three or four times as much as some of the cheaper utility and co-op providers in Washington and Oregon. Initially, it looked good for them too—but in 2000, the "free market" started morphing into an economic prison with a burgeoning death row. The price for electricity, the lifeblood of industry, inexplicably started going through the roof in California in the late spring of 2000, with retail rates doubling and tripling and wholesale "spot prices" for electricity sometimes at ten- or twentyfold what they had been a year earlier.

We know now that a large part of the madness was the result of market manipulation by one company: Enron Corporation, soon to become the poster boy for corporate criminality and misconduct. But in 2000, Enron and its marketing brethren were seen as the fortunate few profiting from a market gone crazy. And Montana, by virtue of its electricity grid being in the same western region as California, got sucked into the vortex of insanely escalating electricity prices.

In the first week of July that year, Montana Resources Company—a huge copper mining company in Butte—shut down its operations and laid off 330 workers because it couldn't pay its electricity bill. Montana Resources had left Montana Power's system in 1998 to buy from another supplier, but its electricity contract with that supplier expired on June 30, 2000. It had been paying $27 per megawatt hour but couldn't find a contract for anything less than $60. The company, which already had been paying about $13 million per year in electricity costs to run the mine, couldn't afford to pay more than double that amount.

One month later, Louisiana Pacific Corporation's fiberboard plant in Missoula announced that it would be closing as well. Its electricity supply contract expired at the end of July 2000, and the company had been paying $25 per megawatt hour. Its supplier? Enron. The new price? Company officials said they could pay up to $110 per megawatt hour but couldn't even get it at that inflated price. The boys from Enron apparently wouldn't even offer a contract at four times the price of the old one.

Late in June 2000, I interviewed a half dozen Montana plant managers who had—or hadn't—waded into the deregulated electricity markets created by the 1997 bill, pushed by Montana Power. My story ran on July 9 in the *Great Falls Tribune*, recounting the Darwinian lottery that deregulation had begun to create for Montana industry, its workers and its citizens.

Montana Refining Company, an oil refinery in Great Falls, ended up paying six times its prior electricity price when it renewed its expiring contract the previous month. "It's a huge, astronomical hit," plant operations superintendent Dana Leach told me.

Dedicated capitalists to the bitter end, these plant managers said they still supported the move to deregulation—even while acknowledging that if current prices remained high, they'd probably have to shut down their plants, idling hundreds of workers. "If we have to pay six times as much for electric energy, that would take all of the profit out of the plant," said Leach of Montana Refining. "There would certainly be a point where we would have to shut down."[14]

Next door in Idaho, which had resisted deregulation, industrial customers of Idaho Power Company still paid twenty-five dollars per megawatt hour. Idaho Power still owned its power plants, which produced most of the power its customers needed, and those customers still paid rates that reflected the cost of production, plus a respectable profit for the utility.

Next in line as a victim of the marketplace were MPC's 285,000-plus residential customers. Their electricity had its price frozen until mid-2002, at the now bargain price of $22.25 per megawatt hour, and no one thought the out-of-control market would last that long. But as Montana's legislature convened in January 2001, the absurdly high prices showed no signs of abating, and Montana businesses and consumers pleaded with lawmakers to somehow bail them out. Yet the same legislature that had passed deregulation four years earlier—and the new Republican governor, Judy Martz—sided with the utilities and power generators and did nothing.

In the end, blind luck and ruthless coincidence—and action by the federal government—finally broke the energy crisis in the West and gave some relief to Montana consumers and businesses. Three weeks after President George W. Bush had refused to consider price caps on power in California, the Federal Energy Regulatory Commission in June 2001 said enough is enough and did what Bush said he wouldn't, stepping in and placing a ceiling on wholesale electricity prices.

Montana's Public Service Commission, controlled by Republicans, put its foot down too, saying it wouldn't accept a Montana Power "deal" with the new owners of the power plants, PPL, for a 50 percent increase starting in 2002.

Next came the September 11, 2001 terrorist attacks in New York and Washington, D.C., which doubled down on a punishing economic recession. Two months later, we had the energy and economic coup de grâce: the exposure and disintegration of Enron, whose market manipulation and financial shell games were exposed by skilled financial reporters. Electricity prices fell back to earth, and Montana consumers saw their getting-soaked days come to an end, with Montana Power residential and small-business customers ending up with a 10 percent, rather than a 50 percent, increase in overall power prices they paid. You might call it small comfort, in the face of what had been many months of economic pain.

THE SAME COULD NOT be said, however, for Bob Gannon, Montana Power and its once invincible telecom superstar, Touch America. By June 2001, Montana Power's stock price had dropped to $10.73 per share, down from its peak of $65 a little more than a year ago, losing more than 80 percent of its value. Some stock analysts said all would be well as soon as the company completed its conversion to Touch America and sold its utility assets to NorthWestern Corporation.

Or would it? On the day the stock hit $10.73, the *New York Times* ran an op-ed piece whose opening line read, "Companies that supply, build and operate fiber-optic networks are burning."[15] The article by New America Foundation fellow Daniel Gross said that while Internet use was growing and would continue to grow, the boom in the fiber-optic cable business was similar to previous American business frenzies like railroads, telegraphs and automobiles. Hordes of companies rushed to cash in on what was obviously a new wave of technology, but many would fail, leaving a wreckage of overreaching companies and bankruptcies, while the strong and few survived.

MPC scheduled a September 14 shareholders' meeting in Butte, at which shareholders were asked to approve the final sell-off of MPC utility assets and convert the company into Touch America. Seven weeks before the meeting, the company reported losses in the second quarter of that year and lowered its earning projections, and the stock dropped again to $7.94 per share, its lowest level in well over a decade.

Then, on August 22, the *Wall Street Journal* ran a lengthy article on Montana Power, complete with a mug shot of Gannon in the *Journal*'s then traditional black-lined illustration style, saying the company's "broadband dream may turn out to be more of a nightmare." It compared the trajectory of Gannon's company to that of another Butte native, motorcycle daredevil Evel Knievel, whose doomed leap over the Snake River Canyon many years before ended with a parachuted plunge into the river. "The joke around [Butte] is that at least Mr. Knievel wore a parachute," wrote *Journal* reporter Bill Richards.

It was a devastating piece, rife with comments from Butte residents saying they couldn't believe how stupid Gannon and the boys had been, taking down a company that had prospered for almost ninety years. The article revealed that New York investment house Goldman Sachs had encouraged Montana Power to ditch the entire utility biz—and got $14.2 million for its advice on the asset sale.

Gannon also scoffed at suggestions that he and the company board had taken the wrong path, predicting that Touch America would emerge as one of the industry's strongest players. And as for the suggestion that Goldman Sachs had taken Montana Power officials for a bunch of rubes? "That's the stupidest thing I've ever heard," Gannon said.[16]

Just days later, the September 11 terrorist attacks shocked the nation and the world. Montana Power delayed the shareholder vote until September 21. At the meeting in Butte, owners of the company dutifully approved the conversion to Touch America.

I was in Butte that day to cover the event and interviewed Gannon at his office in uptown Butte. It was the last time I would speak with him. "It's a new day with a new company on the horizon," he said. "Let's get on with it."

I also chatted with a few shareholders outside the meeting at the Mother Lode Theater. Ray Burns and his brother, Ernest, said they weren't happy when they first heard about the conversion—"I wanted to shoot somebody," Ray told me—but now they were convinced it was a good idea. "They've got a brighter future," Ernest Burns said. "I'm even tempted to go buy a few thousand shares at $5 apiece. This thing today makes it much better for Touch America."[17] For Ernest's sake, I hope he didn't act on that hunch.

Two months later, Montana Power reported a $27 million loss for the year's third quarter, and by December, Gannon was saying that Touch America was in "serious financial trouble," as the state Public Service Commission had yet to approve the sale of Montana Power's utility assets to NorthWestern, which would provide $600 million in cash for Touch America.[18]

But as we would soon find out, it didn't matter. The commission approved the deal a few weeks later and Touch America got the cash, but it didn't slow the company's shockingly swift slide into the fiscal abyss. On its first day as a stand-alone stock, February 14, 2002, Touch America dropped $0.40 down to $3.83 per share. One month later, it laid off thirty employees. Touch America lost another $30 million in the year's second quarter, and on July 31, its stock price dipped below $1, closing at $0.98 per share.

That same day, *Billings Gazette* business reporter Jan Falstad broke the story that while its stock was in freefall, Touch America had negotiated new three-year contracts with its executives, giving them $5.4 million in

MPC stockholders Ray and Ernest Burns in uptown Butte the day the company board approved converting Montana Power to telecom firm Touch America in 2001. *Mark Downey, Great Falls Tribune.*

payouts. Gannon received $2.2 million in July. They said that "change of control" payouts were triggered when Montana Power was finally bought by NorthWestern Corporation in February. Two weeks later, Falstad reported that the same executives, including Gannon, had collected lump-sum pension payments that they were entitled to even though they hadn't retired. Gannon had received a $937,000 payout in March and was still eligible to receive a sizeable pension when he did actually retire.[19]

Sensing that they might be tarred and feathered if they held the first Touch America annual shareholders meeting in Butte, Gannon and company decided to hold it at a conference room in a Minneapolis airport hotel. Gannon ended the meeting after only seventy minutes, with angry shareholders shouting questions as executives and board members exited through a side door. Shareholder Marjorie Schmechel, the daughter of former Montana Power president Paul Schmechel, was among those who tried to question Gannon at the meeting when he unceremoniously ended it. She said later her twenty thousand shares in Montana Power/Touch America had been worth well over $1 million. Now they were worth about $12,000.

By now, the word *bankruptcy* was starting to be mentioned regularly whenever people talked about Touch America. It had all the cash from selling off the Montana Power assets but burned through it like it was being tossed into a blast furnace somewhere in the bowels of the Touch America basement.

On June 17, 2003, Gannon sent out a mass e-mail to 216 employees, telling them their jobs were toast. And the severance package? Nothing, nada, zip. From a workforce that had topped out at nearly 900, Touch America was now down to 162 people. The stock closed that day at fourteen cents per share. Two days later, the company filed for bankruptcy.

Touch America chose Chapter 11 bankruptcy, which is "reorganization," but anyone close to the company knew that it was just a way station along the road to liquidation. The next day, the company told its remaining employees that the end was near and that they'd have a job, at most, for another few months.

Billings Gazette columnist Ed Kemmick obtained a copy of the e-mail Gannon sent to employees on June 17, with its terse announcement that they had been laid off and that it would be permanent. "You can almost hear Gannon's tears hitting the keyboard, can't you?" Kemmick wrote. "Let us try to imagine, if we can, what Gannon's e-mail could have said, in an alternate universe where honor and shame exist."

Kemmick wrote an imaginary e-mail from Gannon that ended with the disgraced CEO saying he was taking his $2.2 million "change of control" payout he received last year and distributing it evenly among the 216 laid-off employees, at $10,185 apiece. "Bob," Kemmick wrote, "it's not too late to do the right thing."[20]

Within weeks, a U.S. bankruptcy judge in Philadelphia accepted Touch America's plan to auction its assets on August 6. Shareholders lost everything. A Canadian firm, 360networks, bought Touch America's fiber-optic network for a mere $43 million, from a company that had been capitalized in the billions just three and a half years earlier. Bankruptcy judges prepared to put a bow on the whole stinking package. Then, at about this time, my boss called me to suggest the story about Gannon's house.

Yes, we did the story. The week after Labor Day in 2003, I met freelance photographer Brian Kennedy at the north end of Flathead Lake, so we could rent a boat and take the pictures. We met on a cool, blustery day at the Echo Lake Café, where we joined former University of Montana journalism professor Nathaniel Blumberg, who had a copy of the newspaper that featured a shot of Gannon's $2.15 million house on Finley Point. We had coffee and chatted before Kennedy and I headed off to rent our boat. An hour or so later, Kennedy was snapping away as I idled the boat on the water not far from Gannon's dock.

Bob Gannon's Flathead Lake mansion on Finley Point, north of Polson, 2003. *Brian Kennedy, Great Falls Tribune.*

The story ran a week later, on the front page of the October 12, 2003 *Tribune*, anchored by Kennedy's photo of the Gannon mansion in all its glory, tucked in the evergreens on the lakeshore, with a speedboat dry-docked for the winter.

"Touch America—Winners & Losers," said the headline, with a subhead that read, "Executives Reap Rewards…'Little People' Pay the Price." Below the shot of Gannon's house, I opened with the story:

> *A $2 million-plus mansion on Flathead Lake. An annual retirement worth six figures. Lump-sum payments totaling more than $3 million the past year. Salaries and bonuses of at least a half-million dollars a year.*
>
> *Sounds like well-deserved compensation for guiding one of Montana's top companies.*
>
> *Perhaps. But this reward is for Bob Gannon, the president and chief executive officer of Touch America, the telecommunications stepchild of Montana Power Co. that is bankrupt.*
>
> *Company records show that Gannon and four other top executives reaped millions of dollars in salaries, bonuses and other payments in the three-and-a-half years that saw Montana Power/Touch America crumble and go broke.*

We took readers through the whole saga, listing the salaries, payouts, bonuses and other windfalls received by Gannon and several other executives. Gannon walked away with his $3 million "change of control" payment, an annual retirement of $226,000 starting at age sixty-five, the lakeside house and two adjoining lakeside parcels valued at $780,000.

We also recounted the fate of Touch America's employees (at least 640 of them out of work and more on the way), its shareholders (who ended up with nothing then but later won a lawsuit that regained a bit of cash), its creditors (about $500 million worth unpaid) and its former employees and retirees (some still had a pension, but any stock they had for retirement was worthless). Montana Power's successor, NorthWestern Corporation, years later also ended up buying back the hydroelectric dams, a portion of the Colstrip-generated power and some of the natural gas wells that were sold, giving customers the privilege of paying for these assets again, at market prices.

Company executives refused to talk to me for the story, and the company provided no help on verifying or supplying any information. But one person who did talk was Dean Conklin, a former newspaperman and former chief spokesman for Montana Power. Conklin, who at times had criticized my early coverage of deregulation, retired from the company in 1999. I'd heard he was willing to give his take on the company's ignominious fate.

"I think the whole state has really suffered," he told me. "The people who really, really took it in the shorts are the people I call the little people—the secretaries, the front-line workers, the supervisors....What you saw was executive greed. I think they just lost their bearings....Some of those bonuses they received were just unconscionable. How could you reward people for just driving the company into a hole?"[21]

Chapter 2

MARC RACICOT

Golden Boy Governor

S itting in the bright, sunny office of Attorney General and Governor-elect Marc Racicot, I asked him what I thought was an easy question. But he didn't want to answer it.

Racicot, a youthful forty-four years old, had just won a close victory over Democrat Dorothy Bradley in the 1992 election to become Montana's twenty-first governor. He had a friendly, open demeanor, and the interview flowed along until I asked why he was a Republican instead of a Democrat. I often asked this question when doing a feature-ish story on political figures, to get a feel for their philosophy and approach to governing and allow them to define themselves politically.

Racicot, however, would not answer it. He said something about how it wasn't a question that really mattered. I insisted that it did. He tried to dodge his way out of it with some platitude about fiscal responsibility, but in the end, he steadfastly resisted telling me what about his personal beliefs made him a Republican or why he had chosen to align himself with a mainstream political party that was popular in Montana. I considered pressing him further but decided to move on with the interview. Nothing from the exchange made it into the story.

It struck me as odd and vaguely annoying, but as I came to know the new governor, it became clear that this gentle evasion cut to the heart of his political persona. He often resisted espousing a hard, partisan position or making a clear statement. That way, he could be all things to all people and, most of all, be perceived as a nice, reasonable guy with whom anyone could agree—if your true position can't be known or clearly defined, it's damn

Governor Marc Racicot at the Montana Capitol after the building's major remodel during his second term in 2000. *Stu White, Great Falls Tribune.*

hard to disagree with it. And even if you do disagree with the guy, heck, he's so darn agreeable and nice it doesn't really matter. If you as a politician have the skill and smarts to pull off this feat, you may be rewarded with soaring popularity ratings.

For Racicot, it worked spectacularly for most of his long and accomplished career. Racicot, a high school basketball star in the northwest Montana logging town of Libby, not only became one of the most popular governors in state history but also climbed close to the pinnacle of national politics, thanks in large part to the relationship he forged with a man who would become president of the United States, George W. Bush.

In the late 1990s, Racicot befriended Bush, a fellow Republican governor at the time, and was in the trenches with Bush during the 2000 post-electoral battle to win the state of Florida, which gave Bush the presidency. Racicot then became chairman of the Republican National Committee during Bush's successful reelection in 2004 and ended up as a high-paid lobbyist for the insurance industry, taking home seven figures as president of the American Insurance Association. He held the job until Barack Obama arrived at the White House, ending an incredible political run for a small-town guy from Montana.

Racicot became governor of Montana a few weeks after I began my first full-time gig as a political reporter, as Capitol Bureau chief for the *Great Falls Tribune*. He was the first top political figure I covered on a week-to-week basis. Like most reporters in Helena, I liked the guy, for he was hard not to like. Young, handsome, well-spoken and disarmingly open, he charmed voters and the media alike. But like any political reporter, I wanted to cover not just the person, but what he was doing on behalf of the public and the state.

Racicot's eight-year stint as governor, in many ways, cemented Republican dominance in Montana, slowly unwinding almost two decades of liberal-leaning policy in the state. The former prosecutor oversaw an explosion in the prison population, supported "deregulation" of utilities, signed bills to loosen water quality standards and squeezed state money for schools and the university system, among other things. I saw a skilled politician with a penchant for concealing or disguising the effects of his actions, and I wanted give the public an unvarnished look at what they were getting. It made for a sometime fractious relationship with Racicot, culminating in perhaps the harshest thing I've ever written about any one politician. But at the same time, I owed Racicot a debt I couldn't repay, for through all of our battles, he basically taught me how to cover a prominent political figure.

RACICOT SHOWED HIS POLITICAL ambition early, running for chief justice of the Montana Supreme Court at age thirty-two. After losing that race, he ran for state District Court judge in Helena two years later in 1982, when he was thirty-four and already a top prosecutor at the state attorney general's office. He would lose that contest as well, but six years later, he would notch his first political win, edging out Democrat Mike McGrath to become attorney general of Montana at age forty, in January 1989.

Three years into his term as attorney general, an unexpected path to the governorship opened up for Racicot. In early 1992, Republican governor Stan Stephens suffered a transient ischemic attack or "mini-stroke" at the age of sixty-two. The stroke briefly felled him at his office. Stephens, who would go on to live a long life, decided that his health wouldn't allow him to run for reelection that year, creating an open seat.

A week after Stephens had bowed out, Racicot—with the blessing of Stephens—announced that he would run for the GOP nomination for governor, paired up with Stephen's lieutenant governor, Denny Rehberg. At the February 6, 1992 news conference announcing their candidacy, Racicot revealed little about what he believed or how he stood on issues facing a state with a looming budget deficit and other financial woes.

"We will strive at each opportunity and on every occasion to produce consensus without disengaging from the values that guide us," he said to questions about his stance on issues. "There will be enough time and enough opportunity for people to hold our feet to the fire and examine us and make up their minds about whether or not we can appropriately serve."[22]

Wow, what did that mean? Racicot's penchant for empty wordiness became an issue in the campaign. Every reporter, editor and TV anchor who interviewed him came away with the same impression: What the heck is this guy talking about? Does he ever say anything definitive?

Reporter David Fenner's lead story in the *Great Falls Tribune* on Racicot's primary election campaign in May 1992 spent its first several paragraphs making fun of the attorney general's circular language, with Racicot seeming to revel in it:

> *Somewhere along Sieben Flats, Marc Racicot pauses to consider his chief flaw….*
>
> *"I'm too talkative," he says. "I talk too much….Right?"*
>
> *His question is directed at campaign manager Glenn Marx, who is driving back to Helena after an afternoon and evening of stumping in Great Falls.*
>
> *"You don't talk too much," Marx replies. "You're incapable at times of zeroing in on precisely what it is…"*
>
> *Racicot interrupts. "I'm verbose. No? Inarticulate? Imprecise?"*
>
> *"No, it's not that," says Marx. "You just take too long to get there sometimes."*
>
> *"That's called circumspection," says Racicot.*
>
> *"Which answer would you like me to use?" the reporter asks.*
>
> *Marx suggests: "He is incapable of a 30-second sound bite."*
>
> *The laughs cease. "I don't speak as precisely as I should. Well, no, that's not it. I'm just too talkative. I talk too much. How would you phrase it?" Racicot again seeks Marx's advice.*
>
> *"It takes you too many words to say what could be said in fewer words," says Marx.*
>
> *"That's verbose," says Racicot, telling the reporter. "I'd go with verbose."*

Racicot's verbosity, however, didn't stand in the way of political success. He won the primary and then the governorship, edging out Democrat Dorothy Bradley, by an eleven-thousand-vote margin, 51 percent to 49 percent.

Marc Racicot in his attorney general office in 1992, the year he ran successfully to become Montana's twenty-first governor. *Stu White, Great Falls Tribune.*

He also came into office facing a state budget deficit projected at $300 million for the next two years, a work-comp system bleeding money and a highway-construction fund in the red. Democrats firmly controlled the state Senate, and yet, in a harbinger of things to come, Republicans had swept away a Democratic majority in the House, gaining 14 seats in the 1992 election to grab a 53-47 majority.

Racicot also had to make good on a campaign promise to try to push through a tax reform package that included a sales tax—something no governor or legislature had done in Montana's 103-year history as a state.

It was a tall order, but Montanans (including many in the legislature, of both parties) desperately wanted the new governor to succeed. They'd grown weary of the backbiting and bickering between the Democrat-held legislature and former governor Stephens and years of scraping together a state budget that barely balanced, battered by a sluggish economy that had never really recovered from the recession of the early 1980s.

Racicot pretty much pulled it off. He and the legislature balanced the budget with a combination of cuts and some minor tax-and-fee increases, passed a motor fuel tax increase to fund highway construction and put in place substantial work-comp reforms, which passed during a dramatic, late-night session on the floor of the Senate on the final day of the legislature.

But the biggest issue of the session—the sales tax reform package—had some unfinished business. Backers of the package knew that the legislature would never simply enact it without a public vote, so they placed it on the ballot in a special election in June, just six weeks after the legislature adjourned. If it failed, an across-the-board increase in state income taxes would automatically take its place to balance the state budget for the next two years. Racicot led the campaign for this proposed historic rewriting of Montana's tax structure.

Montana is one of only five states without a general sales tax. Sales tax advocates—usually aligned with business—had tried to pass one twenty-two years earlier in 1971, and voters crushed it at the polls. The Montana Republican Party suffered politically for its association with the 1971 sales tax vote, losing control of the legislature for most of the rest of the decade and losing the governor's chair for the next four elections. This time, however, both Racicot and Dorothy Bradley, his Democratic opponent, had campaigned for a sales tax package, arguing that it would not only bring needed revenue to the state budget but also help the state's business climate by reducing state income and property taxes.

The tax package imposed a statewide 4 percent sales tax, cut property taxes by an estimated $162 million per year (two-thirds of that went to business) and reduced state income taxes by $63 million.

Racicot campaigned hard for the measure, barnstorming the state in a twin-engine plane on loan from a Billings businessman. I spent a day on the road with the new governor as he pitched the plan. But while the election was still ten days away, I sensed that Racicot already knew it was a lost cause. At the end of a fourteen hour day in the Flathead Valley, the last stop was a roomful of businesspeople who were supposed to be big supporters of the tax redo. Instead, just about everyone who got up to speak trashed it.

"The business climate in Montana is not as horrible as you make it out to be," business owner Mick Seiler told Racicot. "The only avenue I see for the sales tax is another way to reach into our pockets. I never want a sales tax in my state."

Racicot, with typical aplomb, replied, "Obviously there are contrary views, and yours is one of them."

As we drove to the airport to fly back to Helena, Racicot said he was prepared for the tax to go down. If that's what the voters decided, he said, then he'd have to accept the verdict. "I think they're wrong," he said of sales tax opponents. "I'm not sure I'm entirely right. But I'm entirely sure that I'm more right than they are."[23]

TEN DAYS LATER, ON June 8, 1993, the voters spoke—and for sales tax supporters, it wasn't pretty. The proposal went down in flames, by a three-to-one margin.

On election night, reporters contact the winners or losers of an election after its "called" by the Associated Press, which it does when it sees an irreversible trend in the returns. In a wipeout, the "call" by the AP can come pretty darn early, sometimes within minutes of the polls closing—and that's what happened on this night.

Reporters met Racicot in the governor's conference room not long after the polls had closed, asking him how it felt to get creamed. He said he accepted the voters' verdict, but you could see the rejection on his face, knowing that he'd put his personal credibility and reputation on the line and then watched Montana voters kick it down the stairs. No one was surprised. It never had a chance, for a lot of reasons. But I doubt that made it any easier for Racicot to take.

The ignominy for Racicot didn't end with the defeat of the sales tax. Its demise meant that the state income tax increase would take effect, but an emerging conservative, anti-government element of the Republican Party mounted a petition drive to suspend the income tax bill. If they succeeded, a special session of the legislature would have to be called to cut the state budget further, to match up with the lower revenue caused by suspending any tax hike.

Led by University of Montana law professor Rob Natelson, this group, which was a predecessor to the likes of the "Tea Party" movement of the late 2000s, cobbled together an army of volunteers and allies that gathered the needed signatures to suspend the law by September. Racicot had no choice but to call the legislature into special session in early December. To make the budget add up, state lawmakers slashed state funding for public schools, the state university system and several government agencies.

Despite these setbacks, Racicot remained popular and politically unscathed, largely on the strength of his nice-guy personality. A December 1993 poll by Eastern Montana College gave him a 71 percent approval rating. The following year, Racicot and his fellow Republicans would use that popularity to stunning effect in the 1994 legislative elections.

The party widely employed Racicot's face and words to promote GOP legislative candidates across the state, and the party gained huge majorities at the legislature that it would never relinquish during Racicot's entire governorship and that it's rarely lost since. It was also aided by newly drawn districts, which most observers thought favored Republicans. The GOP picked up an astonishing 25 seats in state House and Senate races, turning a 30-20 deficit in the Senate to a 31-19 majority and expanding its majority in the House to 67-33. It was the first time in forty-two years that Republicans in Montana had held both houses of the legislature and the governor's seat at the same time.

As the 1995 legislature kicked off, I wrote a column for the *Tribune* musing about Racicot's spectacular popularity, noting that a recent poll had pegged his approval rating among Montanans at 79 percent. Headlined "What

Makes Mark Racicot So Darned Popular?," the column recounted an experience I'd had a few weeks earlier playing in a charity basketball game that included the governor:

> *The crowd in the Carroll College gymnasium issued obligatory applause as the rosters were announced—until Racicot's name was called. Then they erupted in cheers.*
>
> *Even my own children informed me that if a play came down to a one-on-one faceoff between the governor and I, they might root for someone other than their dad.*
>
> *Which makes one start to wonder: What makes this guy so popular? Is it luck? Talent? Image? Personality? His stand on political issues—or lack thereof?*
>
> *My guess is a little bit of all of the above.*

Yet this column, largely complimentary, evoked a reaction from the governor's office—and a preview of how this governor would react to anything smacking of criticism.

Two days after the column ran, Racicot's communications director, Andrew Malcolm, wrote a letter to the *Tribune* editorial page editor, Eric Newhouse. He began by calling my column a "clever idea" that had a "refreshing dash of humor that doesn't seem to occur to others in the world of Montana journalism." But then he got to the point, which was attacking my suggestion that Racicot's popularity had anything to do with his ability to fog his position on an issue.

Malcolm said he couldn't think of "any significant issue we haven't taken a position on" and attached an entire page listing more than two dozen "controversial issues" on which Racicot had taken a position (without listing what that position was) [24]

We had a good laugh in the newsroom over this letter, admiring it as one of the more artful put-downs from a PR flack. Little did I know this minor exchange was just a warmup for what was to come.

RACICOT PRETTY MUCH CRUISED through the 1995 legislature and got ready to run for reelection the next year. Democrats, sensing he was a shoo-in, struggled to find an opponent.

But he did face a challenge in the Republican primary, from Rob Natelson, the University of Montana law professor who had spearheaded the successful

1993 petition campaign to suspend the state income tax increase. Natelson had been touring the state, giving speeches about how Racicot had betrayed conservative Republican principles and was a "closet liberal Democrat" who wanted to grow government, contrary to the desires of most Republicans in the heavily GOP legislature.

Racicot countered with his own series of traveling stump speeches, touting his administration's record. He labeled Natelson as just another whiny politician who created controversy for the sake of controversy. In one speech, he called Natelson's criticisms "rhetorical artillery shells" that "could destroy the fragile fabric of our special Montana civility." So, if you criticized Marc Racicot, you just weren't being civil.[25]

After reading accounts of these speeches, I decided to fact-check what each man was saying. I asked both Racicot and Natelson to provide me with copies of their stump speeches.

I went into the story expecting to discover that Natelson was the one more often stretching the truth. I'd been covering his anti-government spiel for a couple of years and thought him prone to exaggerating facts and figures to make a point. Yet as I parsed the words of each man, I came to a different conclusion. In a story that ran December 3, 1995, on the front page of Sunday's *Tribune*, I announced my verdict:

> *A Tribune analysis of Racicot' statements in recent speeches reveal some that could be considered false or misleading, although Racicot administration officials defend them as accurate.*
>
> *For example, Racicot has said his 1996–97 budget contained "no new programs," although it had scores of new initiatives, such as a multimillion-dollar state building construction-and-maintenance program.*
>
> *Andrew Malcolm, communications director for the governor, says the initiatives are expansions of existing programs, rather than entirely "new" programs.*
>
> *And Racicot often has said the 1996–97 state budget increased only 2.3 percent, while not always making it clear that he's talking about annual growth of the general fund, which is 35 percent of the state's entire budget.*
>
> *The entire 1996–97 state budget—including federal funds, fuel-tax revenue and other money—has increased about 10.5 percent over the two-year period.*

The story continued with a detailed breakdown of ten statements by each man, dissecting whether and why they were accurate or not. I thought it a rather mild, but pointed, criticism of the governor. The Associated Press picked up the story, which ran in newspapers across the state—and several of them also wrote editorials, calling out Racicot for misrepresenting his record.

Racicot came unglued. He and Malcolm went straight to the *Tribune* publisher with their complaints about the story. Racicot penned a three-page, single-spaced letter calling my piece "grossly inaccurate." Publisher Barbara Henry gave the letter to our editor, Jim Strauss, who forwarded it to me for review and a reply. An excerpt:

> *Despite our timely provision of detailed explanation in response to your reporter's inquiries, he has chosen to omit and misrepresent our positions and statements. In fact, when an administration spokesman met with your reporter two days before the article's publication to provide good-faith answers to the reporter's numerous questions, answers which clearly contradicted your reporter's presumptions, the reporter admitted that he had already written the story and was merely seeking a few details to plug into the article. As evidenced by the resulting article, he clearly ignored most of the information provided to him. Hardly professional, let alone accurate or ethical. Despite the article's reference to "speeches," the reporter was working from an advance text of my Oct. 5 speech to the Great Falls Pachyderm, which the reporter did not attend. Indeed, this reporter has not been seen at one of my speeches in a very long time.*

Racicot's letter never referred to me by name, always calling me "your reporter" or "the reporter." His allegation about me saying I had already written the story two days earlier was false. And as for the nonsense about not witnessing the speech firsthand—he and Malcolm knew from the beginning that I was working off prepared text.

Yet when I got to the second page, a sentence in Racicot's diatribe made me flinch: he said I had inserted a wrong year when accusing him of saying falsely that he'd balanced the budget without raising taxes that year. Had I? I grabbed a copy of the speech.

Sitting alone at my desk in my Jackson Street office in downtown Helena, my stomach felt like it had just fallen through the floor, the basement and perhaps Earth's crust. It was the most horrible feeling a journalist could have—finding out that, yes, I *had* made a mistake, in a story where accuracy was the entire point.

The speech point I had analyzed, and put in the story, said, "We successfully balanced the budget [in 1993] with, I must add, NO new general revenues."

I had inserted the year 1993 for clarity's sake because he didn't mention the year in the text and that's the year I thought he was referencing—and he had said this same thing about that same year, 1993, in previous statements. But he actually had been referring to 1995, when they did balance the budget without new revenue. The text of the speech had been somewhat confusing, but upon a close read, it was clear: I had screwed it up.

We agreed to run a correction of this point, as well another relatively minor point where I had not mentioned that he used the latter part of the speech to clarify an earlier misleading statement.

Strauss, who had become the *Tribune* editor just weeks earlier, wrote a reply letter to Racicot, saying we would correct the errors. But Strauss stood by the rest of the story and told the governor that he, too, found parts of the speech to be misleading and called out Malcolm for alleging that I'd done a slipshod job on the piece:

> *I was disappointed to read that someone told you Mike said he "had already written the story and was merely seeking a few details to plug into the article." In this instance, I will use the word "false" to characterize that statement. Mike told Andrew Malcolm of the article he was working on more than 10 days before it was published. He met with him twice and also faxed a copy of the points he was analyzing.*
>
> *In addition, Mike met with* [the governor's budget director] *Dave Lewis three times. He closely reviewed all information he was given. He even asked for an extended deadline to complete the reporting. It seems you are not happy with the work of one of my staffers. I am not happy with the work of one of yours. I don't want to spend any more time on personnel matters in a letter.*

Racicot wasn't satisfied. He sent another letter, complaining that the correction should be lengthier, more contrite and displayed more prominently. He also told Strauss that the *Tribune* had shown it didn't understand the law or state budget processes. By now, Strauss had clearly had enough. He wrote back again, calling Racicot's denigrating comment a "cheap shot" and letting the governor know that the conversation had come to an end.

But it hadn't. Racicot replied with yet another lengthy, single-spaced letter, four days before Christmas, calling our correction "completely inadequate and an unmitigated disappointment." Dripping with condescension, Racicot's letter castigated Strauss for just about everything he had written in

Racicot on his 1996 reelection campaign brochure. *Author's collection.*

his previous two letters and said that our major offense, for which we hadn't atoned, was that we had "deleteriously impacted" his integrity.[26]

So, there we had it. By suggesting that Racicot, like many politicians, sometimes engaged in embellishing the facts to bolster his reputation, we were smearing his integrity. Racicot simply couldn't stand being made to seem like just another politician. And he wasn't— he was a highly skilled politician who had accomplished some good things in his first three years as governor. But that didn't get him a free pass from criticism or scrutiny or a license to say whatever he wanted to say, no matter the accuracy or context.

The story made me a hero among the conservative, Natelson-supporting wing of the Republican Party, who hailed it as the first time the mainstream press had called B.S. on a governor they saw as a liberal traitor. Some of my fellow journalists also congratulated me for taking on the task—although, in reality, I blew it. I had taken my shot, and because of the error, I had missed—95 percent of the story was spot on, but when 5 percent is not, the story's target and his or her supporters will use that 5 percent to tarnish the entire effort as circumspect, and they did.

And it didn't affect Racicot's political career one bit. He would go on to crush Natelson in the 1996 Republican primary and cruise to general election victory with 80 percent of the vote over a token Democratic candidate. Racicot came into his second term riding higher than ever—and aiming for things much, much higher.

RACICOT BEGAN NOSING AROUND the national political scene in mid-1998 and attended the Iowa Republican Party's "First-in-the-Nation Gala," where potential GOP candidates for president in 2000 tested the waters and their speaking points. But it was someone who *didn't* attend the Iowa event who would give Racicot an entry into the higher echelons of national politics: George W. Bush, then the governor of Texas.

He and Racicot had forged a relationship through their roles as governors, getting to know each other at meetings of the national or Republican governors associations. Later that year, Bush invited Racicot to accompany him and two other GOP governors on a trip to Israel, sponsored by the National Jewish Association—clearly a testing ground to see how Racicot might hold up on the national or international stage. Within months, it was official: Racicot had joined the inner circle of Bush's likely presidential campaign as an informal adviser and someone who could drum up support among fellow Republican governors. Racicot gushed to reporters about his new friend and fellow governor.

"He [is] a man of uncommon character and principle," Racicot told Chuck Johnson, in an interview from Dallas, where Bush was kicking off his presidential campaign. "He's thoughtful and strong. He's the right candidate at the right time, doing the right thing for the right reasons. He has an insurmountable amount of energy and patience. It's quite inspiring to see people react to him. His sensitive and thoughtful ways are just as inspirational."[27]

When asked if he might end up in Bush's cabinet should he become president, Racicot would say he expected nothing and was just doing the right thing.

I wrote my own story on Racicot's involvement in the Bush campaign in August 1999, breaking little new ground, but when I asked Racicot how Bush's stands on issues would improve the country or help Montana, or which of those stands Racicot found particularly attractive, he repeated what he had told other reporters about Bush being "thoughtful," "sensitive" and a man of "common sense and decency."

On election night in November 2000, Racicot found himself in Austin, Texas, at Bush campaign headquarters, standing right next to Bush strategists as they tracked votes in critical Florida. Racicot also would become a key player in the unprecedented drama of deciding the final outcome in Florida and, of course, the presidential election.

Eight days after the November 7, 2000 election, Racicot was back in Austin, providing legal advice to the Bush team on the vote-counting controversy in Florida. In an interview with me, he outlined what would become the Bush strategy for blocking a widespread, manual recount and preserving Bush's razor-thin margin in Florida. An initial, electronic recount of ballots had left Bush with a 537-vote lead, a mere 0.009 percent margin out of the nearly 6 million votes cast and counted. Democratic candidate Al Gore Jr., as was his right under Florida law, sought a manual, hand recount of the votes in four counties, all of which leaned heavily Democratic and had tens of thousands of voters.

Racicot maintained that if people knew the details of the proposed vote recounting in Florida, they'd realize it was "nonsense" to believe that a hand-counting of electronically counted ballots would lead to a more accurate result. Hand-counters in Palm Beach County were being asked to determine whether dimples in unpunched "chads" indicated a vote, he told me. "You introduce so much subjectivity."[28]

Racicot didn't mention that many Florida counties had different types of ballots and that in one, a hand-count had shown that ballots where someone had marked it for Gore and also written "Al Gore" in the write-in spot had initially been thrown out. The hand-count determined that the voter clearly had intended to vote for Gore and counted it as such.

Racicot, however, argued that since America (and Florida) had chosen largely to rely on machine-counted votes, the results from the machine count should be the final outcome (giving Bush the presidency). Gore and his supporters had chosen a few counties where they felt they could pick up votes and sought a hand count, and that's not right, he said. "I think they know that the evidence is such that it won't carry the day," he told me.

Three days after he spoke with me, Racicot vaulted into the national spotlight, taking the lead for the Bush campaign at a November 18 press conference in Austin and on subsequent appearances on *Fox News Sunday*, *The Today Show*, *Good Morning America* and other nationally broadcast news shows and giving interviews to reporters for the *New York Times*, the *Baltimore Sun* and other big metropolitan newspapers.

At the news conference, Racicot continued in the same vein he had taken with me, saying that the manual recount process was a joke and aggressively denouncing efforts by the Gore campaign to conduct the recount. He even said that voting machines make mistakes but that because they make mistakes randomly, their result should be considered more reliable and that a machine doesn't "search for an advantage" as a hand-counter might. "When people read those ballots, the results are incredibly arbitrary," he said. "And that would be true even if those that were judging the ballots were perfectly neutral, and we know that they're not....I think when the American people learn about these things, they're going to ask themselves, 'What in the name of God is going on here?'"[29]

The *Baltimore Sun* noted Racicot's earnest, somber tone, remarking that he had been chosen as the front man who could "level a charge that is too harsh for a presidential candidate to make but deliver it with enough dignity and credibility to be taken seriously."[30]

Of course, the views espoused by Racicot and the Bush team ultimately prevailed. On December 8, the Florida Supreme Court voted 4-3 to order a manual recount of disputed ballots in all Florida counties, but the next day, the U.S. Supreme Court granted Bush's request to block the recount. Three days later, on December 12, a divided Supreme Court overruled the Florida high court, saying the different vote-counting standards in different counties violated the equal protection clause of the U.S. Constitution. The 5-4 decision said there wasn't time to establish a unified standard and that Florida should be allowed to certify the original vote. Republican Secretary of State Katherine Harris did so, and George W. Bush was the next president of the United States.

Racicot, back in Montana, met with reporters one last time as governor, just days after the Supreme Court decision. He couldn't run for reelection because of term limits and his term ended in two weeks. Several of us who'd covered the governor from the beginning sat around a table with Racicot in a small room at the capitol within the complex of offices that made up the governor's east wing digs.

Racicot talked about his experience in Florida and how he was convinced that the Supreme Court had done the right thing. He said it was futile to try to accurately count some of the disputed votes, which involved the infamous "hanging chads," the partially dislodged pieces of punch-hole paper in a ballot that were supposed to be entirely punched to record a vote, or the "dimpled chad," where the re-counters had been asked to decide if the punch-hole paper had been indented enough to indicate a vote, even though it hadn't been punched out.

As we exhausted our questions, we all realized that it was probably the final time we would get to engage Racicot as governor. We said we were sure he'd miss his weekly sessions with the capitol press corps and our attempts to cut through the Racicot rhetoric and determine what it meant. Racicot chuckled and told us, no, he might not miss it, but he came the closest I'd ever seen to admitting that his verbal gymnastics weren't just a charming idiosyncrasy, prompting me to write several days later:

> *As anyone who's ever met Racicot knows, he can be disarmingly personable. He almost never gets mad or strident in public, and after you hear him speak, you leave thinking not only that he's a great guy, but also that he probably believes everything you do....*

The author interviewing Racicot during his second term as governor. *Author's collection.*

One Racicot quality that can't go unmentioned: His smooth, almost hypnotic speaking style. Some might call it an incredible asset, while others say it skillfully masks the fact that he's not really saying anything.

Or, as one Republican legislator recently put it to me: "He's a great messenger. I'm just not always sure what the message is."

In an interview with a group of Capitol reporters several days ago, Racicot openly joked about these rhetorical skills.

"There's been times when I've looked out at you guys and your eyes are glazing over and I can see you thinking, 'Well, it sounded OK—but what the hell did he say?'"

We all laughed. "And," Racicot continued, a sly smile on his face, "that was by design." We laughed again, and so did he. And as we left his office that day, we probably thought he was a great guy who believes in just about everything we do.

Now that George W. Bush was headed to the White House, we figured that Racicot had to be near the top of the list as a cabinet appointee, possibly attorney general. But the speculation was over almost before it even began—and Racicot, for all we know, may have gotten one of his first tastes of power politics on a national scale.

On December 20, Racicot announced he had taken himself out of the running for U.S. attorney general. Racicot, who had five children, the youngest of whom was a sophomore in college, said he needed to "take care of [some things] in terms of addressing the needs of my family" and that the job of attorney general would take up too much of his time.[31]

The following day, however, the *Washington Times* reported that conservatives within the party had opposed Racicot's appointment. Ten days later, the *Washington Post* had a lengthy, detailed story on how conservatives had lobbied against his appointment, questioning his commitment to fighting abortion and promoting "school choice."

Yet Racicot insisted that the decision was his alone, and within weeks, he did what we all thought he would do: land squarely on his feet. He snagged a position at the Washington, D.C., office of the Houston-based law firm Bracewell & Patterson, a job that also kept him close to Bush and the national political stage. Lawyers at Bracewell had worked with Racicot on the Florida recount, and the firm had a stable of well-heeled and well-connected corporate clients and offices in Texas, Washington, D.C., London and Kazakhstan.

Racicot told Bob Anez of the Associated Press in Helena that he would be specializing in environmental and "natural resource" issues, which mainly meant energy. Racicot had become a lobbyist, peddling influence for corporate clients, including one soon to become a poster boy for corporate deception and malfeasance: Enron Corporation.

Enron, in the late 1990s and early 2000s, was a big promoter of "utility deregulation," which meant, essentially, breaking down the monopolies of utilities and allowing independent energy traders, like Enron, to sell power into the utilities' territory at unregulated prices. Enron and other traders marketed wholesale power to large industrial buyers, like manufacturing plants. Enron, based in Houston, was the biggest corporate campaign donor to Bush, giving nearly $2 million to him during his political career.

By early 2001, however, the promise of a brave new world of competitive electricity sales had lost its luster. Wholesale electricity prices in California, which had deregulated, hit untold heights, affecting the entire western market. Utilities and industrial consumers that hadn't locked up enough supply were looking at prices four, five, six or even twenty times what they'd been paying just a few short months before.

The *Wall Street Journal* reported in May 2001 that Enron had hired Racicot to lobby western officials to resist any efforts to rein in deregulation. Racicot and Enron ignored my calls asking what they were trying to accomplish, as western states got pummeled by the high power prices.

Just two weeks later, the Federal Energy Regulatory Commission finally stepped in and capped wholesale prices—against the wishes of President Bush. Financial reporters also had begun investigating Enron's business practices, and it all unraveled that fall, with Enron eventually filing for bankruptcy in December—at $63 billion, the largest U.S. corporate bankruptcy to date. Later, it was revealed that Enron and its energy traders had played a key role in ginning up the western electricity crisis in the first place. They had used elaborate schemes to create phony shortages that drove up the price of electricity in times of high demand, juicing their profits and ripping off millions of citizens and businesses in the West, including Montana. Observers later estimated that the crisis cost California alone somewhere between $40 billion and $45 billion.

A week after Enron filed for bankruptcy, I reported in the *Tribune* that Racicot's firm had been paid $360,000 by Enron for his work on its behalf during the first six months of 2001—and another $300,000 to represent a half dozen other corporate clients. None of the industries who had hired Racicot would tell me what he specifically did on their behalf, and Racicot didn't return my call asking the same question. I got my information from lobbying reports filed with the U.S. Senate. The reports didn't indicate how much of that money actually ended up in Racicot's pocket.[32]

Racicot's lobbying, however, soon made the news beyond Montana, exploding into a national issue when Bush tapped Racicot to head the Republican National Committee in late 2001. Upon his appointment to the new job, Racicot announced he would forego his $150,000 salary as RNC chairman because he planned to continue his work as a lobbyist at Bracewell & Patterson. That decision elicited a storm of criticism in the national press, with most of the stories prominently mentioning Racicot's stint representing Enron.

Within weeks, Racicot had retreated, saying he would no longer work as a lobbyist while serving as RNC chairman—but would still continue to "practice law in other forms."

During the brouhaha, Racicot and a Republican Party spokesman had suggested that Racicot's lack of experience in Washington, D.C., had led to a certain naïvete, perhaps explaining his failure to anticipate the criticism. I couldn't believe that, once again, Racicot and his handlers had chosen to play the "earnest young man from Montana" card and wrote as much in a column for the *Tribune*:

> The idea that Racicot is some sort of rube in Washington, who doesn't
> know the size and shape of hardball, is a real laugher. Just check out his

*duty in Florida in November 2000, when he was public front man for the
Bush campaign's scorched-earth legal tactics to get Bush declared president.*

*If that wasn't hardball, I don't know what is. No doubt Racicot is
polishing up his bat, getting ready for the next series of pitches coming his
way in the coming months.*

For all the speculation about whether Racicot was up to the job at the
RNC, he clearly knew a few things that others didn't, for he had great
success. Republicans won the U.S. Senate in the 2002 election, giving
the GOP control of Congress and the White House, not unlike when
Racicot ran Montana and helped enable the Republican takeover of the
reins of power.

President Bush also must have liked the job Racicot performed as
RNC chair, for seven months later he chose Racicot to chair his 2004
reelection campaign, ignoring howls of protest from the religious right,
which still thought Racicot a closet liberal, particularly on the issue of
civil rights for gays. Racicot, as chairman of the RNC, also had talked

Racicot as Republican National Committee chairman, with Republican U.S. Senate
candidate Mike Taylor of Montana, 2002. *Mike Dennison,* Great Falls Tribune.

about expanding the party's appeal to minorities, saying that the party risked "swimming against the tide of history" by building a party appealing mostly to white voters.[33]

Racicot kept a relatively low profile during the 2004 campaign, appearing on TV talk shows and the like and mixing it up with Democratic opponents when called to do so. You never saw the partisan-warrior rhetoric you might expect from someone running a campaign for president of the United States, and during the waning days of the campaign that Bush would win, barely, Racicot told Lee Newspapers' Washington, D.C., correspondent that after the campaign, he intended to go back to work for Bracewell & Patterson.

For whatever reason, however, that plan didn't work out. It wasn't until seven months after the election that Racicot landed his next job, installed as chief executive officer of the American Insurance Association. Once again, Racicot had become a lobbyist, this time on behalf of the property-and-casualty insurance industry. He held the job for the remainder of Bush's term, taking home almost $4.5 million in salary in his two and a half years on the job and another $3 million in "employee benefits," including retirement funds and contributions to a deferred-compensation plan. While Racicot raked in his insurance industry cash, he also carried out the occasional political errand for his Republican pals, such as denouncing third-party attacks on U.S. Senator Conrad Burns, who had started his 2006 reelection campaign, or campaigning for the confirmation of Samuel Alito to the U.S. Supreme Court. It was on one of these political errands that I had my last remarkable interaction as a journalist with Racicot.

Racicot, back in the state for the Christmas holiday in 2005, had been called on by Republican National Committee chairman Ken Mehlman to visit various media outlets in Montana to defend Burns and belittle accusations that Burns was connected to the scandal involving lobbyist Jack Abramoff. He also defended the Bush administration's record on Iraq, praised the president and said Alito should be a shoo-in for confirmation on the Supreme Court.

I had joined the Lee Newspapers State Bureau in Helena just four months earlier and was the only reporter in the office that week. The editor of the *Helena Independent Record* asked if I could sit in on the conversation between the paper's editorial board and Racicot and write up a story on what he had to say.

We heard the pro-Burns and pro-Bush pitch, but I also asked him what he thought of the current proposal by Montana cities to buy the state's largest electric utility and convert it to a publicly owned utility, in the wake of the failures of deregulation. Racicot said he opposed it—it was better to have a "competitive enterprise" running a utility, he said—and went on to say that he still thought the 1997 deregulation law was a good idea, despite its messy aftermath. That aftermath included the financial collapse of Montana Power Company, higher utility rates, the wiping out of the savings of many and few "competitive" options for the average utility customer.

I could barely believe my ears. I asked him again: Are you telling us, that despite all the damaging things that utility deregulation wrought upon Montana and its citizens, you still support it and would do it again? Yes, he replied, saying that the negative fallout had more to do with other economic forces. He also repeated the debunked claim that utility deregulation was a nationwide force put in motion by Congress and that Montana was merely getting ahead of the game and trying to control its own destiny when it passed the 1997 law.

I put his comments within the body of my story that ran December 31 in Montana's Lee newspapers (the *Billings Gazette*, *Missoulian*, *Independent Record*, *Montana Standard* and the *Ravalli Republic*). But I felt like I had to do more.

The next week, I did a story comparing the current rates of the major electric utilities in the Northwest to those now being charged in Montana. NorthWestern's rates for its 300,000 Montana homeowner customers had become the highest in the region, at 8.83 cents per kilowatt hour—a 50 percent increase since the passage of the 1997 deregulation law, eight years earlier. I also wrote a column aimed directly at Racicot that began:

> *If you read last weekend's interview with former Montana Gov. Marc Racicot, you can be forgiven for choking on your coffee when you read this statement on utility deregulation:*
>
> *"If somebody said to me today, would you be deregulated or not after what you've seen occur, I'd still say we should be deregulated," Racicot told a newspaper editorial board.*
>
> *That's right. The governor who supported and signed Montana's infamous 1997 utility deregulation bill and resisted attempts to undo the damage says if he had the chance to do it all over again, he would.*
>
> *The former governor, now the head of a national insurance lobby, also opined that "there are a lot of myths surrounding deregulation and what happened" and that doomsday scenarios are "not supported by the evidence."*
>
> *Sorry, but the only mythology on deregulation I heard that day came out of Racicot's mouth. And if it's evidence you want on the folly of utility deregulation, it's easily found.*

Before sending the column out to the papers, I asked my new boss, Chuck Johnson, whether it was too harsh. It was the first column I'd written for Lee Newspapers, and I wasn't sure what editors of the respective papers would think of the style of commentary I'd produced at the *Tribune* for the past thirteen years. I also worried that readers might see it as overly biased. Chuck gave it the OK, saying it was hard-hitting but justified and well supported with the facts.

The day after it appeared, e-mails from readers poured in like a flood—and all but a few supported me and cheered me on. On any given story or column, if you got four or five notes in response, that was a lot. On this one, I got seventy e-mails, from readers all across the state (and outside the state). I'd never had, and never would again have, a reader reaction to anything I wrote that even came close.

Racicot wrote a reply column that most of the papers used, terming my piece a "front-page editorial filled with sarcasm and personal invective" and said its "unprofessional" tone was "both troubling and disappointing." He repeated some of his prior arguments and said the solution to Montana's energy woes was to encourage more energy development.

I didn't speak again with Racicot for nearly seven years, after he had moved back to Montana. I called his wife's cellphone (the only number that I had) to see if he wanted to comment in the obituary of his close friend, former attorney general Joe Mazurek, who'd died at age sixty-four from early-onset Alzheimer's disease. Racicot called me back and spoke eloquently about his friend and the tragedy of the disease. He was as cordial as ever, and I quoted him one last time, the final time that I wrote some of the thousands of his words I'd written.

Chapter 3

JUDY MARTZ

"Bad Press" Became Her Middle Name

E arly on the morning of August 16, 2001, a tipster called me at the *Great Falls Tribune* Capitol Bureau with the news: a vehicle had plunged off a mountain road north of Helena and Montana's House majority leader, thirty-two-year-old Paul Sliter, was dead.

I immediately started making calls, to the sheriff, the county attorney, the Montana Highway Patrol and, finally, the office of Montana governor Judy Martz—for word was that her chief policy adviser and former campaign manager, twenty-seven-year-old Shane Hedges, had been driving the vehicle. His sport-utility vehicle had tumbled off the Marysville Road late the previous night and rolled down a steep wooded embankment. Sliter had been thrown from his seat during the accident and under the rolling vehicle.

Information came slowly that morning, for investigators knew they had to be cautious on a fatal accident that had killed one prominent person and could harm the reputation of many others. By day's end, however, we knew that Hedges, Sliter, four top appointees of Governor Martz and two of her political consultants had gathered for dinner and drinks at the only restaurant in remote Marysville the previous evening; that well into the night, Hedges and Sliter had gotten into Hedges's SUV to leave the restaurant; and that moments later, someone had lost control of the vehicle before it rolled off the road.

In the following days, weeks and months, we would learn plenty more. Hedges had been drunk when he climbed behind the wheel that night and would be charged with negligent homicide, to which he would plead

Judy Martz visiting a timber mill in Deer Lodge, Montana, during her 2000 campaign for governor. *Stu White*, Great Falls Tribune.

guilty less than a month later. Investigators suspected that some of Hedges's colleagues attempted to tamper with crash scene evidence to make it look like he hadn't been driving or drinking. And the governor herself had removed Hedges from the hospital the night of the accident, against the wishes of the Montana Highway Patrol, which wanted to interview him. She took him to the governor's mansion, where she also decided to wash his bloody, soiled clothes before investigators had a look at them.

For Montana's first woman governor, this fateful August night marked the beginning of the end of her brief political career—just nine months after she had won a narrow victory over her better-funded Democratic opponent, Mark O'Keefe. The fatal crash involving one of her most trusted and savvy advisers, as well as members of her Cabinet, unleashed a torrent of negative news coverage that would dog her administration for months, before she'd had much chance to establish a political persona of her own. She never really recovered. Two years later, with her approval ratings at a dismal 20 percent, Martz would announce that her first term as governor would be her last, saying she wouldn't run for reelection in 2004.

But even without the tragic occurrence of that August 15, 2001 crash, I'm not sure Martz's political fate would have turned out much differently. Martz won her governorship largely on the coattails of her popular predecessor, Republican Marc Racicot, who made her his lieutenant governor in 1995 and supported her election in 2000. Racicot, perceived by most as a moderate Republican, had skillfully shepherded the implementation of a pro–big business and fiscally conservative agenda in Montana—deregulating utilities, slashing business property taxes, weakening environmental protections and undercutting education funding. Martz, from the more conservative wing of the party, favored the same policies but lacked the political skill or shrewdness to cloak the harder edge of these initiatives in the velvet gloves so deftly employed by her predecessor. Where Racicot was a gentle nudge, Martz was a wrecking ball.

When asked by reporters after her election whether she intended to be a "lap dog" for industry, she said yes, without hesitation. She embraced the tobacco industry, pooh-poohing criticism over her decision to scale back spending on anti-smoking programs and signing a bill that overturned the City of Helena's indoor smoking ban. She blew off an invitation to a rally of more than one thousand teachers and other public school employees at the state capitol as they protested her proposal of no increase in state funding. Instead, she attended a prayer breakfast at the state women's prison.

She got caught taking part in a clandestine, corporate-funded political action committee that had hired and paid her fallen adviser, Hedges, as executive director, after he had been sentenced for negligent homicide. She advocated and got passed a state income tax cut that favored the highest tax brackets. And she constantly and openly feuded with political critics and the Montana press, at one point refusing access to prominent political reporters in the state.

Yet for all her missteps and political blunders, I harbored some sympathy and respect for Montana's first female governor, who inherited the hangover from some dubious policies of her predecessor and who endured a steady stream of bad luck.

A disastrous, multimillion-dollar new computer system at the state Revenue Department had made revenue collection a mess. Utility deregulation had mushroomed into a full-fledged crisis, with industrial plants and homeowners facing huge, out-of-control price increases for electricity. The economy had begun to falter, in the midst of the brutal, two-year bear stock market and tech-sector meltdown of 2000 and 2001, and then dropped off the cliff after the terrorist attacks of September 11, 2001, just nine months into Martz's term as governor.

Martz managed to muddle through the electricity crisis, which largely resolved itself, and she had the courage to scrap the Revenue Department's failed computer reboot before it hemorrhaged even more taxpayer money. She also clawed the state back to financial respectability, agreeing to some badly needed minor tax increases, and later signed into law the income tax cut, which condensed and simplified Montana's previously multi-bracket system.

Democrats excoriated the income tax change for its slant toward the wealthy, but it marked a major accomplishment for Republicans who had long criticized Montana's system for its high marginal rates, which, before the change, topped out at 11 percent. Martz's proposal chopped the top rate to 6.9 percent for everyone earning more than $16,700 in taxable income (adjusted upward each year for inflation; for 2018, it was $17,900). Still, in the end, those successes couldn't overcome her own stumbles and shortcomings, which, for the most part, were entirely her own.

MARTZ BURST ONTO THE Montana political scene in July 1995, when Racicot chose her as his new lieutenant governor. She replaced Lieutenant Governor Denny Rehberg, who had stepped down to run for the U.S. Senate. His departure led to much speculation in the press about who would replace him, but nobody had even mentioned, let alone knew, the name of Judy Martz.

Racicot unveiled his choice in Martz's hometown of Butte, a Democratic stronghold where "Republican" is practically a swear word. Martz was something of a local hero, a former Olympic speed skater (at the 1964 Winter Olympics in Innsbruck, Austria) who worked tirelessly on local causes, from youth programs to the chamber of commerce to housing projects to an Olympic-class ice skating rink called the High Altitude Sports Center. She and her husband, Harry, ran a local garbage collection business. She also had been, for seven years, the Butte field representative for Republican U.S. Senator Conrad Burns.

Martz had almost zero experience in state government, and reporters wondered why Racicot had picked her. We guessed that Racicot, seen by many Republicans as a closet liberal, wanted to burnish his credentials with both the Burns Republicans—a more conservative strain—and the burgeoning religious right, for Martz was one of its own.

She and Racicot cruised to victory in the 1996 election, and Martz spent a rather uneventful four years as lieutenant governor—until she decided to run for governor, as the Republican heir apparent to Racicot. She got going on the campaign early, announcing in mid-1999 that she and Karl Ohs, a

Judy Martz with U.S. Senator Conrad Burns. She worked for Burns in Butte before becoming lieutenant governor. *National Association of Farm Broadcasters (NAFB)*.

Campaign brochure for Governor Marc Racicot and Judy Martz, his running mate, 1996. *Author's collection.*

popular, soft-spoken state representative, would run as the GOP ticket for governor and lieutenant governor in 2000. In the general election, she faced Mark O'Keefe, the Democratic state insurance commissioner and a former outfitter who'd married into a wealthy family.

On an October day during the 2000 campaign, I traveled with Martz for a campaign profile piece and got a taste of what would become her trademark style: brash, outspoken, engaging—and a little nasty toward her critics.

At the high school in Anaconda, Montana, she visited with an auditorium of students, one of whom asked why she had signed a shovel sent to support federal land-use protesters in Jarbridge, Nevada. He said the protest had threatened public officials and that the shovel would be used to illegally open a road closed by the U.S. Forest Service. "Your interpretation of that is absolutely incorrect," Martz said sternly to the student, Warren Dobney. "Do you think I, as a public official, would invite violence on me? That is an absolutely incorrect statement, and naughty on you!"[34]

I talked to Dobney afterward, and the exchange between him and the governor ended up leading my story in the *Great Falls Tribune*. He said he didn't think Martz had answered his question and then corralled her onstage afterward for some one-on-one. Martz told me later that she explained to Dobney what she had meant and told him that she "forgave him."

"And he said, 'I forgive you, too—let's start over,'" she said.

MARTZ STARKLY REPRESENTED WHAT'S always been a significant part of Montana's Republican Party: unabashed advocacy for business, disdain for any government regulation and a yearning for what they perceived as a positive Montana of the past, where industrialism ruled and things like environmentalism and other liberal causes were footnotes. This strain of the GOP in Montana had been leavened somewhat in the previous two decades by an acknowledgement that government had a legitimate role to play, through services like public schools, an affordable university system and necessary checks on corporate power. But with Martz as the party's standard-bearer, those goals seemed to take a back seat, as she said that economic development was her top priority—and if that meant giving corporations and business a blank check, so be it.

The contrast between her and O'Keefe, her Democratic opponent, couldn't have been starker. He was a Pennsylvania native with a master's degree in environmental studies who openly spurned the state's major corporations, saying he represented the wider public and would bring them to heel on its behalf.

Come election night, most of us in the media thought that O'Keefe would pull it out, in part because he'd used some of his personal wealth to easily outspend Martz on the campaign—but we also expected it to be close. As early returns came in, O'Keefe staked out a steady but slim lead, which he held for the first two hours after the polls closed at eight o'clock that night.

But that evening would become a long nightmare for Democrats, both in Montana and the nation. Their fortunes slowly evaporated in every major race in the state that night, and in the presidential race as well, with national broadcast networks backtracking on their earlier calls of Florida going for Al Gore instead of George W. Bush. As returns from rural counties in Montana trickled in, O'Keefe's early lead shrunk and eventually disappeared.

Martz won by sixteen thousand votes, taking 51 percent of the vote to O'Keefe's 47 percent. Libertarian Stan Jones won the remaining 2 percent. Martz won forty-six of the state's fifty-six counties, trouncing O'Keefe in the rural areas and beating him in four of the state's eight most populous counties, including Yellowstone (Billings), the largest, and Gallatin (Bozeman), the state's fastest-growing one.

She led what was a Republican sweep that evening, a night that Democrats thought they had a legitimate chance to win all the state's top races: governor, U.S. Senate and U.S. House. Instead, they narrowly lost them all. Martz had successfully continued a more than decade-long Republican winning streak in Montana, as the GOP extended its hold on the governor's seat to twelve years and easily kept control of the legislature.

Less than a month after the election, Martz made the first of her verbal blunders. Erin Billings, a reporter for Montana's Lee Newspapers State Bureau, interviewed Martz in early December for a story she was preparing for Stateline.org, a newly formed organization of statehouse reporters. Billings told me years later that during the interview, she asked Martz about charges that she would be a "lap dog" for industry. Martz told Billings that, yes, she would be a lap dog for industry if that's what it took to help the state's economy.

Billings said when she told her boss, Chuck Johnson, about what Martz had said, Chuck told her to write it up for the Lee papers right away. It made headlines the next day. That same week, Martz spoke at the annual meeting of the Montana Taxpayers Association, a business lobby, where reporters,

Martz sworn in as Montana's first woman governor by Supreme Court chief justice Karla Gray, January 3, 2001. *Wayne Arnst, Great Falls Tribune.*

including me, asked her about the "lap dog" comment. To our surprise, she didn't back away from it at all and said that she was glad to be the "lap dog of industry."[35]

Later that month, the Lee newspapers did a poll, and one of the questions asked whether people approved of the lap dog comment. The response was "mixed," as they say, with 43 percent saying they disapproved and 41 percent saying they approved.[36] It would be one of the better poll results Martz would see in the coming months and years.

As Martz took over as governor in January 2001, the biggest issue facing the state was a daunting electricity crisis. Western power markets had spiked beyond all reason, and many of the state's industries—which had helped push through utility deregulation four years earlier—faced financial catastrophe because they now had to pay unregulated, market rates for power. Residential consumers also faced a badly timed deregulation deadline, as a four-year freeze on rates was about to come off—just as power rates were inexplicably going through the roof.

On the next-to-last day of the legislature in April that year, scores of lobbyists, lawmakers, political staffers and members of the media crowded into the governor's conference room in the east wing of the capitol for a meeting with Martz over two key utility bills, including one to set up temporary, regulated rates to help businesses and consumers weather the electricity market storm. The previous day, a legislative committee had gutted the bill. Most of the people in the room had supported the measure and pressed Martz on what she would do.

With reporters and TV cameras looking on, Martz refused to say and lectured or castigated anyone who questioned her. When labor leader Don Judge said that inaction would allow power producers to continue to charge outrageous prices, she snapped at him: "What makes you feel you are more concerned than any person in the room, Mr. Judge?" "This is not a Montana problem," she continued. "This is a regional problem....If I were the Tooth Fairy and could wave my wand, I'd say give us back our 2.2-cent power."

When a lobbyist for AARP, the consumer group for senior citizens, asked if she planned to veto either of the two bills, she said, "Do you think I would tell you the answer to that now?"[37] Well, I thought, you *are* the governor and the legislature is ending tomorrow—why wouldn't you tell us what you plan to do about the most pressing issues facing the state?

The session ended a day later with virtually no real corrective action by the legislature and Martz saying that she had "chosen the path toward market-based solutions," which meant hoping and praying that the electric producers would somehow drop their prices.

In the end, two government agencies independent of Martz took steps to end the crisis. The Federal Energy Regulatory Commission in June 2001 capped wholesale electricity prices in the region. Also that summer, Montana's Public Service Commission, controlled by Republicans, faced down Montana Power and its major supplier, PPL Montana, until the price caps tamed the market, leaving consumers with a manageable increase in their rates, about 10 percent.

We would learn later that the likes of Enron Corporation and other energy traders had illegally gamed the western electricity market to create fake shortages and extract huge profits, at the expense of unsuspecting consumers and businesses throughout Montana and the region. Hundreds of Montana workers had lost their jobs as their companies closed or scaled back operations because they couldn't pay exorbitant electric bills—and Martz had done little to assist them.

LESS THAN FOUR MONTHS later, the political lull of summer was shattered with the events of August 15, on the dirt-and-gravel Marysville Road northwest of Helena.

Hedges, Martz's chief policy adviser and former campaign manager, and Sliter, his friend and the current Montana House majority leader, had spent the evening having dinner at the Marysville House, a restaurant and bar in a funky former mining town just below the local ski hill. Also at the dinner were Martz's chief of staff, Ed Bartlett; state commerce director Mark Simonich; state agriculture director Ralph Peck; Leo Giacometto, a Martz appointee to a regional power council; and two Virginia political consultants who'd worked on Martz's campaign.

Sliter and Hedges left the restaurant at about eleven o'clock that night in Hedges's new Ford Explorer, with Giacometto a few minutes behind. They hadn't gone far when the vehicle went up a bank on the left side of the road, overturned and then rolled down the steep, twenty-five-foot embankment on the right edge of the road. Sliter, not wearing a seat belt, had been thrown from the vehicle as it rolled. My story on the wreck led the *Tribune* on August 17:

> MARYSVILLE—*A one-vehicle rollover near this historic mining town killed House Majority Leader Paul Sliter, who was on his way home from a dinner party late Wednesday with members of Gov. Judy Martz's cabinet.*
>
> *Also in the vehicle was Shane Hedges, the governor's chief policy adviser. Authorities said Thursday they're investigating who was driving and whether alcohol was involved, but were tight-lipped about other details.*

Six days after the crash, prosecutors charged Hedges with negligent homicide, revealing that his blood-alcohol content was 0.15 percent—one and a half times the then legal threshold for drunkenness. Within days, Hedges announced that he would plead guilty, saying through his attorney that he was "accepting responsibility for his actions." The next day, he resigned from his job as Martz's chief policy adviser.

At his sentencing hearing, Hedges broke down as he told the judge that he and Sliter, his best friend, had big plans for the future, "and now everything's gone....A lifetime's dreams was dashed in a single moment....I really miss him badly...and I'll look in the mirror for the rest of my life and know that it's my fault that he's not here."[38]

The judge sentenced Hedges to a six-month stay in a pre-release center, fined him $6,000 and gave him a six-year deferred sentence, which would be wiped from his record if he committed no other crimes during that period. As negligent homicide sentences go, it was more lenient than most, but not extraordinarily so—especially when the victim's family supports it. Sliter's widow, Elaine, told the court she would remain friends with Hedges and that he should not be treated like a criminal. Nearly two hundred people also had

House majority leader killed in rollover

Headline on the author's story on August 15, 2001 traffic accident that killed House Majority Leader Paul Sliter; a top Martz aide was driving. *From the* Great Falls Tribune.

written the court—many of them political figures from Republican Party circles—praising Hedges and asking for leniency.

While Hedges took responsibility for his actions that caused the fatal August 15 wreck, the reaction and actions of Martz in the days and weeks after the accident seemed odd, to say the least. For several days after the accident, Martz had Hedges stay with her at the governor's mansion, calling him "my son"—but said she asked him nothing about the accident and didn't want to know about it.

She also said Montanans didn't want to hear about it, that she wasn't a witness and that it would be improper for her to comment. Not until months later did she reveal that prosecuting attorneys had advised her not to talk to Hedges about the accident because that might make her a witness. Still, we wondered why the governor wouldn't want to know the circumstances of the accident and evening that had taken the life of the House majority leader and involved members of her Cabinet and inner circle.

Martz also allowed Hedges to remain on the state payroll while he took a leave of absence, including after he was charged with a felony. When Hedges finally resigned, Martz told Associated Press reporter Bob Anez that she saw no reason why he should resign, that she was "sick" over losing him and that he was welcome to come back and work for her if he wanted to.[39]

By now, reporters had started hearing rumors about strange goings-on the night of the accident, at the hospital and the accident scene, involving Martz and other members of her administration. At the sentencing hearing in October 2001, for example, it was revealed that Hedges initially lied to investigators about who was driving his Ford Explorer that night, saying three times that it had been Sliter. He later admitted to being the driver, in the face of investigative evidence. Lewis and Clark County attorney Leo Gallagher, however, said the accident report and other investigative material would remain sealed because it was considered "confidential criminal justice information."

Fourteen Montana news organizations sued to gain access to the records, arguing that the public's right to know outweighed any privacy interests of the public figures involved. Martz, realizing the media likely would win the lawsuit, tried to preempt some of the impact of what they might find, granting an extraordinary interview with Anez and Lee Newspapers' Kathy McLaughlin in the first week of January 2002.

Martz called the two reporters over to her office in the capitol and proceeded to tell them that on the night of the accident, after she had taken Hedges from the hospital to the governor's mansion, she had washed Hedges's bloodied, dirty clothes and didn't realize she'd done anything wrong until authorities came two days later to collect his clothes as evidence.

"I was never told not to do anything with them," she told Anez and McLaughlin. "A mother does that kind of stuff. If something's dirty or got blood on it, you try to get it off and you clean it up. I never even thought about it, you know, being anything wrong with it. If I had to do it over again, I wouldn't have."[40]

Anez, like any reporter hearing this news, promptly called Gallagher, the prosecutor, and asked if Martz had destroyed vital evidence. Gallagher said no, that investigators had been able to get what they needed despite the fact the clothes had been washed. Investigators wanted to obtain fiber from the clothing to see if it matched fibers on the crash vehicle's driver's side seat belt, to determine who'd been driving. They were able to get the fibers anyway. Gallagher did, however, suggest that it had been a "poor decision" by Martz to wash the clothes before police collected them.

The lawsuit by media organizations ended several weeks later when a judge approved an agreement among the media, prosecutors and Sliter's family to release four hundred pages of investigative documents. The trove included transcripts of interviews with witnesses and Hedges, reports by the highway patrol and sheriff's office, medical records and some investigative subpoenas. It didn't paint a pretty picture, as I reported in a story that led the *Tribune* February 14 edition:

> *Three witnesses at last summer's fatal traffic accident involving governor's aide Shane Hedges say they believe people at the scene initially tried to conceal Hedges' involvement, according to investigative documents released Wednesday....*
>
> *They said people at the scene initially insisted Sliter was the only person in the vehicle. One of the witnesses said they believed Hedges was hiding in the trees and bushes near the crashed vehicle, others said it appeared someone wanted to drive Hedges away before law enforcement officials arrived.*

The documents also revealed that the governor had taken Hedges from the hospital despite a highway patrolman's specific direction not to. Martz said it was a misunderstanding and that she thought Hedges had been cleared by medical personnel to leave. On the day of the document release, Martz said she had cooperated "in every way possible" with law enforcement and then got in a dig at the media: "I sincerely hope that those interested in opening and rehashing this accident realize, first and foremost, the incredible loss to the individuals and families involved."[41]

Believe me, we did. No one in the media took any pleasure in having to go to court to get the records on a tragic accident that involved people we knew, and we didn't win any friends doing it. But, as explained by my editor, Jim Strauss, in the paper that day, the accident involved state officials "at the highest level." With rumors running rampant about what happened that evening, the press and the public should see the evidence firsthand, he wrote.

Montana has some of the strongest open-government and public-record laws in the nation. Media in the state have a long tradition of insisting on rigorous enforcement of those laws, as well as the constitutional provisions that underpin them. Our newspaper didn't join the lawsuit that led to release of the documents because it felt the case should have been argued on straight constitutional grounds, without any negotiating over which documents should be released. The agreement called for blacking out the details of Sliter's injuries and the names of witnesses who were not public figures.

Stories on the documents made headlines in newspapers across the state, and any way you spun it, the governor came out looking none too well. Ed Kemmick, a reporter and columnist for the *Billings Gazette*, summed it up in a devastating piece that ran a few days after the document release:

> *So, now we know that our governor acted against the wishes of the Highway Patrol, apologized to the Highway Patrol, then hired Highway Patrol officers as her personal bodyguards, paying them with money pulled from the recently established governor's Office of Economic Opportunity.*
>
> *This is not criminal, perhaps, but it is crazy. Do we really expect businesses to invest in a state whose morally dull leaders appear to be on the verge of a meltdown?*
>
> *A considerable number of people have accused the press of ganging up on the governor, or of exploiting a personal tragedy for partisan purposes. One can only wonder if these latest reports will suggest to them that the*

*governor and members of her inner circle don't need to be attacked by
anyone outside that circle.*

    They have become their own worst enemies.

Gang-up or not, it didn't take long for the next big story on Martz to
surface. Less than a week later, McLaughlin reported in Lee Newspapers'
dailies that the governor was chairing a new "stealth" political action
committee that had raised $191,000 from corporate interests—and that
Shane Hedges, while serving his sentence at the pre-release center—was the
group's executive director. Sliter's widow, Elaine, also served as the group's
secretary-treasurer.

A politician or group of like-minded politically active people setting up
their own corporate-funded PAC is hardly news in the post–*Citizens United*
world now, but in 2002, such political money pools were somewhat rare. The
group, called the Montana Majority Fund, had been formed in May 2001 to
raise money to further "Republican causes."[42]

A list of its donors reads like a who's who of corporate big boys
operating in Montana. AT&T, Burlington Northern–Santa Fe Railroad,
PPL Montana, Anheuser-Busch, Delta Airlines, Enron Wind Systems,
Philip Morris (the tobacco giant), NorthWestern Corporation and several
large in-state construction firms and construction firm owners. Its clear
intent was to operate as an "issue advocacy" group that eventually would
promote Republican candidates and somehow skirt Montana's ban (which
has since been voided by *Citizens United*) on corporate money being used to
advocate for candidates. It was all perfectly legal, but the relative newness
of this mode of campaign spending and its clandestine nature made it
a story. It also didn't help that Martz never responded to McLaughlin's
several attempts to contact her.

The president of the fund, Mark Baker, a Helena attorney and longtime
Republican operative, said he set up the fund and that Martz was merely
an honorary chair who had helped with some of the fundraising—like
appearing at an event at a golf club in Palm Springs, California.

Baker said he hired Hedges to be the group's executive director because
Hedges was supposed to get a job while serving his sentence at the pre-
release center. The group reported paying Hedges $5,100 for about two
months of work—and also paid the cost of extending his health insurance
after he resigned from state government.

Democrats in Montana had a field day with the news, calling the fund
a "slush fund" that took advantage of campaign finance loopholes. "Here

we have a national movement for campaign-finance reform and against the stench of soft money and we have the Republicans going out and rolling in the manure," said Senate Minority Leader Steve Doherty of Great Falls.[43]

As the drumbeat of negative press continued for Martz, she and her supporters did what beleaguered politicians often do: blame the media. McLaughlin, in particular, was relentless in her coverage, as she followed the money trail of the Montana Majority Fund and reported on Martz's telephone calls from her office to some of the fund's donors.

In response to a story McLaughlin had written on Martz personally calling Majority Fund donors, Martz called McLaughlin to tell her that the coverage was hurting the state and hindering economic development. McLaughlin responded by writing a story about Martz calling her. It ran in papers statewide the next day:

> *An audibly agitated Martz called the Lee Newspapers State Bureau on Wednesday to take issue with an article detailing her dealings with two California businessmen who own property in Montana. The story reported that both men said they gave money to the Montana Majority Fund—a GOP-linked political committee that Martz headed until a few weeks ago—but they weren't trying to gain favor with the governor by doing so.*[44]

Martz said the press had to realize that the governor must work with people who do business in the state, otherwise they'll never want to help Montana with economic development. One of the businessmen she'd called was Tim Blixseth, a multimillionaire real estate mogul who was building a private, gated ski and golf community near Big Sky, Montana. The Yellowstone Club had its own golf course and ski hills, with chair lifts, and the development had some issues with state environmental regulators. When asked what state business or economic development she'd been discussing with Blixseth, who'd given $47,000 to the Majority Fund, Martz wouldn't say.

"We do not tell the media every single thing that's going on with businesspeople, because we're asked not to," she said. But the calls to Blixseth were "totally explainable," she said, calling him "a good man doing good business in Montana." More than a decade later, Blixseth ended up in jail for several months for contempt of court during a lengthy legal battle over the bankruptcy of the Yellowstone Club. Montana authorities in 2018 said that he still owed the state more than $70 million in back taxes.[45]

Several weeks later, Martz told a business group in Kalispell that she would no longer grant interviews to certain reporters, citing their "misleading" stories. The *Kalispell Daily Inter Lake* first reported her comments, and the Associated Press picked up the story. It didn't take long to figure out which reporters she meant: Bob Anez at the AP in Helena and Kathy McLaughlin, as well as perhaps McLaughlin's colleagues at the Lee Newspapers State Bureau.[46]

One week later, the AP's news editor, John MacDonald, had a private meeting with the governor to talk about her refusal to meet with Anez. The stories written by Anez, a veteran reporter, were distributed to dozens of newspapers, TV stations and radio stations across the state that were members of AP, a news cooperative. If he didn't have access to the governor, hundreds of thousands of Montana citizens wouldn't get the unvarnished take on her words. Unbeknownst to most of us, Martz had been refusing to talk to Anez for more than a month. While Anez was certainly an aggressive reporter, his colleagues in the media knew him as funny, outgoing, relentlessly fair and without bias. Martz, however, didn't see him that way.

MacDonald met with Martz for more than an hour on May 29, 2002. He prepared a two-and-a-half page memo that summarized the meeting. He said there was no convincing the governor that Anez was not "out to get" her and that when he told her that Bob wasn't going anywhere and that she should try to start with a clean slate, she replied, "Not with him." The memo continued:

> *She was often angry and defensive. When I politely told her that the AP takes complaints about bias and unfairness seriously, she responded "no you don't." (keep in mind I was the one who suggested the meeting)*
>
> *When I said that painting all reporters as liberal was insulting, she said "I don't care if you're insulted."*
>
> *When I inadvertently interrupted her, I apologized and said "I'm sorry. I interrupted you." She leaned back in her chair, folded her arms and said "Go ahead, you seem to have an answer ready for everything."*
>
> *At one point, after I reminded her that none of her complaints had ever been passed to Bob or me, she said she had no idea how to get a hold of me. I reminded her that Mary had my number, then I slipped a business card from my wallet and handed it to her. She folded it and TOSSED it to Mary.*
>
> *Basically, Martz doesn't like Bob. Period. In her words, she "can't stand" him. She referred to him as "immoral," as "an enemy," that he is "slick," and said he "walks around here like he owns the place."*

She believes, and couldn't be convinced otherwise, that Bob has a liberal agenda, that he "takes liberties" with the truth and that he "attacks my person" in his stories.

Martz eventually patched things up enough with Bob to resume talking to him but still saw him as the enemy—as evidenced by a bizarre story he told me years later.

In the waning days of the Martz administration, he wandered by the lobby of the governor's office and saw Martz standing there. She said hello and told Bob she wanted to show him something. She led him into her office, opened up the top drawer of her desk and pulled out an Altoid Mints tin box. Inside the box, which she opened, was a cinnamon gummy bear, but it did not have the head of a cinnamon gummy bear. Martz (or someone) had replaced the gummy bear head with a tiny, photographic picture of Bob's head, attached to the bear's body.

"Bob," said the governor, "you don't know how many times I've wanted to take out that bear and bite that head right off."[47]

As I read (and wrote some of) the litany of stories on Martz's political follies, I could look down the tunnel toward the end of Martz's first term and see the only light was an oncoming train. Any reelection campaign was a year or more in the future, but anyone with any political sense could see she was finished. In a year, she'd absorbed more negative coverage than most politicians get in an entire career.

In September 2002, a poll by the Lee Montana papers showed that Martz's approval rating had sunk to 23 percent—the total of respondents who thought she was doing a "good" or "excellent" job. Yet it struck me as somewhat unfair that Martz found her approval ratings in the sewer when she was carrying on the same policies as her predecessor, Marc Racicot. I expressed that thought in a column that ran in the *Tribune* on October 7, 2002:

OK, here's a political pop quiz: Which Montana governor is a friend to large corporations, is the bane of environmentalists and carries the banner for timber and mining interests?

Which Montana governor promotes tax cuts as economic development, agrees to scant increases in state education funding and strongly favors utility deregulation?

Governor Judy Martz in an interview as the 2003 Montana legislature began. *From the* Great Falls Tribune.

If you said Judy Martz, you're technically correct. But I'm not talking about her. I'm talking about her predecessor, Marc Racicot.

Yet, if polls are to be believed, there is one huge difference between these two governors: One was wildly popular and the other is not....

It's ironic, isn't it? Republican Martz, who wouldn't even be governor were it not for Marc Racicot, gets blamed for every ill effect of the very policies her and fellow Republicans promoted and carried out for the past decade.

Political scientists I quoted in the column expressed what I'd come to believe: that Martz's clumsy style and forthright promotion of the conservative agenda gave a hard edge to policies that had been delivered more subtly by Racicot. They also noted that policies like "cut government," "no new taxes" and other messages of austerity didn't sound very reassuring when the economy was imploding and people were in need.

MARTZ CAME INTO HER final legislature in 2003 facing a gaping hole in the state budget, caused by the dramatic drop-off in tax revenue due to the post-9/11 recession and the two-and-a-half-year cratering of the stock market.

Martz started the session by proposing no increase in funding for the university system (meaning student tuition would go up to cover rising costs), no raises for state employees, a small increase in state funding for public schools and a pledge not to raise taxes. The leaders of her own Republican Party in the legislature said they wouldn't go along. She finally relented on the "no new taxes" pledge, agreeing to some selected sales tax increases to help ease the budget cutting.

But the session's action also had a major win for Republicans and Martz: the revamping and lowering of the state's top income tax rates. The package also included a substantial deduction for capital gains income, which primarily benefited Montana's wealthiest taxpayers.

The tax cut's impact was delayed for two years, so if the alleged benefits didn't materialize (such as the GOP prediction of luring more wealthy people to the state), future legislatures would have to deal with the budget consequences. A year after it took full effect, a Department of Revenue study quietly revealed what most people had surmised about this tax change: its benefits flowed overwhelmingly to wealthy taxpayers, while those in the middle-income strata saw their tax bills decline by a few bucks.

But Martz had balanced the state budget in a difficult environment—and, including the tax cut, her administration could claim some legitimate victories, such as pulling the plug on the Revenue Department's ruinous new computer system that had been installed by the previous administration. Martz's revenue director, Kurt Alme, and some courageous Republican legislators worked together to ditch it, stopping the hemorrhaging from a system that most thought had cost the state at least $100 million.

These successes hadn't improved Martz's political stock, however. Three weeks after the legislature adjourned, I wrote how people were practically falling over themselves to get into the 2004 governor's race, knowing that Martz was about as vulnerable as a politician could be.

Democrat Brian Schweitzer, who'd lost his 2000 challenge to U.S. Senator Conrad Burns, had already declared himself a candidate for governor, and some Republicans had indicated they would challenge Martz in the primary. That spring, Montana Lee Newspapers paid for a poll that showed Martz with an approval rating of only 20 percent—and only 18 percent of those surveyed said they would vote to reelect the governor. In a supposed matchup against Schweitzer, the largely untested Democrat would beat Martz by a 2-to-1 margin. In the same poll, President George W. Bush got a 68 percent approval rating, and he had just invaded Iraq.

Martz made the inevitable announcement on August 13, 2003, that she would not run for reelection in 2004. She told AP's Bob Anez that she had accomplished what she set out to do and her biggest disappointment was that her record had been distorted by the media, making it impossible for

Martz says she won't run again

Great Falls Tribune headline, August 14, 2003.

Montanans to know "that all I had in my heart was what was best for this state." She also said that her elderly mother did not want her to run, as she was tired of reading news accounts of her daughter's alleged missteps as governor.

"She hated the media," Martz said of her mother.

As MARTZ'S FINAL MONTHS as governor wound down, I did a farewell piece for the *Tribune*, but I chose to do it in midsummer, five months before her term ended. As I told Martz, if I waited until the final weeks, the story would just get lost in the crush of post-election coverage about her successor and the incoming 2005 legislature.

I interviewed Martz in her capitol office in late July, accompanied by a photographer who took a series of great photos of an animated Martz. The story led the front page of Sunday's paper on August 1, 2004.

The sixty-one-year-old Martz spoke about how she had no plans to slow down in her final months as governor, working still to bring business and other development to the state. At some point in the interview and story, however, I had to ask about, and Martz had to confront, the political woes that had become the dominant narrative of her time as governor.

Martz told me how the fatal accident involving Hedges had truly hurt her and how much she missed both Hedges and Sliter. She also bristled at my suggestion that perhaps she could have handled the aftermath differently and publicly disciplined those involved in the affair. "People are easy to judge and they're easy to criticize, but they don't have a clue what they're talking about," she said.

As for the media and coverage of her administration, Martz had nothing good to say. "When I came into this job, [I thought] because you're honest, because you're a morally good person, because you're a hard worker, that the media will not attack you and almost try to destroy who you are," she said. "I've got news for whoever's governor: It will happen to them, too."

As I left the interview and, later, as I wrote the story, I thought how those who brave the world of politics are convinced they are doing the right thing for the right reasons, to help advance the state and their fellow citizens. For Martz, it had to have been a lonely four years, feeling as she did that her good intentions went ignored, while the negative news piled up and the media, in her eyes, morphed into an attack dog. As she put it to me that day, "I just tried to concentrate on what was right and best for the most of the people in the state of Montana."

Chapter 4

CONRAD BURNS

"It's Not 'Senator,' It's 'Conrad'"

Cass Chinske, a Democrat and environmental activist and former city councilman in the Democratic stronghold of Missoula, Montana, staked a campaign sign in his front yard in 1994 for the reelection of Republican U.S. Senator Conrad Burns, an avowed enemy of just about every environmentalist in the state.

"I'm still not forgiven for that," Chinske said twenty years later. "And I try to explain it to all my Democratic friends."

Chinske spent fifteen months in federal prison for a 1991 marijuana bust in Missoula—but if not for Burns, Chinske's bust and prison term would have been a lot rougher. Burns used his influence as a U.S. senator, not once but several times, to help Chinske survive the brunt of a federal criminal justice system intent on making him an example to those who might not fully cooperate with prosecutors.

Three years before the drug bust, Chinske—frustrated with Montana's Democratic U.S. senator, John Melcher, whom Burns beat in an upset victory in 1988—had provided some surreptitious campaign help to Burns. Burns returned the favor by, among other things, enabling Chinske to prevent his home from being permanently confiscated by the Justice Department. "Senators have power," Chinske said. "He was watching my ass. He was being a truly honorable friend."[48]

Burns's favor to an unlikely friend never made the newspapers in Montana. Years after I heard about it from Chinske, I had planned to approach Burns and write about it, once he left office. But in the wake of his defeat for reelection in

Conrad Burns, early in his eighteen-year career as U.S. senator. *National Association of Farm Broadcasters (NAFB).*

2006, Burns bitterly blamed the media and just about anyone but himself for his loss, singling out one of my close colleagues for particular scorn. I couldn't bring myself to write something positive about him.

In many ways, my attitude embodied the public's and the Montana media's Jekyll-and-Hyde view of Burns, at that time the only Republican U.S. senator in Montana history to win reelection (twice) by the voters.

Burns, a gregarious, wisecracking farm broadcaster from Billings, was a funny, engaging politician who relished the fact that he was treated more like a regular guy than a U.S. senator. "I love Montana because it's not 'senator,' it's 'Conrad,'" he told me as he campaigned for reelection in Billings in 2006.[49]

Burns's "aw shucks" persona, burnished by years as a livestock auctioneer and a broadcaster on his own Northern Ag Network, made him a popular guy, particularly in rural Montana. He also made sure you knew how much federal money he had brought to the state, in rural and urban areas alike, financing everything from rural water systems in northeast Montana to fuel cells at a Billings hospital to research grants for Montana State University in Bozeman. In all three of his reelection battles, this fiscal conservative spoke with pride about bringing home the federal bacon—and how Montana's mostly rural residents sure as hell deserved it.

Yet for all his likability, Burns created his fair share of political enemies and generated plenty of negative press. Burns would say that the "liberal" press of Montana was biased against him and didn't treat him fairly, especially in his final election, which he lost in 2006. But Burns did plenty on his own to earn the bad press that certainly played a role in his political demise.

He reportedly uttered the occasional racist or insensitive joke or comment, including the word *nigger*, and sometimes overplayed his image as a country bumpkin (which he wasn't). In an election year, he publicly dressed down a group of firefighters who had just spent days battling a range wildfire in southeastern Montana, accusing them of screwing up the job. And last but not least, Burns became embroiled in the 2005–6 scandal of uber-lobbyist Jack Abramoff, who went to prison for ripping off his Native American tribe clients, giving illegal gifts to members of Congress and their staff and making campaign donations to representatives and senators who allegedly cast votes on bills favorable to his clients.

Burns received more campaign donations from Abramoff, his associates and lobbying clients than any other member of Congress—$150,000 over four years—and took some votes that appeared directed at favoring Abramoff's clients. While Burns was never officially accused of violating any law or ethics rule in relation to the case, his staff apparently had enough of a relationship with Abramoff to prompt Abramoff himself to finger Burns in a devastating 2006 *Vanity Fair* article on the scandal.

"Our staffs were as close as they could be," Abramoff told the magazine, saying he and his associates got "every appropriation we wanted" from an appropriations subcommittee chaired by Burns. "I mean, it's a little difficult for him to run from that record."[50]

The article's revelations prompted University of Virginia political scientist Larry Sabato to remark, "I wouldn't say that [Burns] is necessarily toast, but you can smell the bread burning."

The allegations dogged Burns for his entire 2006 reelection campaign, which he lost, but not by much. Despite bearing the Abramoff cross and toting some other considerable political baggage, Burns lost by a mere 3,562 votes, out of 406,505 cast.

I met Burns in his first campaign for U.S. senator in 1988, when he was a Yellowstone County commissioner and the Republican challenging veteran incumbent Democrat John Melcher. Like Burns, Melcher was from eastern Montana and had professional roots in agriculture. Melcher was a former veterinarian from Forsyth, Montana, who often went by "Doc," among friends and foe alike. Burns officially got into the race in January of that year, just ten months before the election, an unheard-of short interval today, when U.S. Senate candidates in Montana sometimes start their campaigns as long as two years before the election.

I covered the race for the Associated Press, where I'd been working as a reporter since 1985 in Helena. Burns, fifty-three years old, had hired his own campaign manager, but when it looked like the race might be tightening, national funders and Republican Party people brought in a new one: Denny Rehberg, a thirty-two-year-old state representative from Billings who would go on to become Montana's lieutenant governor and a six-term U.S. congressman representing Montana. Rehberg brought a new professional intensity to the campaign and was relentlessly upbeat, constantly talking up how Burns was mounting a serious challenge to Melcher. Several days before the election, I chatted with Rehberg, who said that all of their internal polls showed a tightening race and that they were "just where we want to be at this point." He said their polls showed Burns either with a slight lead or within the margin of error of the poll, meaning Burns was no more than a few points behind.[51]

I remember thinking, "What a load of bull." Conrad Burns, a rookie candidate, actually beating John Melcher, an entrenched incumbent? It wasn't going to happen, and this fast-talking Republican state representative saying it would wasn't going to make it happen. I know I wasn't alone in thinking that way, among reporters covering the race.

Two days later, Burns, Rehberg and the voters of Montana proved us all wrong—and surprised even Burns himself, as he confided to the *Billing Gazette* five years later. Burns ran close to Melcher most of election night on November 8, 1988, and when the rural returns starting coming in, Burns began edging past him. I was at the office from early in the evening until the end, when the AP's bureau chief, John Kuglin, called the race around midnight. I telephoned Melcher, who was in Missoula. His twenty-year Congressional career had come to an end, but he didn't seem angry or bitter. He told me he "never really had a good feel" for the race.

"I always like to win, but I enter all these things realizing that voters may not approve," he said. "And if they don't, you have to accept that."[52]

The final count was relatively close, but nothing like a razor's edge. Burns defeated Melcher by 14,000 votes out of 364,000 cast, or 52 percent to 48 percent. In Montana, that's a close but solid victory.

Burns wins Melcher Senate seat

Great Falls Tribune headline, November 9, 1988.

When I talked to Burns the next day, I asked him if he thought it would be a steep learning curve, going from the Yellowstone County Commission to the U.S. Senate. What he told me became the lead of my day-after story: "There's no real difference. We're just dealing with more zeroes [in the budget]. The responsibility's the same."[53]

The *Washington Post* immediately picked up on this comment, as one of its reporters called Burns to ask him, essentially, did you really say that? Is that what you think? Burns told the *Post* reporter he'd been quoted out of context.

ONCE BURNS MADE IT to Washington, it didn't take long for his mouth to get him in trouble. On his first day there, in the presence of reporters, he cracked, "There's some awful good folks up there [in Montana]. Some of them can read and write." Burns was just being his usual wise-ass self, poking fun at where he came from and probably getting in a subtle dig at the mindset of the eastern press, which would be only too eager to presume that people from Montana and in Montana were hillbillies or worse.

But some in Montana thought Burns seemed a little too willing to play to the eastern image of Montana, chewing tobacco, picking his teeth with a pocketknife and cracking wise with his Missouri drawl, which is where Burns grew up. After the comment, the *Bozeman Daily Chronicle* wrote in an editorial that Burns was making Montanans look like "bumpkins."

The *Chronicle* also broke the story some six years later on the first of Burns's racially charged comments that made it into the media. Burns, running for reelection in the fall of 1994, had stopped by the *Chronicle*'s old downtown office to chat with the editorial board. He'd been talking to Dan Burkhart, the assistant managing editor for the *Chronicle*, and launched into an anecdote about how a rancher from the tiny Montana town of Absarokee had asked him, "Conrad, how can you live back there [in Washington, D.C.] with all those niggers?"[54]

Burkhart told me twenty years later that when he heard Burns say the word *niggers*, he thought, "Did he just say that?" So we asked him later (after the editorial board meeting), "What did you say to him?"[55]

Burkhart, who knew the rancher, asked Burns how he responded, and Burns laughed and said, "I said, 'It's a hell of a challenge.'" Burkhart said he decided a story was in order and assigned it to reporter Gail Schontzler, who was covering the Senate race between Burns and Democrat Jack Mudd.

Conrad Burns yuks it up at a ribbon-cutting ceremony. *National Association of Farm Broadcasters (NAFB).*

Schontzler, who also recalled the incident with clarity twenty years later, said she wasn't looking forward to confronting Burns about the comment and telling him the *Chronicle* planned a story, but she did it—and also gave Burns a talking to. "I said, 'You're one of just 100 people elected to the U.S. Senate—you can't say things like that,'" Schontzler told me. "He said, 'I wasn't saying it. I was just repeating what somebody else said.'"[56]

The *Chronicle* ran the story the next day. The Associated Press and other media then started calling Burns, asking him to explain himself. He later issued a statement apologizing and said that he regretted telling a story "which could have been interpreted that I share racist views."

Ken Toole, president of the Montana Human Rights Network, a group formed to fight white supremacists in the state, wasn't about to let Burns off the hook. He said Burns's response to the rancher essentially affirmed what the rancher had said about Washington and was "as racist as the original remark."

Toole noted that Burns was one of several senators who voted to renew a patent on the Confederate flag insignia for the Daughters of the Confederacy, despite protests from the only African American U.S. senator at the time, Carol Moseley Braun of Illinois. The *Washington Post* also wrote a harsh editorial condemning Burns several days later, saying that any difference between Burns and the rancher he had quoted "seem pretty small."[57]

Not two weeks passed before another story surfaced about Burns mouthing off about black people, this time cast as saying the word *nigger* himself, reported by the *Billings Gazette* and the Bozeman paper, just three days before the November 8 election in 1994. Two passengers on a flight with Burns said they'd heard him tell other passengers a joke about a black farmer and a mule and use the phrase "Mississippi nigger."[58]

I asked Burns about it on the Saturday before the election, meeting him at a private air terminal in Helena as he was doing a last-minute campaign fly-around. "It never happened," he told me. "I don't know where these guys are coming from, and I just think it's last-minute political garbage." He also remarked that "I think it's Ken Toole who's pedaling that bicycle," noting that Toole was a supporter of Burns's opponent, Jack Mudd.[59] The reporting on these statements seemed to have no effect on the election, for Burns won easily.

Some five years later, just days before announcing in 1999 that he would run for reelection to a third term, Burns, during a speech to farm equipment dealers in Billings, called Arabs "rag heads" as he talked about oil prices and the United States' dependency on foreign oil.

The *Billings Gazette* broke the story when it got a copy of an apology that Burns had sent to the Montana Equipment Dealers Association and to "the people of the Radisson Northern Hotel" for using the term. He said he shouldn't have used it.[60]

Brian Schweitzer, Burns's Democratic opponent for the upcoming 2000 election and a farmer, chastised Burns for the comment as well, alleging that the comment may have led to Pakistan canceling a 300,000-metric-ton order of American wheat.

Schweitzer ran an aggressive, professional campaign against Burns in 2000 and appeared to be on the verge of defeating him. In fact, Burns's handlers told me later that on Election Day in 2000, they had gone to him before the polls had closed and told him to be prepared to lose. Exit polling that they'd conducted or seen indicated Schweitzer would eke out a close victory.

But the polling turned out to be wrong. Similar to his upset victory in 1988, Burns benefited from a strong showing in rural Montana, winning in forty-four of the state's fifty-six counties and holding his own or winning in a few cities, such as Bozeman, Kalispell and his hometown of Billings. He defeated Schweitzer by 13,500 votes out of 410,000 votes cast, a similar but slightly smaller margin than when he beat Melcher in 1988.

YET ONE OF HIS last foot-in-mouth episodes might have been the most damaging of all, likely playing a role in his 2006 loss to Democrat Jon Tester. This time, his comments had nothing to do with racism.

On July 23, 2006, Burns was in Billings's Logan Airport when he encountered members of an elite firefighting unit from Augusta, Virginia. They'd been battling a ninety-two-thousand-acre brush and forest fire near Billings and were awaiting a flight home. Burns had been in the area over the weekend and met with ranchers affected by the fire, some of whom weren't happy with the firefighting efforts.

Burns accosted the firefighters, who'd been working long hours and getting paid, at most, twelve dollars per hour and eighteen dollars per hour for overtime. He told them they'd done a "piss-poor job" fighting the fire and were "wasting a lot of money and creating a cottage industry." Somehow, U.S. Forest Service officials heard about the exchange quickly and called state Department of Natural Resources and Conservation public information official Paula Rosenthal to the airport to talk to Burns.

When she got there, Burns unloaded again, according to her report, saying, "See that guy over there? He hasn't done a God-damned thing. They sit around. I saw it up on the Wedge fire and in northwestern Montana some years ago. It's wasteful. You probably paid that guy $10,000 to sit around. It's gotta change."[61]

One of my colleagues at the time, Lee Newspapers State Bureau reporter Jennifer McKee, got her hands on Rosenthal's report and wrote it up in a July 27 story that appeared in all five of Lee's dailies, in Missoula, Billings, Helena, Butte and Hamilton.

But the story didn't end there. The Associated Press picked it up, and Internet bulletin boards for firefighters quickly filled up with comments blasting Burns. Once again, Burns had to apologize, saying that he wished he had "chosen my words more carefully" and that he should have directed his criticism at those in charge of managing the firefighting effort rather than at those trying to put out the fire.

Yet while Burns racked up press hits for putting his foot in his mouth, he also managed to fashion an impressive career and play a central role in a revival of the Republican Party in Montana. Democrats had controlled Montana politics for most of the 1970s and held the governor's office through 1988. But coinciding with the election of Burns, Republicans at least equaled the sway of Democrats in the state and stayed on that plane or higher until his defeat. He'd also brought some $2 billion worth of projects and other federal money to the state since getting elected and was one of the first senators to recognize the power and potential of the Internet.

Burns, who predicted the rise of the Internet, speaks with Microsoft cofounder Bill Gates. *National Association of Farm Broadcasters (NAFB)*.

In the early 1990s, not wanting to be known simply as an "ag guy," Burns started promoting telecom reforms that would expand broadband access before most people had any idea what it meant.

I wrote perhaps the first widely distributed story on this effort, as a reporter for the Associated Press in Helena. Burns was an early backer of a bill that would have required telephone companies to prepare a plan to build a nationwide broadband network by 2015, while removing a prohibition on telephone companies owning video programming and other services. I'm not sure I believed his predictions of a world where fiber-optic lines would bring the world to one's doorstep, but the opening to my January 1992 story on Burns's push reads like a prophecy of the future:

> *Doctor appointments without ever leaving your home. Cable TV provided by the telephone company. Rural students routinely tapping into libraries in major cities.*
>
> *Sound improbable? Not to U.S. Sen. Conrad Burns, R-Mont., who is pushing hard for a new bill that would mandate sweeping changes in the nation's telecommunications industry.*
>
> *In recent months, Burns has produced television ads promoting the bill, arranged a junket for Montana newspaper publishers leery of his plan and sent two of his aides on a lobbying trip across the state.*
>
> *He's also wooing educators, doctors and others with the promise of telecommunications development that could bring business and services to rural America.*

"If a state like…Montana can develop a superior broadband communications infrastructure, they will be in an excellent position to compete globally for new industry," he said in a Senate floor speech introducing the bill.

Consumer groups, newspapers and broadcasters fought the bill, saying it would set up telecoms as potential monopolists who could not only build the fiber-optic line that transmitted the information but also control the programming on it. Burns eventually withdrew his support for the bill, but he continued to promote the idea of advancing telecommunications as a way of bringing the world to rural America. He helped guide millions of dollars in earmarks and private donations, mostly to Montana State University, for research. In 1993, MSU established the Burns Technology Center, named after the senator, to develop and spread the concept of distance learning across the state and elsewhere. By the time Burns was gearing up for his final campaign, he would brag about federal money he'd brought to the state and how MSU had become a major center for technology and science research.

YET BY THE TIME of Burns's third try for reelection, something had happened that came to overshadow anything innovative or good the senator had ever done: the Jack Abramoff scandal.

Washington Post reporter Susan Schmidt, who would win a 2006 Pulitzer Prize for her work unearthing the scandal, wrote the first stories on Abramoff in early 2004, revealing that four Native American tribes in Michigan, Mississippi, California and Louisiana had paid Abramoff and his associates an astonishing $45 million over three years for lobbying services, when the tribes seemed to have few issues before Congress that demanded such expensive attention.

Burns's name in connection with the scandal didn't surface until March 2005, when Schmidt wrote about a $3 million federal grant from a program intended for impoverished Native American tribal schools. It had gone to one of the richest tribes in the country, the Saginaw Chippewas of Michigan, who also happened to be an Abramoff client.[62]

Schmidt reported that Burns, as chairman of the Senate subcommittee that oversaw the budget including the grant program, had pressed hard for the Chippewas to get the money, over the objection of Interior Department officials. She also noted that Abramoff, his associates and the tribes he represented had given $137,000 to Burns's political action committee and campaign since 2000 and that the Abramoff lobbying team had "strong connections to Burns' staff." The story said that Burns's then chief of staff, Will Brooke, and a subcommittee staffer under Burns had been treated to a trip to the 2001 Super Bowl in Florida, courtesy of a corporate jet leased by Abramoff.

A spokesman for Burns defended the senator's action on the grant by saying Burns had merely responded to requests from the Michigan delegation to secure the money for a Michigan tribe. The Saginaws, who wanted the money to build a new school, operated a large gambling casino north of Detroit and had enough money to pay each tribal member $70,000 per year from gambling profits.

One month later, as Capitol Bureau chief for the *Great Falls Tribune*, I wrote the first story by a Montana reporter toting up what Burns had received from Abramoff and his associates. Federal Election Commission records showed that Abramoff, two of his associates, his lobbying firm and five Native American tribes he represented had given $140,500 to Burns and his political action committee, Friends of the Big Sky, from 2001 to 2004. The money accounted for 30 percent of all donations to Burns's PAC in 2001–2 and 6 percent of its donations in 2003–4.

The five tribes also gave $13,000 to Burns's reelection campaign fund, making the Abramoff-related total giving to Burns $150,500, more than any other member of Congress had received. I also reported that Abramoff and company had given some money to the other members of Montana's Congressional delegation, but not nearly as much.[63]

Burns spokesman J.P. Donovan told me that it wasn't that big of a deal, as Abramoff and his buddies had "cast their money out on the waters," giving to many people, and Burns was just one of many. In the broader context, it wasn't that much money—one half of 1 percent of the $2.2 million Burns had raised for his campaign at that point. But he had taken in *more than any other member of Congress*, a distinction he would hear many times during the ensuing campaign.

By now, Montana reporters were paying attention to this story, but the national press continued to have the edge on breaking elements. In late November, the *Wall Street Journal*, quoting anonymous sources, said that Burns was part of the U.S. Justice Department investigation into Abramoff, who'd already been indicted. Donovan told the *Journal* that the Justice Department had not contacted Burns and that Burns had not hired a defense attorney. "We would be more than happy to help out in any investigation should we be asked," he told the *Journal*.[64]

Chuck Johnson, who by then was my boss at the Lee Newspapers State Bureau (which I joined in September 2005), wrote a story about the *Journal* story. The *Washington Post* also reported that Burns was among the few lawmakers involved in the Justice Department probe into Abramoff-related activities. Burn objected strenuously to the Montana press picking up national stories citing anonymous sources, saying we were violating our journalistic principles. He had a point, but it's hard to ignore a story on the front page of the *Wall Street Journal* or other prominent national papers.

Soon, however, our office began breaking its own stories on the scandal. My colleague, Jennifer McKee, who wrote most of the stories, told me years later that she and Chuck, who was also her boss, decided in the fall of 2005 that they were tired of getting beat on the Burns-Abramoff story by the national press and stepped up their game to look into some of the allegations themselves.

I joined the Lee Bureau right about that time, and although I didn't report these stories directly, Chuck Johnson, Jennifer and I spent many hours in our office across the street from the state capitol building, sharing in the discussion on how they would be reported and written.

In one of her first big stories on the Burns-Abramoff scandal, McKee reported on December 3, 2005, that in 2001, Burns had voted against an obscure bill that Abramoff had been hired to kill. He did so within a month after an Abramoff associate had donated $5,000 to Burns's Friends of the Big Sky PAC. The bill would have tightened regulation of garment manufacturers on the Northern Marianas Islands, a U.S. commonwealth. It was opposed by clothing manufacturers who had been accused of exploiting Chinese workers on the islands.

Burns had supported the bill (which died) a year earlier, but in May 2001, he voted against it and asked specifically that his vote be recorded in committee, instead of having an unrecorded voice vote. In speaking to McKee for the story, Burns said that he couldn't remember why he had voted one way and then another four years earlier but that he was sure it wasn't because of any donation to his PAC. He also said he didn't recall why he asked for the recorded committee vote.[65]

Four days later, Mary Clare Jalonick of the Associated Press in Washington, D.C., expanded on the story, reporting that Burns and his staff had met eight times with Abramoff's lobbying team and collected $12,000 in donations at about the time he voted in committee against the bill in 2001. The bill had passed the committee but never saw action on the Senate floor.

Jalonick said the AP had documented how more than four dozen lawmakers, from both parties, had taken actions favorable to Abramoff clients around the time they got big donations from the lobbyist and his clients. The same day Jalonick's story appeared in Montana newspapers, Burns, obviously feeling the heat, was in Kalispell, speaking to a TV reporter, when he said he wished that Abramoff had "never been born," that he was a "bad guy" and that Burns hoped he went to prison "and we never see him again."[66]

The stories now had become a form of Chinese water torture for Burns and his campaign. Although an individual story might have only a tidbit of new information, each story repeated and summarized all the previous scandal-related information that referred to Burns, cementing in the minds of the public a connection between Abramoff and Burns. It was a no-win situation for the senator, for once your political brand is sullied by scandal, it's darn difficult to scrub out the stain—even if you didn't do anything or very little wrong.

Within weeks, on January 3, 2006, another bombshell dropped: Abramoff decided to plead guilty to conspiracy, fraud and tax evasion and agreed to help federal prosecutors with their investigation. Burns issued a statement blasting Abramoff as a liar and a thief and repeated a pledge that he and his office would fully cooperate with federal investigators.

Burns officially launched his reelection campaign a few days later and sat down with McKee, Chuck Johnson and me for an interview on January 9 as part of his campaign launch. We met in a windowless basement conference room in the building that housed our office, with Burns's campaign manager, Helena attorney Mark Baker, sitting in. One of the first things we asked him about were the Abramoff allegations, which he said were based on "half-truths and innuendo." He then ripped into us for repeating the *Wall Street Journal* and *Washington Post* reports about the investigation, based on anonymous sources.

"Until I am or am not [charged], what makes it a story?" he asked. "Just [my] opponents. You take the word of one opponent and you know it's all a bunch of garbage. It's not what you throw against the barn door, it's what sticks….The Democrats said they were going to run a smear campaign and they're doing it." Burns, seventy at the time, added that he'd never been more energized for an election battle than now: "Take it to the bank. Make book on it."

During the interview, he directed many of his critical comments at McKee, who had been writing most of the stories about the Abramoff scandal. Late in the interview, as we talked issues other than Abramoff, we asked Burns about his support for the war in Iraq. Burns said it was important for the United States to maintain a position of influence in the Middle East and spread American values in Arabic countries, where, he said—and pointed his finger at McKee—"women like you are treated like *chattel!*"[67]

This remark didn't make into the story that McKee wrote that day, but we laughed about it later, wondering what prompted Burns to say what he said and the way he said it. Did he think he was sticking up for women? Was he telling Jennifer that she should feel lucky to live in America and that he was protecting her, and she should be more appreciative, rather than writing all of those mean stories? We'll never know.

THE SCANDAL UNLEASHED ITS full fury two months later, in the form of the devastating *Vanity Fair* article in which Abramoff spoke freely about his associations with various lawmakers and political figures, specifically fingering Burns as someone he'd influenced and telling the magazine that "every appropriation we wanted, we got" from the subcommittee that Burns had chaired.

Burns's office tried to deflect the damage, first by calling Abramoff a "pathological liar" and then by giving a tortured explanation of how Abramoff's allegations couldn't be true because only senators, not lobbyists, can submit requests to a committee and therefore his entire quote was circumspect. As Montana State University political scientist Jerry Calvert told the *Great Falls Tribune* upon hearing that logic, "That's pretty nuanced."

Stories on the *Vanity Fair* article made the front page of every major newspaper in Montana. Some ran an Associated Press story out of Washington. The *Great Falls Tribune* did its own story, and Jennifer McKee did a story for our papers, not only reporting on the *Vanity Fair* revelations but also recounting her own extensive catalogue of stories on the links among Burns, his staff and Abramoff's lobbying firm and clients.

Burns and his reelection race had become the story we talked about every day in the bureau's morning news meetings. Chuck, Jennifer McKee and I all had our individual beats and other races to watch that 2006 election year, but the Burns race, with its national implications, had become *the* story, and we treated it as such, with each of us ready to step in and cover whatever aspect needed covering. We not only had the Abramoff scandal hanging over

Abramoff says he got 'every appropriation we wanted'

Coverage of the damning March 2006 *Vanity Fair* article on Burns's connection with disgraced lobbyist Jack Abramoff. *From the* Great Falls Tribune.

the race like a twisted vulture, but also the fact that party control of the U.S. Senate hung in the balance. The Burns race might be the one that decided whether Democrats seized control from Republicans. Having all three of us on the story also allowed us to play "good cop, bad cop," substituting in one reporter when the other might have fallen out of favor with the subject to be covered. As far as Burns and his campaign were concerned, McKee pretty much had claimed the "bad cop" moniker for life. So, when it came time to travel with Burns for campaign coverage, that job fell first to me, in late April, when Burns was contested in the primary.

On-the-road coverage was a tradition among Montana's leading political reporters, who often spent a day on the campaign trail with the major candidates in the biggest statewide races. Everything was on the record, and the stories gave us an unvarnished look at the candidate and his or her persona.

I joined Burns in Billings, his home turf, where he attended a cable TV exposition and a few other events before driving north some 125 miles to Lewistown, where he was to attend a fundraiser for a local shooting range. For most of the trip, I sat in the front seat of Burns's pickup truck while he drove, and his campaign spokesman, Jason Klindt, sat in the rear seat of the extended cab. I filed my story for our Sunday papers on May 6:

> Roundup As Conrad Burns hurtles along U.S. Highway 87 in a Chevy Silverado at 80 mph, he makes a grand gesture toward the miles of unbroken prairie south of here.
>
> "I'm a man of this land," says the three-term U.S. senator from Montana. "We are in my element right now. These people need the shot."
>
> The "shot," in his words, is the policy—and the money—that he can bring to bear for rural America.
>
> As Burns campaigns for his fourth consecutive term as Montana's junior senator, he says this role is his reason for pressing on at age 71.
>
> "I want to get some things done that I've started," he says, mentioning huge rural water projects in eastern Montana and other economic boosts for

the state. "I started it, and I want to finish it. I could've retired, but this state is really important to me."

Yet Burns, the only Republican to win re-election as U.S. senator in Montana, is facing a rocky road in his bid for another term.

Democrats and the media have been relentless in reminding Montanans that Burns is a figure in the Jack Abramoff lobbying scandal, possibly under investigation by the U.S. Justice Department. From 2001–2003, Burns received more campaign money than any other member of Congress from Abramoff, his associates and lobbying clients.

Burns has adamantly denied any wrongdoing, says he doesn't know Abramoff, and says he is returning that $150,000 or giving it to charity....

He's also one of Congress' staunchest supporters of President Bush, whose popularity is flagging nationwide. From the Iraq war to Social Security privatization to health care, Burns seldom strays from the Bush view of the world.

Those few paragraphs, for me, captured Burns and all his warts, from his down-home charm, determination and attachment and dedication to rural Montana to his ego, stubbornness and embrace of a conservative, corporate agenda.

While Burns got a kind reception just about everywhere he went that day, you could sense that, for the first time in a long time, he was swimming upstream in an electoral battle. At the Lewistown shooting

Conrad Burns visiting the Grace Treatment Home in Great Falls during his 2006 reelection campaign. *Robin Loznak,* Great Falls Tribune.

range fundraiser, for which he'd taken a 250-mile trip to speak, the president of the shooting range's board told Klindt that Burns could speak for "three to five minutes" at the very end of the banquet. The applause seemed polite rather than enthusiastic. Burns's campaign workers stood in the banquet entryway, handing out blue "Conrad Burns" stickers to people as they came in the door. Many accepted, but more than a few declined. As we drove back to Billings that evening, Burns said some were suggesting he should pull out of the race because he couldn't win. "I'm not backing out of this race," he told me. "There's just no reverse in my transmission. I'm sorry."

Burns easily won the June primary election, setting up a fall showdown with Democrat Jon Tester, a farmer and state senator who won something of an upset victory in the Democratic primary.[68] Mere hours after the primary elections had been called, Burns and his campaign came out swinging, calling Tester an "unabashed liberal" who would be more comfortable as a senator representing New York or Massachusetts.

Burns also did something that no incumbent who felt comfortable would do. he immediately agreed to a pair of debates with Tester and asked for more. Burns knew that he was not starting from a position of strength. One could even have said the race was Tester's to lose, but knocking off an incumbent is never easy. Polls consistently showed Tester with a lead, sometimes by as much as eleven points, but every reporter covering the race knew it would be close. A poll two weeks before the November 7 election had Tester leading, 46 percent to 43 percent, and our newspapers' own poll, taken just days before the election, showed the race as a dead heat, with Burns and Tester each polling at 47 percent.

While Tester seemed to have the upper hand for most of the race, you could feel a tiny momentum shift back the other way that final week. Were Montanans really ready to send another Democrat to Washington, D.C., and turn out their affable, wisecracking farm boy, just because the eastern snobs thought he might have treaded a bit too closely to ethical boundaries? National Republicans must have seen something in the polls, too, because, after all but abandoning Burns for the final months of the campaign, they jumped back into the fray in a big way.

The National Republican Senatorial Committee, which hadn't bought a TV ad in Montana for twelve weeks, opened its pocketbook for $310,000 worth of TV ads the last week, and President Bush and Vice President Dick Cheney scheduled campaign stops in Montana that final week to talk up their man in Montana.

Burns, Tester go head to head

By GWEN FLORIO
Tribune Capitol Bureau

WHITEFISH — They agreed on a couple of things — no amnesty for illegal immigrants, for instance — mangled a few words, accidentally contradicted themselves as well as one another.

Republican U.S. Sen. Conrad Burns and his Democratic challenger, state Sen. Jon Tester, featured clear and sharply worded ideological differences that will be repeated and refined through Nov. 7 in one of the most closely watched races in the country. The loss of

"If we cut and run ... we'll end up like Vietnam."

"The war in Iraq is not fighting the war on terror."

U.S. Sen. Conrad Burns

State Sen. Jon Tester

federal spending.

"Win," said Burns, in response to moderator Greg MacDonald's question about what the strategy should be in Iraq.

"There's no substitute for winning, and we are. But it'll be a long, long pull."

Tester, on the other hand,

saying that "if we cut and run ... we'll end up like Vietnam." U.S. involvement in that country lasted a decade, with 58,000 Americans killed, before ending in 1973; the United States is now Vietnam's largest trading partner.

Burns held up the differ-

Great Falls Tribune headline on summer 2006 debate between Burns and Democratic challenger Jon Tester.

On the day of the election, I was at the Great Falls hotel where Tester held his election-night party. Tester clung to a narrow lead for much of the night, but the race wasn't called until the next morning, as we waited for votes to be counted in a few key counties. He ended up beating Burns by a mere 3,500 votes—and became the Democrat whose victory gave his party a 51-49 majority in the Senate. A photograph of Burns that ran the next day in papers across the state said it all: Burns, briefcase in hand and grimace on his face as he departed the Billings hotel where his election-day party had been held, pointedly ignoring Montana Public Radio reporter Hope Stockwell as she walked beside him, extending a microphone.

When he did talk to reporters after the election, he chastised them. In Washington, D.C., he told a group of reporters that they'd been dishonest and that they should go read the 109th Psalm in the Bible. They did, and the AP reported the Psalm's opening passage in its story that day: "Hold not thy peace, O God of my praise; for the mouth of the wicked and the mouth of the deceitful are opened against me: They have spoken against me with a lying tongue." If we had any doubt about how Burns felt about the press, the Bible itself had settled it.[69]

Burns made sure that we in Montana knew how he felt too. During the 2007 Montana legislature, which started the following January, I was working in the office on a Saturday with Chuck Johnson when I heard what I thought was a familiar voice coming in the door. There was Burns, who sat down in a chair opposite Chuck's desk. We shook hands and I sat down next to him, expecting some reminiscing and perhaps a chat about what Burns might be up to.

But Burns had come by primarily to harangue us and the media in general for our coverage of the 2006 campaign. He asked if we had any ethical standards at all, said the Republican Party was the party of Abraham Lincoln and asked how the media could suggest that Republicans didn't like black people or had anything to do with racism (I didn't recall that we had). I left after a few minutes, but Chuck told me later Burns had remained for almost an hour, complaining about how the press had screwed him. It wasn't the last time he would come by our office to deliver similar soliloquies. Sometimes he'd just telephone and tell us directly what he thought about us, and it wasn't complimentary.

YET FOR ALL THE times that Burns acted less than admirably, I knew he could be a fine person—and nothing spoke to that more than what he did for Cass Chinske more than two decades earlier, when there was nothing in it for Burns other than simply being loyal to a friend.

I knew plenty about Chinske's tangle with the feds over marijuana before I ever learned what Burns did for him. In 1991, when I worked for the Associated Press in Helena, I did a story on how the U.S. Drug Enforcement Administration and federal prosecutors had gone on a tear against marijuana growers in western Montana. Chinske had yet to be arrested, but his name had been mentioned as a possible suspect. Toward the end of my interview with the head DEA agent for Montana, he bragged about how they'd arrested a slew of pot growers and then blurted out something that shocked and shook me: "And that Cass Chinske? We're going to bust that guy, too. We're taking that guy down."[70]

I half-expected him to say, seconds later, that his comment was off the record or that I couldn't report that information. But he didn't. The silence in our conversation hung there for a moment or two. I felt a little bit threatened and a little bit scared. He knew I knew of Chinske, a former city councilman and prominent environmentalist. By telling me, a reporter, this information, I felt like he was almost daring me to report it or tip off Chinske on what was going to happen—which, of course, might be interpreted as abetting him.

Yet I doubt Chinske needed me or any other reporter to tell him the feds were out to get him, as they'd already busted a bunch of growers in Missoula and Chinske was growing marijuana in the basement of his house. He knew people were being pressured to finger him. They arrested him in mid-1991, and Chinske did something that few federal drug defendants do: he refused to cooperate, to turn on others, to get a better deal. He pleaded guilty, but that was it. Soon, he was headed off to federal prison.

Within twenty-four hours of getting arrested, Chinske says he got a call from Washington, D.C. It was Burns. "He said, 'You're in a lot of trouble, because I made some calls,'" Chinske told me in an interview some twenty-two years later. "He said, 'I'm worried about you, and I'm going to be in Missoula in a few days, and I want to have breakfast with you.'"[71]

Burns met Chinske for breakfast, alone, at a hotel in downtown Missoula. He told Chinske he didn't want to see him go to prison, but Chinske told him it was inevitable. Burns asked what he could do. Chinske told Burns that if he could do anything, it would be to somehow stop the feds from confiscating his house, which he had built himself and hadn't been financed by drug money. Prosecutors had already seized it, arguing that it was part of the drug operation. Burns ultimately helped arrange a deal so Chinske could buy his home back from the feds with what money he had left before he was sent to

Cass Chinske in front of his Missoula home, which was saved from seizure in part with Burns's help after Chinske's 1991 drug arrest. *Mike Dennison.*

prison. "I can't tell you how ultimately important it was for me, to have my reintroduction into society and have my home to come back to," he said.

Burns's help didn't stop there. Chinske thought he had an agreement to be sent to a low-security prison in Oxford, Wisconsin, so he could be near his sister, who was dying of cancer, but federal marshals arranged to send him to a high-security federal prison in Englewood, Colorado. "I told my probation officer, 'This is going to be turned around tomorrow; you're not going to fuck with a judge's order,'" he told me. "The next morning, my orders were cut to go to where I was supposed to go."

He went to the Wisconsin prison, but several weeks later, he was dragged out of his cell in the middle of the night, shackled and sent to Terre Haute, Indiana, where he was strip-searched and put in a maximum-security cell. Within hours, he was flown to an even higher-security prison in El Reno, Oklahoma. His only way of communication with the outside world was a collect telephone call, and Chinske said it was six or seven weeks before he even felt safe enough to try to leave his cell to make a telephone call. He called collect to Burns's office in Missoula, where a staffer took the call only because she recognized his voice. He told her what had happened. Within twenty-four hours, he was on an airplane, heading back to Wisconsin.

Chinske's sister died while he was in prison, in May 1992. An hour after her death, Chinske said he was called into the office of the warden, who handed him a thirty-six-hour pass to go to his sister's funeral. "[Burns] did those kind of things for me," Chinske said. "He never forgot our friendship."

Chinske first told me parts of this story in 1996. I had called him for a piece I was researching on Democratic U.S. Senator Max Baucus because I knew Chinske had been one of the first people to support Baucus in the 1970s. Chinske told me that when he got arrested, he never got a call or any help from any powerful Democrat—not Baucus or anyone else—and that the only person who offered to help was Burns.

"We were kindred spirits," Chinske said of Burns, years afterward. "I'm on the pro-environmental side, he's on the con side, and we both got big mouths. He sent my family and me a Christmas card. And he said, if you have anything you need, you can always call. He never forgot."

THE LOYALTY AND AFFECTION that Burns's friends and allies felt for him was front and center the last time that I reported on him, in person, at a tribute at the state Republican Party annual convention in Billings in June 2010.

Burns had suffered a stroke just seven months earlier and walked with a limp, but he hadn't lost much in the way of political pointedness or humor. "We can't let the government take over this great health-care system," he said, complimenting his physical therapist who helped him recover from the stroke and dissing President Barack Obama's Affordable Care Act, which had passed three months earlier. "It works because you've got great people with heart, and I've never seen a compassionate bureaucracy."[72]

Dwight MacKay, who had served with Burns on the Yellowstone County Commission in the 1980s and later became one of his top staffers, said that Burns had always said, "If you can't have fun doing something, then don't do it," and that every day with Burns was nothing if not fun.

Finally, Burns stood to address the crowd. He told how, in the early 1980s, he had been part of a horse team that was to escort then-president Ronald Reagan into Billings and that he'd been waiting for more than an hour when Reagan's presidential limousine pulled up. Reagan got out, walked up to Burns and said, "Hi, I'm Ronald Reagan."

"I said, 'No shit,'" Burns told the crowd. "He looked around and he said, 'Boys, we *are* in Montana.'"

But his story wasn't finished. Several years later, Burns had traveled to Washington, D.C., and went to the White House as part of a group of local officials meeting with Reagan. Burns said he waited in the West Wing for a while and then was ushered into the Oval Office.

"I said, 'Mr. President, I'm Conrad Burns,'" he recalled. "And Reagan said, 'No shit.'"

Chapter 5

BRIAN SCHWEITZER

Montana's Dynamic Democrat

As Brian Schweitzer rode shotgun in a 4x4 pickup on a highway between Helena and Bozeman, Montana, while campaigning for governor in 2004, I leaned forward from the back seat of the cab to ask why he—a farmer, a gun lover, a businessman—had chosen to be a Democrat.

"I've always figured that I'm for the little guy," he said. "Everybody ought to have a fair shake, and if they're not getting a fair shake, I'm going to get them one."[73] Then he told me when he was a kid at school, he couldn't stand it when he saw bullies picking on weaker kids and that he'd sometimes be the one sticking up for the bullied on the playground.

I'd often recall this story as I heard Schweitzer's critics malign him as the very thing he said he despised—a "bully" who liked shouting down and humiliating his foes—and as I witnessed Schweitzer sometimes bear out those critics, employing a take-no-prisoners approach to getting his way and punishing his political enemies.

During that same truck ride in October 2004 during his first gubernatorial run, Schweitzer also talked about how he had "a skill of bringing people together" and that he'd use that skill as governor to advance the state. "I'm a good communicator," he told me. He had the "communicator" part down cold. He wasn't just good—he was great, and he would use that skill and an uncanny political sense to become one of the most popular and successful politicians in Montana's recent history.

Brian Schweitzer on a radio talk show during his 2000 run for the U.S. Senate. *Stu White, Great Falls Tribune.*

But while he could and did fashion some bipartisan victories—he had to, as Republicans controlled the legislature for most of his governorship—he could be a divisive political figure as well. He reveled in skewering the opposition and squashing anything or anyone who might challenge him or steer the political spotlight away from him (including some in his own party).

This penchant for political theater and needling his opponents reached its zenith during the 2011 Montana legislature, when he vetoed forty-four bills, all but two sponsored by Republican lawmakers. He didn't just veto the bills with a pen—he made a special branding iron forming the word *VETO* and literally branded replicas of many of the bills, setting them ablaze on the capitol lawn in full view of a stable of TV cameras and turning the spectacle into a national story.

Clever, brash, boastful, calculating, self-centered, charming, shrewd and relentlessly entertaining—any and all of these adjectives would apply to Schweitzer on almost any given day. He ran against and almost beat sitting U.S. Senator Conrad Burns in his first campaign in 2000 and was treated by the national media as a potential presidential candidate fourteen years later, until the wheels came off with some cringe-worthy comments referencing gays and prostitutes. In between, he served eight years as governor.

It was hard not to admire Schweitzer's innate flare for political showmanship, his rhetorical skill and a sharp mind that could master the details of complex policy and then spit them out for the TV cameras without missing a beat. It was also hard to resist the sheer personality of Schweitzer, who would usher reporters into his capitol office at a moment's notice and share a knowing laugh (often at someone else's expense). Or he might just call you up on the phone, out of the blue, to shoot the breeze about what you'd covered that day or the day before, announcing himself on the phone with, "Hey, it's Brian," or, later on in his term as governor, not even saying his name. He'd just launch into a monologue the moment you answered the phone, knowing that within seconds you'd know who it was. He'd take you into his confidence, and it could be flattering.

Schweitzer rarely faced critical press in Montana and had many national reporters in thrall as well, producing a steady diet of mostly positive stories about whatever he chose to talk about it. Yet the apparent political end for Schweitzer came at the hands of the media in June 2014, when the former governor spoke a little too freely to the wrong reporter. He compared a U.S. senator (California's Dianne Feinstein) to a streetwalker and said then U.S. House Majority Leader Eric Cantor and southern men seemed "effeminate" and that Cantor had set off Schweitzer's personal "gaydar." The comments appeared first in a lengthy feature article in the *National Journal*, a respected D.C.-based magazine on national politics, then went viral on the Internet and made front-page headlines across Montana—not in a positive way.

SCHWEITZER IS THE RARE political superstar who came out of nowhere, bursting onto the scene in early 1999 with a political stunt that had many of us in the Montana press corps dismissing him as a rookie grasping for attention.

He announced his challenge to two-term U.S. Senator Conrad Burns by dumping $47,000 in cash onto a table in the capitol rotunda and then holding a news conference, saying the cash represented all the money Burns had accepted from tobacco-company lobbyists. Some in the press corps dutifully covered it and left the event wondering, "Who is this guy?"

Schweitzer was a mint farmer from Whitefish, in northwestern Montana's Flathead Valley. His only experience with anything remotely political had been a 1993 appointment to the three-person Farm Services Agency state committee, which oversaw the $300 million annual budget of federal farm subsidies in Montana. It was a low-level presidential appointment, and he'd been recommended for the post by Democratic U.S. Senator Max Baucus. Schweitzer had never run for political office until the Senate bid. He was forty-three years old.

Although the tobacco money toss somewhat underwhelmed, Schweitzer made a bigger mark with another series of political stunts on a real issue: the high price of prescription drugs in the United States. Schweitzer, with the help of his parents, organized a series of bus trips from Montana to Canadian pharmacies in the fall of 1999. The buses carried scores of Montana senior citizens, who, when they arrived at the predetermined Canadian drugstore, bought their prescription drugs at much lower prices than they paid at Montana pharmacies.

I climbed on the first Schweitzer bus ride, from Great Falls to Milk River, Alberta, as a reporter for the *Great Falls Tribune*. Some forty senior citizens joined Schweitzer; his brother Mike, an anesthesiologist; and his parents for the 135-mile trip to the small agricultural town just across the U.S.-Canadian border. It made headlines in every major newspaper in the state, including the *Tribune*, which ran my lengthy story with photographs.

One woman told me she paid about ten dollars for a three-month supply of the diabetes drug Glucophage, which would cost her ninety-three dollars in Montana. Schweitzer used the trip to call on Congress to take what he said should be an obvious solution, to remove the restriction on importing prescription drugs from where prices are cheaper, like Canada and Mexico.

A week later, I wrote that Schweitzer had seized an issue with the potential to propel this rookie candidate to prominence:

> *Schweitzer, a Democrat, is the little-known challenger to U.S. Sen. Conrad Burns, R-Mont. He may be a political neophyte and a long shot to unseat Burns, but it looks like he's found one issue that has some serious political legs.*
>
> *"With one busload of senior citizens, we've already done more for the communities of Montana than all of Congress has done in the last six years," he said. "This is about Montanans pulling together and solving the problem here in Montana."*
>
> *For his part, Burns said through a spokesman that the issue is "something that we're going to look into."*[74]

Schweitzer's approach to the prescription drug issue had all the elements that would become his hallmark: the populist tackling big industry on behalf of the ripped-off little guy, with an easy, doable solution that stalled only

Schweitzer points to a prescription drug price chart during his 2000 campaign for U.S. Senate. *Stu White, Great Falls Tribune.*

because evil corporations (and their political handmaidens) had blocked it. Schweitzer saw himself as a crusader and clearly loved the role.

Some of Schweitzer's crusades succeeded, some didn't—but on this one, he nearly rode it all the way to the U.S. Senate.

In May 2000, a state newspaper poll showed Burns with a twenty-four-point lead over Schweitzer. By the final week of October, Schweitzer had made it a dead heat. On the day of the election, Burns's handlers told him late in the day to be prepared to lose because exit polls had indicated Schweitzer would win a narrow victory.

Those polls turned out to be wrong. Lifted by a late run of votes from rural counties, Burns won the day, defeating Schweitzer by 13,652 votes out of about 411,600 that were cast, 51 percent to 47 percent. Burns no doubt benefited from a Republican wave in Montana in the major races that day. George W. Bush beat Al Gore in the presidential race in Montana by twenty-five points, and Republicans won the open governorship and U.S. House seat.

Schweitzer, however, didn't seem cowed by the loss. He told our paper that "Don Quixote" may ride again some day—and clearly wasn't ruling out a political future.

At the state Democratic Party Convention in Butte the next year, Schweitzer recalled a conversation he had after the 2000 election with a man who didn't vote for one Democrat. "He said, 'Your party is not pro-family,'" Schweitzer told convention-goers. "He said, 'Your party is trying to take away my job.' And he said, 'Your party wants to take away my guns.'"[75]

Schweitzer had hit precisely on the Achilles heels of Democrats in Montana: they were seen as the party that favored abortion and a secular society ("not pro-family"), that backed environmental policies that threatened mining, timber and other natural resource jobs ("take away my job") and that wasn't strong enough on gun rights, a sacred issue for many in the state.

He would spend the rest of his career trying to undo or overcome these perceptions about his chosen party. On energy and the environment, Schweitzer stood up for regulation and renewable energy but openly feuded with mainline environmental groups to establish his pro–natural resource industry cred. He would appear in campaign ads toting his hunting rifle or firing any of a multitude of firearms. And on the "anti-family" tag, he wouldn't change the party's stance on abortion or private religious schools, but he would try to turn the tables on that argument, urging Democrats to paint Republicans as the true anti-family party.

He called the GOP servants of tobacco, big energy and drug makers, saying that Republicans stood by these industries' efforts to rip off or addict America. "What is pro-family about these tobacco companies reaching out and trying to get your kids and my kids to light up for the rest of their lives?" he said during the 2001 speech in Butte.

It soon became clear that Schweitzer had his eye on the governor's race in 2004, and by mid-2003, he had declared himself in. The current Republican governor, Judy Martz, had suffered a remarkable run of political bad luck and was deeply unpopular. She announced in August 2003 that she wouldn't run for reelection. Republicans chose Secretary of State Bob Brown as their nominee.

I traveled with Schweitzer during the campaign as a *Tribune* reporter for our "on the road" profile pieces on major candidates and both times saw the Schweitzer we had come to know in the 2000 Senate race: gregarious, engaged and relentlessly energetic. On our trip in late September, I joined him shortly after 8:00 a.m. at the state two-year vocational-technical college in Helena. He told me later he'd already been up for almost four hours. He said he got out of bed at 4:15 a.m. to read the day's news and quickly ticked off the times that each major paper would begin to post its stories for the day on their websites. He campaigned relentlessly, as portrayed in my story:

> *At a highway construction stop on U.S. 287, something catches the eye of Democratic gubernatorial candidate Brian Schweitzer.*
>
> *"Look, there's a Schweitzer sticker on that truck," he says, pointing to the pickup stopped in front of his own truck near Toston.*
>
> *Schweitzer bounds out of his passenger seat, runs to the pickup and reaches into the cab to shake hands with a man and woman he's never met.*
>
> *As traffic resumes, Schweitzer climbs back into the cab—but not before a good-natured exchange with the construction flagman, who says Schweitzer just lost a vote because he didn't shake his hand, too.*

But on that trip, I also got into an unexpected argument with Schweitzer. For on-the-road coverage, reporters want a day that gives us time to do some interviewing as we drive, and that presents multiple opportunities to see the candidate actually campaigning. Everything is on the record.

Our day began in Helena and continued in Bozeman, where it was scheduled to end with an evening fundraiser at a private home. Yet following an afternoon meeting with Montana State University officials, I heard Schweitzer telling his driver how they would arrange for someone else to take me back to Helena before the fundraiser. I told Schweitzer I wasn't going back to Helena because I was going with him to the fundraiser.

"No you're not," Schweitzer said. "That wasn't part of the arrangement."

"Oh, yes it was," I replied. "The deal is that I spend the entire day with you, including the fundraiser." Schweitzer continued to insist otherwise and didn't relent until I told him that if he wouldn't let me go to the fundraiser, I would make that refusal a big part of the story.

The fundraiser was at the home of a prominent, wealthy environmentalist outside Bozeman—and would be attended by scores of environmental activists. Schweitzer did not want me witnessing him sucking up to a roomful of environmentalists, who would be expecting him to make a speech about his environmental stands and credentials. He told me that he'd be making some statements that played to the crowd but that he didn't want to be portrayed as a wild-eyed environmentalist. I told him if I reported any of his comments at the fundraiser, I would do so accurately and in the proper context.

He gave the environmentalists what they wanted—he said he was a "hell no" against oil and gas development on the Rocky Mountain Front, a wild

Schweitzer picks up some seed in Townsend, Montana, while campaigning for governor, 2004. *Mike Dennison,* Great Falls Tribune.

and scenic area in northwest Montana—but he also said he saw the need to develop coal and natural gas in the state. When someone asked him where environmental protection ranked among his priorities, Schweitzer said people told him on the campaign trail that jobs, education and healthcare are their top priorities, while conservation issues usually rank a bit lower. He also spoke to almost everyone in the room and raised $6,000 at the event.

As we rode home to Helena in the dark that night, Schweitzer sounded as confident as ever, but he knew the race was a long way from being over. "We're in the seventh-inning stretch," he said. "There's a lot of balls to be batted and a lot of balls to be pitched. We'll find out in the ninth or 10th inning."[76]

Republicans, who had controlled the Montana governorship since 1989, threw every piece of mud they could muster at the genial Schweitzer. He pitched it right back, however, and in the end prevailed. While President George W. Bush shellacked Democratic challenger John Kerry in Montana and the state's GOP congressman, Denny Rehberg, cruised to victory, Schweitzer scratched out a victory of his own. He won with 50.5 percent of the vote to Brown's 46 percent; third-party candidates accounted for the final 3.5 percent. Schweitzer would be the first Democratic governor in Montana in sixteen years—and hold the first public office of his life.

Schweitzer told me years later that Martz wouldn't allow him or his people any office space in the capitol during the transition and that he didn't set foot in the governor's office until after he was inaugurated on January 3, 2005. When he walked into the governor's corner office, he said the office key was sitting on a table.

"I held up the key and threw it in the garbage, and said, 'That door will never be closed while I'm governor,'" he said.[77]

MONTANA DEMOCRATS ALSO WON a majority in the state Senate that election—the only outright majority they've won in a legislative house in Montana since 1992—but could do no better than a 50-50 tie in the Montana House. To get any part of his agenda through the legislature, Schweitzer had to peel off at least one Republican in the House, and he set about trying to do just that, to the great irritation of GOP leaders, who already were smarting from being out of power for the first time in a decade.

Schweitzer would invite a select few Republican legislators into his office to talk from time to time or over to his state "mansion" (a large but soulless '70s-style house two blocks from the capitol in Helena) for social occasions. He even took them on the governor's state airplane when he flew from Helena to their district for some type of official event. GOP leaders accused Schweitzer of "working behind our backs" to cut deals. Schweitzer would just laugh when asked about his lobbying efforts and say, in so many words, why wouldn't I do what I'm doing?

The battle came to a head on the House floor in mid-April when Democrats prepared to ram through three key measures on Schweitzer's and the Democrats' agenda: a freeze of business property tax rates (stopping a potential cut to zero), a bill mandating that utilities buy a minimum amount of renewable power such as wind or solar and a measure to encourage ethanol production in Montana. Each one passed by razor-thin margins—including the tax freeze bill, which sneaked through on a 51-49 vote, with one Republican joining all 50 Democrats to move it forward.

Republicans were beside themselves. Their floor leader, Mike Lange, a Republican and union member from Billings, called the wind power mandate an "abomination" during the floor debate and said he wanted to "kick it right in the governor's teeth with [the wind bill]....So vote no." It passed 54-46.[78]

It also didn't take long for the GOP to start complaining that Schweitzer was a "bully"—an accusation that, at first, seemed mostly ironic, for Republicans in Montana had long practiced their own brand of muscle-bound, wedge-issue politics to get their way and build legislative majorities. Yet the more we came to know and observe Schweitzer the more this particular label appeared to have some truth to it.

House Republican leader Roy Brown, a Billings oilman who would later run against Schweitzer for governor in 2008, said halfway through the 2005 legislature that the governor would threaten to personally campaign against freshman Republican legislators if they didn't back some of his key proposals. "I've never heard of a governor who used the bully pulpit of his office to do that kind of thing to an individual freshman legislator," Brown told a reporter. "It's just not proper."[79]

GOP legislative leaders demanded a meeting with the governor, and he agreed—while also inviting the press to sit in. Once everyone shuffled into the governor's office in the east wing of the capitol, Schweitzer proceeded to lecture the half dozen Republican leaders for twenty-five straight minutes, without letting any of them utter a single word. He then terminated the meeting by thanking them and saying, "I appreciate the opportunity. I have a meeting at eight o'clock. We'll see you later."

State Senator Bob Keenan of Bigfork, a Republican who had been Senate president before Democrats won the majority in 2004 and was now Senate minority leader, said Schweitzer had subjected them to "a 10-year-old temper tantrum."

Schweitzer, interviewed later by Lee Newspapers State Bureau chief Chuck Johnson, feigned surprise at the Republicans' anger. "They all just sat there," he said. "I don't know why they didn't step in with anything."[80]

A few weeks earlier, Keenan also took a shot at Schweitzer that the governor considered personal, although it was a legitimate point to raise: why did the governor allow his brother Walter to work as an unpaid "volunteer" in the governor's office, using a state telephone and appearing to conduct official business for the governor?

Keenan confronted Schweitzer about his brother during a meeting when reporters were present, saying it raised questions about nepotism and the appearance of impropriety. Schweitzer, clearly annoyed, said his brother wasn't getting paid and cut Keenan off, ending curtly with, "We'll look into it. Thank you."[81]

THE STORY OF WALTER Schweitzer, however, didn't go away. Walter and his wife, Cindy Palmer, and their two daughters had moved from north-central Montana to Helena after Brian was elected, living in a house not far from the capitol and the governor's mansion. Walter had worked on his brother's campaign and now showed up at a lot of key meetings as an apparent representative of the governor—without being on the payroll.

I left the *Tribune* Capitol Bureau in September 2005 to join the Lee Newspapers State Bureau, and one of the first stories that my new colleagues, Chuck Johnson and Jennifer McKee, talked about was a piece on Walter Schweitzer and his role in the administration. The *Missoula Independent*, a weekly paper, beat us on the story, but *Independent* writer John Adams relied mostly on unnamed sources, and the governor's brother wouldn't talk to him.

Still, we thought the story should be told in the mainstream press and suspected that Walter couldn't get away with not talking to reporters who wrote for the biggest daily papers in the state. As we began work on the story, we heard talk about Walter being a "heavy" for his brother and the administration, doing the dirty work of telling people they were fired or ostracized in some way. Yet as we checked out these rumors of political retribution and roughhousing, the culprit often turned out not to be Walter but the governor himself dealing out political punishment or pain to his perceived enemies. When I interviewed the governor for the story on December 6, 2006, I asked him about these accusations.

Schweitzer became both defensive and dismissive, saying he wasn't the usual Democrat who just rolled over in the face of political opposition and that people who called him a bully or heavy-handed were just upset that they couldn't get their way anymore. "There seems to be no shortage of people criticizing me," he said. "I've been governor for two years; I'll be governor for two more. I have an activist agenda. The clock is ticking. I'm not here to just spin the wheels and go through the motions. I have a lot to accomplish."

He said critics and political enemies were just looking for an angle to undermine him publicly and that labeling him a bully or a bad person was one of those angles. "When people tell lies or tell untrue things, or spread untrue things to third parties, there's really not a lot we can talk about," the governor told me. "I don't want to engage them if they're going to do that."

Those comments didn't make it into our story on Walter, which ran in our papers four days later. We felt the story should focus mostly on the governor's brother. The story relied on a few unnamed sources, but most spoke on the record, as Democrats and Republicans frankly discussed Walter's role as adviser to his brother. Walter spoke to us, too, agreeing to an interview at our office across the street from the capitol. He was funny, charming and rarely ducked a question:

> *Walter said there's no mystery about his political work or his political desires: He wants his brother to succeed as governor and believes Gov. Schweitzer's agenda is good for the state.*
> *"Basically, Brian's interests and mine parallel, and that* [interest] *is Montana," he said. "My accountability is whether or not he's successful."*

The governor told us Walter "doesn't have a role in my administration" and was there mainly to help with his reelection effort for 2008. Walter called himself a "volunteer intern" and said he'd been involved in politics his entire adult life, going back to the 1980 U.S. Senate campaign of Colorado Democrat Gary Hart.[82]

Whatever Walter's true role in his brother's administration, it pretty much ended after our story. He still lived in Helena with his family but stopped showing up at meetings in the capitol and seemed to fade from view as an informal adviser to the governor. We could only assume that the two of them decided that Walter's involvement was a potential liability they no longer wanted.

YET WHILE SCHWEITZER WOULD never claim to be everyone's friend, he had a remarkable run of success early in his governorship. He pushed through historic tax credits to encourage wind power development and the bill mandating more renewable energy from utilities. In a two-day special session in late 2005, he muscled the legislature to pass the largest two-year increase in state funding for public schools in fourteen years, aimed at heading off a court decision declaring the level of state school funding unconstitutional. He helped negotiate a statewide indoor smoking ban, which even included bars (starting four years later), beating the notoriously powerful tavern owners' lobby. And he did it all while balancing the state budget without any tax increases, as a wave of good economic news ballooned the budget to a surplus of nearly $1 billion midway through his second term.

As the 2006 elections approached, Schweitzer and Montana Democrats found themselves in prime political position. Republican president George W. Bush's popularity had cratered, and the Schweitzer administration had a string of successes under its belt. It seemed a golden opportunity for the governor and his party to deliver some knockout blows to Montana Republicans, who'd ruled the political roost for nearly fifteen years.

They did take out U.S. Senator Conrad Burns, who would lose a squeaker to state Senate president Jon Tester. But that electoral success didn't translate to the legislature, where Republicans managed to gain an unusual one-seat majority in the House, setting the stage for one of the most poisonous, volatile legislatures I'd ever cover.

It would start with seemingly nothing to fight about, as Montana had a $1 billion surplus in its budget. But it would end with an infamous profanity-laced tirade by a Republican leader and a bitter split in the Republican Party that defined Montana politics for the next decade and beyond.

The GOP maintained its 50 seats in the 100-member House, but one Democrat lost her race to a candidate from the far-right Constitution Party, giving the GOP a 50-49 majority. That one-vote margin gave the GOP the power to appoint all committee members and the committee chairs and have the committee majorities—no small edge in a closely divided legislature. Democrats ended up with a 26-24 majority in the Senate. Schweitzer made a plea for bipartisan cooperation in his January 2007 State of the State address to the legislature, but eighty-eight days into the ninety-day legislature, it hadn't happened. The two sides were locked in a budget standoff, with Republicans insisting on using the surplus to slash taxes and Schweitzer pushing to fund government programs he thought had been shorted during the GOP reign of the 1990s and beyond.

Two days before the scheduled end of session, Schweitzer thought that he had brokered a deal with House Majority Leader Mike Lange, with a mix of tax rebates and spending increases. The House gaveled itself into session that morning of April 25, 2007, and quickly broke for party caucus meetings. My colleague, Chuck Johnson, went to the GOP caucus, and I stayed on the House floor. Twenty minutes later, House Republicans started trickling back onto the floor, signaling their meeting was over.

One of them, Representative Jesse O'Hara of Great Falls, walked by me and said, "Well, Mike, you really missed the news today," and then, with a beaten look on his face, just shook his head.

"What happened?" I asked. O'Hara said Lange, the majority leader, had lost his cool, that it would be the all over the news and the papers and that Republicans would look terrible.

2007 LEGISLATURE

Lange to gov: 'Stick it'

TRIBUNE PHOTO/ROBIN LOZNAK

House Majority Leader Michael Lange stands in the House chambers in Helena on Wednesday. Earlier in the day, Lange called Gov. Brian Schweitzer, a Democrat, "that S.O.B. on the second floor," and accused the governor of trying to bribe him.

House majority leader goes off on profane tirade

Montana House Majority Leader Mike Lange, after his obscenity-laden tirade aimed at Governor Schweitzer, 2007. *Robin Loznak,* Great Falls Tribune.

"Aw, don't even worry about it," I said, flicking my hand in a "who cares" gesture. "By the end of the day, everything will change, and we won't even be talking about what happened at a 9 a.m. meeting."

"Oh, I think you'll be talking about it," O'Hara replied.

Boy, were we. Chuck Johnson practically ran up to me moments later, with the look of someone who had just seen something so astonishing that it rivaled anything he'd seen in decades of reporting.

Lange had unleashed a profanity-filled broadside at the governor, telling them Schweitzer had tried to "bribe" Republicans with his budget offer. "So my message to the governor is to stick it up your ass," he shouted to the caucus. "That's my message to him—stick it up your ass!"

Lange didn't stop there. He said Schweitzer could go "straight to hell," called him an "S.O.B. on the second floor [of the capitol] that thinks he's going to run this state like a dictator" and accused Democrats of negotiating like "radical socialists" in the Soviet Union, North Korea and "Red China."

In an interview afterward with a TV reporter, Lange said he meant everything he said and was "not budging off one comment of it, not one word of it. I meant the truth, and that's not showmanship, that's called dignity and honor."[83]

Another TV reporter had caught most of the tirade on tape—including many House Republicans actually clapping in approval of Lange and some who chanted "Stay 'til May," meaning they wanted to continue the budget impasse past the end of the session and force an additional, special session of the legislature. Our newspaper chain bought a copy of the tape for $100 and posted it on our websites. It quickly became a sensation on YouTube.

Schweitzer immediately began portraying himself as the rational man inside an insane asylum: "I just have to shake my head and say this session will be remembered as 51 flew over the cuckoo's nest," he told reporters, referring to the House Republican majority (it was actually fifty, with the Constitution Party representative, a former Republican, making it fifty-one). "This is theater of the absurd."

Newspapers across the state condemned Lange, who later would be removed from leadership by his own caucus, run for U.S. Senate, lose badly and, many years later, go to prison for distributing methamphetamine.

House Republicans, however, still wouldn't crack on a budget deal. On the final day of the session, Senate Democrats discovered that House Republicans planned to pass a bare-bones budget and adjourn. Instead, the Senate beat them to it, abruptly adjourning and ending the session without passing a state budget. I'd never seen that happen—and never would again.

Chuck and I wrote a double by-lined story that led all of our papers the next day:

> *The 2007 Legislature stumbled to a messy end Friday, as lawmakers left town without agreeing on a state budget, forcing a special session later this spring.*
>
> *The final moments Friday played out much like the rest of the regular session, with Democrats and Republicans blaming one another for the crash-and-burn ending that left the state without a budget, school funding or tax cuts for the next two years—despite a record $1 billion surplus.*

Montana's constitution requires the legislature to pass a balanced budget every two years. The state's next two-year budget period would begin in two months, on July 1. Without a budget, government would have to shut down.

TWO WEEKS LATER, SCHWEITZER called lawmakers back to Helena for a special session to make another stab at approving a budget. Unbeknownst to the media, a dozen mostly renegade Republicans had been meeting secretly with Schweitzer administration officials to craft a tax-and-budget bargain that would pass the legislature, cutting most of the GOP leadership out of the loop.

On the first day of the special session, May 10, Chuck Johnson and I heard talk of the meetings, later dubbed the "log cabin" sessions because they'd been held in a rural log-wall lodge owned by Representative John Ward, a moderate Republican from Helena. We wrote a story on the meetings the next day.

Scott Sales, the Republican House Speaker, wasn't invited to the log cabin sessions, where moderate Republicans and Democratic leaders agreed to a budget package that included $230 million in tax cuts and $50 million less in spending than had been approved by the Democratic Senate, more state money for schools, money to create full-day kindergarten at Montana public schools, tax breaks for green energy projects and a tax incentive bill for coal, oil and gas.

The coalition that hammered out the deal pushed it through the special session in six days, over the objections of Republican conservatives, including Sales. Schweitzer had achieved most of what he desired—and driven a wedge into the Montana Republican Party.

Representative Scott Mendenhall of Clancy, one of the conservatives, summed up how they felt on the final day of the special session: "We have squandered a record surplus. We have grown government by record numbers. We have absolutely caved in and given this executive branch—that is, by all accounts, a bully—everything he wants."[84]

Yet the "bully" remained popular among a consistent majority of Montanans. He cruised to reelection in 2008, defeating Republican State Representative Roy Brown of Billings by an almost two-to-one margin.

DEMOCRATS, HOWEVER, STILL COULDN'T manage to win the Montana legislature, and two years later, Montana Republicans took advantage of discontent with President Barack Obama and low voter turnout in Montana to take a firm control of the legislature that they had not relinquished ten years later. They picked up an astounding 18 seats in the state House, turning a 50-50 House into a 68-32 majority for the 2011 legislature and also increased their majority in the Senate to 28-22.

For much of Schweitzer's second term, he also found himself dealing with the aftermath of the country's 2008 financial meltdown, which meant scant funds for any new initiatives. One of his few notable late-term accomplishments brought him back to the issue that launched his career: healthcare. Using excess money from the state employees' health plan, he opened the first of a series of health clinics in late 2012, where state workers could get primary care for no charge, as a benefit of their state healthcare coverage. The clinics were modeled after similar centers in Canada's single-payer system, which Schweitzer admired, where citizens could get primary care and basic health testing free of charge, supported by taxpayer-financed health coverage.

Republican legislators denounced the idea and said that Schweitzer didn't have the authority to proceed without legislative approval. But just as he had on many other ventures, he ignored them and said the clinics would be funded by the state employee health plan, which the executive has the power to administer. By the time legislature met again in 2013, the contract to run the clinics had been awarded to a Tennessee-based firm that ran similar clinics across the country.

Several weeks before Schweitzer's final day as governor, Chuck Johnson and I interviewed him for his farewell profile. I wrote the story, leading with how he rammed his historic school funding proposal through a special session the first year as governor:

> *If nothing else, it's a fine example of Schweitzer in all his ragged glory: A governor who made an impact, especially on education, who wrestled the Legislature into submission, who did it with a style and flair that may never be matched—and who probably ticked off a fair number of people while doing it.*

The story's lead photo was a shot of Schweitzer using his "VETO" brand to set a vetoed bill afire on the capitol lawn. We also had plenty of comments from Schweitzer's detractors, who had more to say about his style than the political substance of his reign:

Schweitzer blows out the flames during his "branding veto" of several facsimile Republican bills on the state capitol lawn, 2011. *Rion Sanders,* Great Falls Tribune.

"He could have stood on his own good work without having to run everybody else down," said former Senate President Bob Story Jr., of Park City. "He didn't have to be beating on legislative staff all the time or ridiculing the Legislature.…He couldn't share the credit or the glory."

Senate President Jim Peterson, R-Buffalo, who helped negotiate a budget deal between Schweitzer and legislative Republicans last year, said Schweitzer ruled with an "iron hand," resisting the ideas of others and ensuring that the spotlight would always be on him.

"He's a hard guy to deal with; he likes to divide and conquer," Peterson said. "Now, on the other hand, I have to respect him for his ability to change the face of the state.…For me, the guy is amazing to watch, but hard to like."

Schweitzer had his defenders, among them Eric Feaver, the president of MEA-MFT, the state's largest labor union. Feaver said the people who criticize Schweitzer are simply too thin-skinned and envious of his political skills. "They are no contest for his skills to fence, to debate, to quip," Feaver told me. "I'm going to miss him, plain and simple."

Schweitzer was his usual brash self in our interview and denied that he had ever "bullied" anyone—but then proceeded to rhetorically thrash corporate lobbyists and anyone who takes their money. "I've never been particularly interested in somebody's opinion when they've been paid to have that opinion," he told us. "That's not their opinion. That's the opinion of corporate headquarters that told them this is what we want to get done.… And I'll tell you what: It doesn't worry me a damn bit that these lobbyists are glad to see me go. And I never built a relationship with them, and I'm proud of that.[85]

SCHWEITZER LEFT OFFICE IN January 2013 but wouldn't stay out of the news, and for a brief moment, it looked as though he would jump back into politics full-force.

In April, Montana's veteran U.S. senator, Democrat Max Baucus, surprisingly announced that he would retire the following year, ending a thirty-six-year stint in the U.S. Senate. Schweitzer's name was the first on everyone's lips as Baucus's likely successor.

By June, we'd heard that Schweitzer had all but announced his candidacy, lining up staff, donors and consultants to propel his bid. I started drafting a story saying Schweitzer would run. Montana State University political scientist David Parker, who had solid connections in both major political parties, told me his Democratic sources believed Schweitzer would run, and U.S. Senator Jon Tester had told NBC White House correspondent Chuck Robb that he would "bet the farm" on it. My own sources were pretty adamant, too, that Schweitzer was in, and we prepared a story to run on June 16, a Saturday, that said just that.

Yet I still hadn't talked directly to Schweitzer, who had not returned calls. On the Friday evening before the story ran, however, he finally called, reaching me on my cellphone at home. He confirmed that he had been actively exploring the run for U.S. Senate but said he hadn't made up his mind. "The question is, can you make a difference?" he said to me. "I don't know that a lot of people back there are even trying to make a difference.… That's a demerit."[86]

Upon hanging up, I had an odd feeling. Schweitzer had pulled our leg on more than one occasion, but this time, his comments had the feel of sincerity. I sent a note to our papers, inserting his comments into the story and adjusting the lead paragraph. Instead of saying he would run, the lead said he "looks very much like a candidate," attributing both named and unnamed sources.

Less than four weeks later, he pulled the plug on it all, announcing that he wouldn't run. Schweitzer said he'd polled his family and that none of them wanted him to do it, although we never thought Schweitzer had ever let anyone dictate what he might do. We also heard speculation about other reasons but never confirmed any of it.

His pass on the race all but guaranteed that the U.S. Senate seat held by Baucus would pass into Republican hands for the first time in one hundred years. Montana Democrats had no one else with Schweitzer's talent and popularity, and 2014, an off-year election, was already shaping up as a Republican year. Montana's newly minted Republican U.S. representative, Steve Daines—who initially had wanted to run for the U.S. Senate in 2012 before opting for Montana's lone House seat and winning—had been waiting to see what Schweitzer would do. With Schweitzer out, Daines was in. He would coast to victory in 2014 and the U.S. Senate seat he'd coveted in the first place.

But Schweitzer wasn't done grabbing headlines—and, for all I know, may never be. In late 2013, a full two years before the 2016 Iowa presidential caucuses, Schweitzer showed up in Iowa, saying he planned to visit all ninety-nine counties in Iowa and pointedly criticizing the likely Democratic and Republican frontrunners for the 2016 presidential nomination.

A burst of publicity followed—or, more likely, had been arranged already. Within the next week or so, Schweitzer appeared on ABC's *This Week with George Stephanopoulos*, MSNBC's *Morning Joe* and on CNN's *Anderson Cooper 360*. He appeared periodically as a cohost on CNN's *Crossfire*, and NBC signed Schweitzer up as a contributor, even setting him up with a makeshift studio in his Georgetown Lake home so he could broadcast from there. Reporters for national print and online publications started visiting Schweitzer's lakeside home, playing up the irresistible (to them) angle of the folksy, entertaining Democrat in the wilderness, ready to shake up the national Democratic establishment party.

Yet it all came crashing down on June 18, 2014, with the publication of a story in the *National Journal*. The piece by Marin Cogan started out like most Schweitzer features written by East Coast–based reporters, with an anecdote of Schweitzer the colorful rural politico, chain-sawing an overhead beam at his gate so an NBC boom truck could make it up the driveway. But it wasn't until well into the five-thousand-word story that Cogan reported the statements that got Schweitzer in trouble.

Schweitzer compared U.S. Senator Dianne Feinstein of California to a prostitute for her support of CIA spying ("She was the woman standing under the streetlight with her dress pulled all the way up to her knees, and now she says 'I'm a nun' when it comes to this spying!"), but then came the kicker: He told Cogan that when he saw U.S. House Majority Leader Eric Cantor of Virginia, his "gaydar" went off and that most southern men seemed "effeminate."

"I'm fine with gay people, that's all right—but my gaydar is 60–70 percent," he was quoted as saying. "But [Cantor's] not, I think, so I don't know. Again, I couldn't care less. I'm accepting."[87]

National Journal posted its story online that evening. Within minutes, social media had exploded. Tweets reacting to the Schweitzer "gaydar" and Feinstein comments lit up my iPhone like a slot machine, roundly castigating or ridiculing our former governor.

Chris Cillizza, then the editor of the *Washington Post* political blog *The Fix*, tweeted, "That Brian Schweitzer for president talk was fun while it lasted."

Schweitzer's political detractors also had a field day. Jim Messina, a Baucus protégé and manager of Obama's 2012 reelection campaign, tweeted that Schweitzer was the "most overrated pol in memory" and that "offensive comments and bolo ties don't get you POTUS."

The next day, I wrote a story for Lee's Montana papers, saying the comments had "set off a media and social media firestorm Wednesday night." I called Schweitzer and left a message, but he didn't call back, instead just posting an apology on his Facebook page: "I recently made a number of stupid and insensitive remarks to a reporter from the National Journal. I am deeply sorry and sincerely apologize for my carelessness and disregard."[88]

Schweitzer sorry about 'gaydar' comment

USA Today

Former Montana Gov. Brian Schweitzer apologized Thursday for making "a number of stupid and insensitive remarks" in a National Journal story.

"I am deeply sorry and apologize for my carelessness and disregard," Schweitzer wrote on Facebook.

Among Schweitzer's comments: He said House Majority Leader Eric Cantor, R-Va., set off his "gaydar" and Southern men are "a little effeminate."

"If you were just a regular person, you turned on the TV, and you saw Eric Cantor talking, I would say — and I'm fine

Schweitzer

Schweitzer's "gaydar" comments make statewide headlines, June 2014. *From the* Great Falls Tribune.

Some professed to be mystified by Schweitzer's comments, asking why he would say something that dumb on the record. But for the reporters who had covered Schweitzer on a daily basis, we had all heard similar off-color or even offensive outbursts from him many times before and gotten too used to it, shrugging them off as Schweitzer being Schweitzer and not reporting them.

This time, however, he mouthed off to the wrong reporter, who printed the comments. In fact, it appeared that Cogan had drafted her entire story before Schweitzer made the most damning comments, about Cantor. They appeared in the story inside parentheses, right after the recounting of Schweitzer's remarks on Feinstein. Cogan said she had called him after Cantor's stunning defeat in the primary election in 2014 and that Schweitzer volunteered his observations about "effeminate" southern men.

Talk of Schweitzer as a presidential candidate pretty much disappeared, and most of the national media stopped calling.

I didn't have contact with Schweitzer until more than a year later, when he congratulated me on getting a new job as a TV reporter and told me he had written a book about energy. He sent me a draft, asking my opinion. Within weeks of starting my new job as chief political reporter for the Montana Television Network in September 2015, David Parker and I had arranged to have Schweitzer as the first guest on our newly fashioned *Face the State*, a half-hour statewide public affairs show that airs on MTN stations on Sunday mornings.

A slimmed-down, goateed Schweitzer showed up for our taped interview on a clear, balmy October afternoon at the KBZK studio west of Bozeman, dressed in blue jeans and a black open-necked shirt. His book, which he'd

Schweitzer on Montana Television Network's *Face the State*, late 2015. *Montana Television Network (MTN).*

had published by the *Philipsburg Mail*, a small-town newspaper in western Montana, outlined his vision of an energy future in America transforming to solar power, smart electricity meters and electric cars, which would have batteries where homeowners could store and resell energy generated by their solar panels. An ebullient Schweitzer fielded our questions about his book and his political future (and missteps—I brought up the "gaydar" comment) with his usual aplomb, dictating and dominating the interview as the experienced pol that he was. As we wrapped up the show and signed off, Schweitzer turned to us with mock incredulity, suggesting we hadn't laid a hand on him.

"That's it?" he said, grinning. "That's all you got? That's the best you can do?"

Yes, Brian, that's it—until the next time.

Chapter 6

MAX BAUCUS

Unassuming Power Broker

A few days after Max Baucus, Montana's veteran U.S. senator, had just pulled off his crowning achievement—getting President Barack Obama's signature healthcare bill through the Senate in December 2009—I was told to do a story on whether he'd been drunk on the floor during the debate.

An anonymous post on YouTube, accompanied by a clip showing Baucus stumbling over his words as he sparred with an opposing senator, had made the allegation. The clip had become an Internet "meme" with 177,000 views, and the conservative online Drudge Report made the video its top story. Conservative readers of the *Billings Gazette* were calling the paper, demanding to know why we hadn't written about the clip and Baucus's drunkenness. They accused us of intentionally protecting the senator because of our alleged liberal bias.

I briefly argued with the paper's editor, Steve Prosinski, against legitimizing this anonymous smear but knew it was an argument I would lose. An Internet sensation and charges of bias were pressure points we couldn't ignore. Baucus's office wigged out when I told them we'd be doing a story, but as I explained, I had my marching orders and that was that.

As I watched the video, I could see how someone who'd never witnessed Baucus speak might conclude he was drunk or on drugs, for how could anyone who was a U.S. senator sound so incoherent if he wasn't impaired, right? But having covered Baucus for two decades, I knew it was just Baucus being Baucus, as ineloquent as I'd often heard him. He was probably dead tired too, having spent, at age sixty-eight, days upon days trying to cobble together the coalition to pass the bill.

I struggled over how to describe the video and convey what I knew to be true and came up with this sentence: "Baucus, whose public speaking style can be halting and awkward, is not slurring his words, but sometimes repeats himself during the five-minute video."[89] Conservative readers went ballistic. My assertion that Baucus "is not slurring his words" elicited a wave of e-mails, online comments and even direct telephone calls from people as far away as Missouri, denouncing me as a Democratic hack who would lie, cheat and misrepresent to cover up the obvious inebriation of one powerful senator.

Senator Max Baucus runs in a five-kilometer race in Great Falls, Montana, 1999. *From the* Great Falls Tribune.

To those who would listen, I explained that his speech patterns that particular day were no different from many Baucus speeches or interviews I'd witnessed or heard during twenty-plus years of covering him. And if they had cared to learn, I could have told them much more about Max Baucus—who never lost an election over a forty-three-year career in Montana politics and who would ultimately spend thirty-six years as a U.S. senator, doggedly etching his mark onto some of the biggest issues and political personalities of the state and country.

As ranking Democrat on the Senate Finance Committee in 2001, he helped cut the deal to pass federal income tax cuts championed by President George W. Bush—cuts that erased a historic budget surplus in a matter of months and plunged the nation into deficit spending it has yet to escape.

Four years later, Baucus and his chief of staff, Jim Messina—who later became deputy chief of staff and campaign manager for President Barack Obama—torpedoed Bush's plans to privatize Social Security, orchestrating a political guerrilla war that obliterated it.

And finally, perhaps his most controversial achievement, he was chief author and Congressional quarterback of the 2010 Affordable Care Act, aka "Obamacare," which ultimately eroded his approval ratings in the aftermath of its passage.

He also routinely brought home the bacon to his home state and fellow Montanans. In addition to billions of dollars to pave Montana's highways and build Montana's bridges and bike paths, he was the force behind bringing special medical coverage to hundreds of citizens of Libby, Montana, who'd been stricken by asbestos fibers from a long-running vermiculite mine.

And Baucus did it all without what most would consider the usual skills of a master politician. At times, it seemed Baucus could barely utter a coherent, complete sentence. His halting speaking style left audiences cold. When he told a joke and no one laughed, he would sometimes say, out loud, "That was supposed to be a joke," which was funnier than the joke he just fumbled.

He looked uncomfortable in a crowd and was far from a natural campaigner, but he rarely shied away from talking directly with voters, including those who wanted to strangle him, such as a roomful of gun owners who castigated him as "un-Senator Baucus" during an encounter in Missoula in 1994, after he'd voted for a ban on the sale of assault-style rifles. During interviews, he sometimes seemed distant and robotic, uttering platitudes that bore only a remote relationship to the question asked.

Yet of all the politicians I've covered, none has matched the resilience, dedication, influence or staying power of Baucus, who had an uncanny knack for being at the center of one huge story after another. His campaigns provided no end of memorable and sometimes bizarre episodes, and his perch on the powerful Senate Finance Committee gave him sway over almost every big-money issue before Congress for more than twenty years. His role in passing "Obamacare" also gave me a front-row seat for covering the huge issue of healthcare reform, right up to and including covering the U.S. Supreme Court, in person, as it heard arguments on whether to uphold the law—a spot I wouldn't have had without the intervention of Baucus.

BORN IN HELENA, BAUCUS grew up on the family's ranch north of town, part of the famed Sieben ranching family. In a 1996 interview, Baucus told me that the "seeds of later public service" were largely sown on a year-long, global trek he made as a college student, hitchhiking north from Paris, France, to start the trip and eventually traveling through most of western Europe, the Middle East, Africa, India, Nepal and southeast Asia. He ended it by flying back to San Francisco and taking a final train to Montana, where his mom picked him up at Garrison, Montana, forty miles west of Helena.

He said he had no thoughts at that time of going into politics but recalled that as he witnessed the poverty and problems of many countries, he thought someone should work toward making the world a better place. Baucus also told me that he learned something on that trip that served him well during his lengthy career in Congress: "There is always a way—there is always a way, to skin a cat. Even if you can't speak the language, you can always get something to eat, find a place to stay....There is always a way."[90]

Baucus earned a law degree from Stanford University and later set up a law practice in Missoula before running for the state legislature in 1972. He said he chose to run as a Democrat because "they were more for change and a little more inclusive, while Republicans were more for the status quo and less inclusive."

After one term in the legislature, Baucus entered a three-way Democratic primary in Montana's former western Congressional district (long before Montana would lose one of its two U.S. House seats, in 1994). The winner would take on Republican incumbent Dick Shoup. In this campaign in 1974, Baucus imagined and pulled off what's become an iconic moment of his career and twentieth century Montana politics: The Walk.

Lonn Hoklin, a University of Montana history student who had signed on as the campaign's research director, told me it was Baucus who suggested walking six hundred miles across the entire district, from south to north. "Some of us were dead-set against him doing it," Hoklin recalled. "We thought it was nuts. But, looking back on it, it was probably a brilliant move."[91]

Baucus began the walk in late March in Gardiner, on the northern border of Yellowstone National Park. On the first day, a blizzard swept through the canyon that envelopes U.S. Highway 89. The temperature then dropped to twenty below zero while Baucus and a campaign staffer slept in a camper on the side of the highway.

The next day, Baucus said he had painful shin splints. He soaked his legs in the hot pools at Chico Hot Springs, some forty miles north of Gardiner, but it didn't help, and by the time he reached Livingston, he was in serious pain. He got in touch with Montana State University track coach Gordon Herwig, who taped up his shins. The walk continued.

Mike Cooney—a college kid who later went on to become a state legislator, Montana's secretary of state, a state senator and lieutenant governor—was Baucus's "advance man" during the 1974 campaign. He said Baucus designed strict rules for the walk: no advancing forward geographically without walking, but going sideways or backward by car to attend campaign events was OK. Cooney said it became a logistical, organizational and strategic nightmare for the staff.

Max Baucus on his 630-mile walk during his campaign for the U.S. House in 1974, south of Livingston. *From the* Great Falls Tribune.

"We really needed him to start talking [to voters] about issues, but the only thing people wanted to talk to him about was the walk," Cooney told me some twenty years later. "How many shoes did you wear out? What about shin splints? How did you go to the bathroom?' It was incredible."[92]

Two and a half months and 631 miles after he began, Baucus completed the walk at the Dirty Shame Saloon in Yaak, in the far northwestern corner of Montana, covering 41 miles on the final day. He used the same pair of shoes the entire way.

INDEPENDENCE AND PERFORMANCE

Four years ago a new voice of independence emerged in Montana . . . Max Baucus. He went to Washington with only one promise: to serve the people he represented. He would challenge the power structure. He would bend to no special interest. He would stand up and speak out. Max Baucus kept his word . . . fighting inflation . . . cutting spending . . . and going back to cut it again. He stayed in touch. He worked to solve problems—of the elderly, of the farmer, of the small businessman. He fought for more sources of energy, and for reform in Congress. Yes, Max Baucus promised very little, but he delivered a great deal. Now he's challenged by an opponent who offers us little more than political promises. On Tuesday we can send to the Senate a voice of independence, of integrity . . . with Max Baucus . . . who's come so far and done so well. We can't let up now.

**That's Max Baucus.
For the next six years we need a
friend like Max in the U.S. Senate.**

Baucus ad during his 1978 campaign for the U.S. Senate. *From the* Great Falls Tribune.

Baucus won the Democratic primary, beating Pat Williams, who would win the seat four years later when Baucus made the jump to the Senate, and went on to defeat Shoup with 55 percent of the vote, becoming part of the huge "Watergate class" of Democrats of 1974. He served only two terms in the U.S. House before deciding to run for the U.S. Senate, taking on Democrat Paul Hatfield, appointed to take the place of Senator Lee Metcalf after Metcalf's death in 1978. Baucus easily defeated Hatfield in the primary and won the Senate seat in the fall—the first of six Senate races Baucus would win. Only one of those races would be considered close.

That one semi-close contest was the first Baucus campaign I would cover extensively, in 1996, as Capitol Bureau chief for the *Great Falls Tribune.* One of my first stories analyzed Baucus's voting record, charting his ratings from various interest groups over the years to see if he had, as Republicans charged, "flip-flopped" his allegiance, voting more conservatively as election time neared.

The analysis found that Baucus had a pretty consistent moderate-to-liberal voting record and, in some instances, did start voting a little more conservatively in election years or the year before. Every time Republicans tried to beat Baucus, they would roll out the "Baucus is a liberal" charge. It just wouldn't stick. Members of his own party didn't consider him a liberal, and I almost never heard Baucus utter anything that sounded remotely populist or anti-establishment. Baucus tacked to the middle on many issues, especially as elections neared, making him very difficult to beat.

Republican Denny Rehberg came the closest that year, losing by 5 percentage points. A Reform Party candidate in the race pulled almost 5 percent of the vote, keeping Baucus just under 50 percent.

During that campaign, a large, manila envelope stuffed with documents showed up in my mail at my downtown Helena office, with no return address. I opened it to find records from Baucus's 1982 divorce settlement with his former wife, writer and journalist Anne Geracimos, and a recent dispute they had over alimony and child support payments. Baucus's only child, Zeno Ben Baucus, from that marriage, was twenty at the time. Baucus had remarried a year after his divorce.

The same packet had been mailed anonymously to a reporter I knew at the *Bozeman Daily Chronicle* and the Rehberg campaign. When I called Rehberg's campaign about it, campaign manager Steve McCarter told me that Rehberg had directed his staff to do nothing with it because "we think we can win the race on the issues."[93]

The records revealed a side of Baucus we'd never seen, as he wrote sarcastic letters to his ex-wife and sometimes scrawled "extortion payments" on the checks that he sent her. My editors and I mulled whether to write a story on it and ultimately did, but neither Rehberg nor Baucus mentioned it again. The subject of Baucus and women, however, would surface against three years later, in a much more severe and public form.

LATE FRIDAY AFTERNOON BEFORE the Labor Day weekend in 1999, the Washington, D.C., political magazine *Roll Call* reported that Baucus's chief of staff, Christine Niedermeier, had accused Baucus of firing her after she rebuffed his sexual advances. I got tipped on the story and immediately called Baucus's office, which was well aware of it. It was almost five o'clock. I also discovered that the Associated Press in Helena was on the story. After a quick consult with my boss, City Editor Dan Hollow, we decided to let AP handle that first breaking story.

But that evening, at about nine o'clock, my home telephone rang—and it was Niedermeier's attorney, who said she'd tried to fax something, but it wasn't going through. She asked me if I planned to write anything. The attorney, Elaine Charlson-Bredehoft, might as well have tossed a hand grenade into my office and asked if I was going to do anything about it. But I wasn't about to start working the story at nine o'clock at night on a Friday, when our paper already had the AP version. Something about the story also seemed a little fishy to me—all served up nicely on a platter, on a holiday weekend, when it would have the run of the papers for several days before the experienced political reporters returned to work and when many people who could respond on behalf of Baucus would be out as well.

The story was splashed across the top of the front page of every Montana newspaper the next day. Both AP and the State Bureau for Lee Newspapers, my competitor, quoted the *Roll Call* story, which was online, labeled a "*Roll*

Fired aide says Baucus harassed her

Lawyer says most of staff demanded dismissal

By BOB ANEZ
Associated Press Writer

HELENA — A top aide for Sen. Max Baucus, D-Mont., has accused him of firing her after she rejected his repeated sexual advances over the last 15 months, the Washington, D.C. publication Roll Call reported Friday.

The article, which appears in the latest edition of Roll Call, said Christine Niedermeier claimed she lost her job as chief of staff because she had confronted Baucus about the alleged sexual harassment and told him to stop.

Baucus denied the allegations.

"They have absolutely no basis in fact," he said in a prepared statement issued here and in Washington. "Prior to making these allegations, I suggested to her that she seek new employment. I regret that her response has been to assert these frivolous charges against me."

Jean Manning, who represents senators in employment disputes, told The Associated Press that Baucus informed Niedermeier last month he planned to fire her because most of his staff had threatened to resign because of her "intolerable management style."

"He had 36 people in the office threatening to quit," she said. "He tried to take appropriate action which was to terminate the cause of the problem."

Manning accused Niedermeier of concocting the sexual harassment claim in an effort to discourage Baucus from firing her. "This was made up after the fact."

Baucus spokesman Bill Lombardi said Baucus, who is in Montana, would not talk with reporters about Niedermeier's charges. Baucus, 58, spent the day Friday driving a tractor.

See BAUCUS, 5A

Sen. Max Baucus

Great Falls Tribune headline, September 4, 1999.

Call Exclusive." Bredehoft did the talking for Niedermeier, saying she decided to come forward after news leaked that she had been fired and that she wanted to set the record straight on why. Bredehoft, who had won some big sex-discrimination and sexual-harassment verdicts in the D.C. area, said Niedermeier recently had confronted Baucus in Montana about his alleged harassment of her and asked him to stop it. It was then that Baucus decided to fire her, Bredehoft said.

Baucus flatly denied the charges. An attorney for Baucus said Niedermeier had been fired because the rest of the staff had come to Baucus complaining about her "intolerable management style."[94]

When I returned to work the next Tuesday, I started calling Baucus staffers, former staffers and longtime associates for a story on what they thought about the allegations. Baucus's office also began offering up its own ideas on who I should talk to, all of whom were former female staffers. I interviewed nearly a dozen people, some on background, and the message from all was pretty much the same: they couldn't imagine Baucus sexually harassing anyone, let alone Niedermeier, his chief of staff. Doug Mitchell, who'd been a prior chief of staff for Baucus and worked then in Helena as a political consultant, said it simply wasn't "in his moral code." Even Republicans who talked to reporters, including Rehberg, said it didn't sound like the Baucus they knew.

"I hope it's not true," Rehberg told Bob Anez of the AP. "Max is a good man. I've always seen him as a perfect gentleman."[95]

Staffers and former staffers also had a universally negative view of Niedermeier, saying she was a tyrant to work for. Jim Messina, who had worked then for Baucus, told me he quit because he could no longer take working with Niedermeier. "It was an unenjoyable and brutal place to work," he said. "I'd turned down a couple of jobs, and finally I couldn't take it anymore….She was the prime example of about as bad a leader as you could get."[96]

Baucus himself wouldn't talk to reporters initially but by Friday decided to break his personal silence. He told me the same thing he told other reporters that day: that the only mistake he made was not getting rid of Niedermeier earlier and that her charges were categorically false. "I'm not crossing my words, I'm not using legalese," he told me. "I'm telling Montanans in a straight-talk way: I never sexually harassed Christine Niedermeier."[97]

Of course, once Baucus lifted his self-imposed moratorium on talking directly with the press, Niedermeier did the same, calling the same reporters on the same day that Baucus spoke with them. She told me that Baucus's office had been dysfunctional and that she'd been the one brought on in 1998 to straighten things out, and that's why people resented her leadership.

I had met Niedermeier briefly, once, but didn't really know her at all and had never spoken with her at any length until that interview. But something about her story just didn't ring true. She struck me as someone with a huge ego—hardly an uncommon trait in D.C. politics—but who also felt compelled to pump up her importance.

The Niedermeier story continued to make the rounds of D.C. publications for the next few weeks, and she filed a harassment complaint with the U.S. Senate three weeks after the story broke but ended up dropping it several months later. A poll conducted by Montana State University–Billings in November 1999 said that only 18 percent of Montanans found the Niedermeier charges credible, and the story just sort of faded away. It didn't even come up in Baucus's reelection campaign three years later. But that 2002 campaign still ended up being one of the most bizarre campaigns I'd ever cover.

As the 2002 campaign season approached, Baucus appeared unassailable. Republicans had no clear, well-known opponent, and Baucus had his usual pile of campaign cash. He also had helped President George W. Bush pass his first round of 2001 tax cuts. To the consternation of many Democrats, Baucus, the chair of the Senate Finance Committee, which wrote tax legislation, supported and voted for the $1.35 trillion, eleven-year cut. He even stood next to the president when Bush signed the cuts into law for a photo-op. For any Republican thinking of tackling Baucus, the race had to look like climbing Mount Everest.

Still, Bush had won Montana by a whopping twenty-six points in 2000, and Republicans won every major race in the state that year. Baucus was the last big Democrat standing in Montana, and in an off-year election, Republicans

Baucus shaking hands with President George W. Bush. Baucus was instrumental in passing Bush's 2001 tax cut through Congress. *From the* Great Falls Tribune.

had a natural advantage with the lower turnout. They also had a candidate ready to step in: state Senator Mike Taylor, a wealthy businessman originally from Lewistown who had made a fortune on barber and hair-styling salons, beauty supplies and ranching. He'd also been the chief sponsor of a 1999 bill that slashed Montana's property taxes on business equipment, to the great pleasure of all business owners.

The race poked along for the latter part of 2001 and into 2002, with Baucus clearly on cruise control, rolling up $5.5 million in campaign funds by June 2002. Taylor had raised only $860,000, and that included $550,000 of his own money. A poll by Lee Newspapers two months before the election showed Baucus up by nineteen points—all of which made the final turn in the campaign even weirder and more unexpected than any of us thought possible.

On the first Friday of October 2002, the state Democratic Party called reporters covering the race and invited them to a news conference held in the basement of the headquarters of MEA-MFT, the state's largest labor union. I joined several of my colleagues as we filed into a room with a TV. Democratic Party staffers handed us a sheaf of documents outlining how Taylor had supposedly mishandled student loan money at his beauty school in Colorado in the 1990s. Then they plugged a videotape into the TV and played the ad attacking Taylor for this alleged indiscretion.

We watched as the videotape rolled, showing a young, bearded man applying face cream and massaging the face of another nicely coiffed man, who was seated. The words "facial demonstration" flashed on the screen and then "Mike Taylor Beauty Corner broadcast 1980's."

Wait a minute, I said—is that *Mike Taylor?* It was, but it looked nothing like the Taylor we knew, a fifty-nine-year-old, somewhat stout businessman who wore conservative suits and ties. The Democratic staffers grinned a knowing grin, and most of the reporters couldn't help but burst out laughing. The Taylor in the ad, twenty years younger, looked like he'd just walked off the set of *Saturday Night Fever*, clad in a colorful polyester shirt with huge collars and an open neck, as well as a gold chain. The bearded, hipster-ish Taylor giving the other man a facial served as backdrop to the ad, which aired the charges against Taylor as perpetrator of a "student loan scam." The party said the ad would begin running that day and that it was a weeklong, $100,000 buy—not an insubstantial amount in Montana at that time.

The ad became the dagger in Taylor's heart. Insiders for both campaigns told me that in the first few days of the ad run, Taylor's poll numbers dropped so far and so fast that it was like nothing they'd ever seen. As one staffer told me, the most devastating blow you can deliver to an opponent is to make him or her appear dramatically different to the public than they've presented themselves to be. It's the easiest and best way to make them appear deceptive and untrustworthy.

Five days later, Taylor delivered his own stunner: he pulled out of the race, saying he'd had enough of Baucus's "sea of sleaze" campaign. He said the ad clearly had insinuated that he was a gay hairdresser and that there was no way to counter it with four weeks until Election Day. "I would have to blanket the airwaves with slime more thoroughly than [Baucus]," he said. "If that's what it takes to win, it is a victory not worth winning. I think I would make a good senator. But I know I'd make a bad liar."[98]

By now, Montana's Senate race had become the butt of jokes nationwide. Conservative radio commenter Rush Limbaugh gleefully accused Montana

Taylor quits Senate race

After the Montana Democratic Party ad in 2002 showing Republican U.S. Senate candidate Mike Taylor as a hairdresser, his poll numbers plummeted, and he temporarily withdrew from the race. *From the* Great Falls Tribune.

Democrats of "gay-bashing," and the *Washington Post* jokingly castigated Democrats for making Taylor look like John Travolta.

Then, twelve days after he'd pulled out, Taylor was back in, saying he wouldn't cave to "gutter politics." No doubt Republican Party officials had told him he had to continue, since he was still on the ballot as the top of the ticket. Not that it mattered. Baucus cruised to victory, rolling up a state record $5.8 million in spending on a single campaign and winning with 63 percent of the vote to Taylor's 32 percent.

Six years later, Baucus would again easily win reelection, crushing another overmatched opponent. Bob Kelleher, an eighty-five-year-old Butte lawyer and perennial candidate who had run for various offices as a Democrat and Green Party candidate, decided that year to run as a Republican for the U.S. Senate and won the primary over a field of nobodies. We hardly even covered the general election campaign, knowing that Baucus had it in the bag.

The big election news that year, of course, was Barack Obama winning the presidency and the Democrats rolling up a sixty-vote majority in the Senate.

Baucus, now sixty-seven years old and still the chairman of the powerful Senate Finance Committee, returned to Washington, D.C., for what would be his sixth and final term as a U.S. senator and to tackle perhaps the toughest, most divisive job of his career: crafting and passing the Patient Protection and Affordable Care Act, soon to be known as "Obamacare."

WHILE THE AFFORDABLE CARE Act became known as "Obamacare," a more accurate name for this complex and never-totally-popular reform would be "Baucus-care," for Baucus and his Senate Finance Committee staff are the ones who imagined it, studied it, pieced it together and hauled it through the political minefield to pass it into law. They worked on it for more than two years and then watched as the ACA became the political club that enabled Republicans, in one devastating election in 2010, to erase the Democrats' historic victories in 2006 and 2008 on the national stage. And they suffered this blowback for a healthcare reform that still left millions of Americans uninsured and did little to control the country's high cost of care.

Baucus and those closest to him told me it was the best they could do politically, that more aggressive reforms like a "public option" health insurer or a single-payer system ("Medicare for all") simply had no chance to bruise their way through the D.C. landscape, where they would be crushed by the powerful healthcare and insurance industries. Instead, Baucus said he was looking for a "uniquely American" solution to the problem (read: *not* a socialized, universal-coverage program like Canada's or countries in Europe).

One of the plan's cornerstones became the requirement that every American who isn't covered by a government plan must buy private health insurance—a concept that had originated with conservative-leaning and Republican reformers. This segment of "Obamacare" would be aimed at the approximately 10 percent of Americans who bought health insurance individually, who had no access to less expensive group health coverage through their employer.

If you didn't make much money and would have trouble affording a private plan, the feds would provide subsidies to help pay for it—paid directly into the coffers of private health insurers. The subsidies would be applied only if you bought the policies on an Internet marketplace, set up by states or the feds.

The plan also would expand Medicaid, the state- and federal-funded program that pays medical bills for the poor, to cover millions of low-income, childless adults, virtually for free.

For the vast majority of Americans already covered by group health insurance at work, it provided basically nothing. As President Obama put it, if you like the insurance you have, you can keep it. But if you didn't like it? You still got to keep it. And most of the plan's components that actually expanded coverage wouldn't take effect until *four years later*, in 2013.

The bill cleared Baucus's Finance Committee on October 13, 2009. The AP's Washington-based office called it "a personal triumph for Baucus, who has weathered criticism from fellow Democrats after his attempt at bipartisanship cratered earlier this fall after months of exhaustive effort."

Republican U.S. Senator Olympia Snowe of Maine provided the only Republican vote in committee for the bill, but she would later desert the effort on the floor. Democrats were going it alone despite having made multiple concessions to all corners of the healthcare and insurance lobbies.

To me, it seemed obvious that the plan was a road map to political disaster for the Democrats. "Obamacare" helped very few people until 2013, four years later, and no one could know for sure if they would be one of those people or to what degree they'd be helped. Despite tons of media coverage, few Americans really knew what the proposal contained or how it would work. It was just too complicated.

I spotlighted the weakness of the plan in a mid-November column, discussing how the reforms did little or nothing to affect or help the 160 million Americans who already had health insurance and quoting both President Barack Obama and Baucus as saying what they thought was a positive (and that turned out to be false): "If you like the insurance you have, you can keep it." My column noted that for many Americans, keeping what we had wasn't exactly a plus.

Two weeks later, on November 30, 2009, the debate on Obamacare began on the Senate floor, with Baucus playing a lead role. I asked to interview Baucus, but the staff wouldn't make him available. Instead, they supplied his scripted comments from the floor. His refusal to talk directly to reporters in Montana that day, as he played a key role in the biggest issue facing the nation, was part of a curious pattern. Baucus often seemed to prefer talking to the national press on the big moments and rarely, if ever, gave a breaking story first to Montana newspapers, which were likely to give him more favorable coverage.

On Obamacare, I didn't interview Baucus directly until nearly three weeks later, a week before Christmas, while the debate dragged on in the Senate and a final vote still hadn't occurred. By now, even some liberal commentators and interest groups said the bill wasn't worth passing because it had been compromised by too many concessions to get the sixty votes needed to crack a filibuster. Baucus adamantly disagreed, telling me, "Clearly, it's much better than no bill." Not exactly a ringing endorsement.[99]

The Senate passed the bill on Christmas Eve, 60-39, without a single Republican vote. It still had to go through the Democratically controlled House and a conference committee, but Democrats managed to get it passed on March 21, 2010, despite Democrats losing their sixty-seat Senate majority in a Massachusetts special election in January.

Baucus spoke to me by telephone the next day, saying he was "very proud of our country and of Congress, for stepping up and doing what's right.…We have to go through a few hoops and hurdles over here, but it's a done deal.…It will stop this broken health-care system that is breaking families and breaking the country....We've got folks out there who can't afford to get sick."[100]

Baucus clearly wanted to help the millions of Americans who faced bankruptcy, financial ruin and the jail of chronically poor health because they didn't have enough money or health insurance to cover costly care. And the bill did end up bringing affordable coverage to millions of Americans without it, despite its corporate-friendly tilt. But it would fall far short of universal coverage, did little to reduce the extraordinary cost of healthcare in America and came at great political cost to Democrats, both in Montana and the nation.

Republicans mounted a full-scale political and legal campaign against the Affordable Care Act, culminating in the 2010 Election Day debacle for Democrats, both in the nation and Montana. Democrats lost their U.S. House majority, which they didn't recover until 2018, and lost eighteen seats in the Montana House, going from a 50-50 tie to a 68-32 Republican majority, the largest one-cycle swing I'd seen in my entire reporting career. The GOP also made it clear that it wanted nothing less than total destruction of Obamacare, battling it in court and in state legislatures around the country in 2011.

TWO YEARS AFTER OBAMACARE'S passage, I would witness the arguments before the U.S. Supreme Court on the lawsuit to torpedo the law. I had arranged to be in Washington, D.C., in March 2012 to cover the two contestants in that year's Montana U.S. Senate race, Senator Jon Tester and his Republican challenger, Denny Rehberg, who was Montana's only U.S. representative. A week after I'd booked my plane and hotel, the news broke that the Supreme Court had scheduled three days of oral arguments that same week on the Obamacare lawsuits.

I immediately called the Supreme Court's press office to ask how I could get a spot to cover the hearings that week. I had to fill out a form online and wait to see if I might get one of the coveted guest media spots. Although I'd covered the issue perhaps more than most reporters in the entire country, I figured my chances at getting one of the coveted slots was a long shot—and I was right. A few weeks before I was to leave, the Supreme Court press office told me I would not be one of the reporters covering the arguments.

That same day, I was talking to Jennifer Donohue, Baucus's press secretary, arranging to talk with Baucus while I was in D.C. I knew he would be attending the Supreme Court arguments, and I wanted to interview him about it. I mentioned to her that the court had rejected my request to cover the arguments myself.

"You talked to them?" she said. "They told you no?" Yeah, I said, telling her about the process that rejected me. "Let us look into that," she said. "We'll talk to them." Within days, the court's media chieftain called me back and told me I would be covering the oral argument.

My seat at the court, courtesy of Baucus's intervention, would be the first of many times that trip that I would see the power and influence Baucus had in Washington. I had planned to do a story on the reputations of Tester and Rehberg in the nation's capital and arranged to talk with Congressional staffers, D.C. reporters and even a U.S. senator or two. When I would call to inquire about Tester and Rehberg, the general response was, "Who?" And when they found out I was a Montana reporter, the next comment would be, "Now, if you want to talk about Baucus, we can talk about him—he's the one who has the power, the one we know about."

On the day of the Supreme Court hearing—Monday, March 26—I showed up at the appointed time in the court's press office, notebook in hand, and took a seat in the crowded press room. Beat reporters for national media outlets such as the Associated Press, National Public Radio, the *New York Times*, the *Wall Street Journal*, the *Washington Post* and more had their own partitioned cubby hole. The rest of us milled around, waiting for the cattle call for the sixty-odd guest reporters. We could bring only a notepad and pen into the courtroom—no recorders, no cellphones and no cameras.

Seats for visiting press are off to the side of the courtroom, some of them behind huge, twenty-foot-tall marble columns draped with vermillion-colored, gold-fringed curtains. I ended up with an assigned seat not behind a column and could see justices Elena Kagan, Samuel Alito, Ruth Bader Ginsburg and Anthony Kennedy. If I leaned forward, I could get a glimpse of Chief Justice John Roberts and Antonin Scalia, but if Stephen Breyer or Sonia Sotomayor spoke, I had to identify them from their voices. I couldn't see Justice Clarence Thomas either, but he hadn't asked a question in six years, so no worry about identifying him.

The regular beat reporters, like Nina Totenberg of NPR, sat several rows in front of us, with a clear view of the justices and the packed courtroom. Armed only with a pen and notebook, I struggled to keep up with arguments and would have had a difficult time writing a coherent news story, instead penning a column on the experience. The important arguments on the constitutionality of the authority of the ACA would be the next day.

Baucus would attend the hearings that second day, and I interviewed him late in the afternoon. It would be the only time I would interview Baucus at his D.C. office. We sat in his own personal conference room, which was probably bigger than the entire office of most congressmen and women.

Baucus, seventy at the time, looked a little tired after a long day. He told me he heard "a lot of tough questions" from the justices, but he expected that and made no prediction on how they would rule. He also said he welcomed the intense media scrutiny that the hearings had lent to the ACA because it would cause people to learn more about its contents: "Most people don't know what's in the bill, and when they do, they're going to say, 'Gee, that's not so bad.'"[101]

Three months to the day from the final day of the Supreme Court oral arguments, the court ruled. I sat at my desk in our downtown Helena office, following *SCOTUSblog* and other outlets on Twitter as the decision was released, read and reported on by Washington-based reporters. In the initial burst of reporting, CNN said the law had been overturned, and I re-tweeted the news on my Twitter feed.

Seconds later, however, *SCOTUSblog* and others got it right: In the now-historic 5-4 decision, with Chief Justice John Roberts siding with the court's four liberal justices, the court upheld the guts of the Affordable Care Act, although it did overturn the mandate for all states to expand Medicaid in 2014, making it optional for the states.

Later in the day, I interviewed Baucus again, by telephone. He sounded neither triumphant nor smug, but merely relieved, and predicted that people would take a fresh look at the law and start deciding it would be positive. "I think this decision will really help these reforms proceed," he told me. "Now the wind is at the back on those who want to make this work."

Well, not really. The comments that day from Rehberg, the only Republican in Montana's delegation, would prove more prophetic, as he said the court's decision didn't change the fact that Obamacare "is still not a good piece of legislation" and that Republicans would continue their quest to undo it.[102]

Rehberg, however, would go down to defeat that year in his attempt to unseat Senator Tester, Obama would win reelection handily and Democrats, thought to be sure losers in their goal to hang onto the majority in the U.S. Senate, would actually expand their majority. Democrats had come back from the political grave, despite the continuing doubts over the Affordable Care Act.

Yet they couldn't sustain the winning streak. Baucus himself predicted the next snafu when, at a budget hearing before his Senate Finance Committee in April 2013, he told U.S. Health and Human Services secretary Kathleen Sebelius he had grave concerns about whether the online "marketplaces" to sell subsidized insurance polices for individuals would be ready by October 1. "I just see a huge train-wreck coming down," he said. "The administration's public information campaign on the benefits of the Affordable Care Act deserves a failing grade. You need to fix this."[103]

Baucus's statement made headlines across Montana and the country, and he must have had inside information on what was going on, for the initial launch of the Internet health insurance exchanges that fall would be a disaster. But he also knew something else when he uttered those comments: he could afford to be frank, for he would end his political career soon.

ON THE MORNING OF April 23, 2013, less than a week after the "train wreck" stories, *Billings Gazette* editor Steve Prosinksi e-mailed me to say the national press was reporting that Baucus would not run for reelection in 2014.

My boss and colleague, Lee Newspapers State Bureau chief Chuck Johnson, was sitting next to me. He then told me Baucus's people had called him the night before, at home, to tell him Baucus had an important announcement the next morning and that he would be calling Chuck at 10:00 a.m. It was probably 9:15 a.m. when we got the note from Steve. True to form, big news on Baucus had been leaked to the national press before we got it at home.

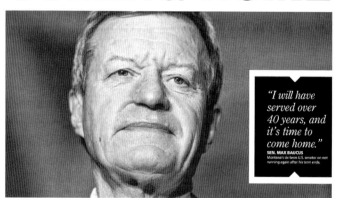

Baucus, on the cover of the *Great Falls Tribune*, the day after announcing in April 2013 he would retire from the U.S. Senate in 2014.

Baucus, seventy-one, had spent the last thirty-four-plus years of his life as a U.S. senator and become one of the most powerful men in Washington, and he was calling it quits.

We wondered aloud why Baucus had chosen to bail on his forty-year career in Congress. But the answer seemed obvious to me, and Baucus pretty much spelled it out in his interview with Chuck, saying it was simply time to retire. "I just don't want to die with my boots on," he said. "I'm a Montanan. I'm coming home to Montana. It's my home."[104]

Yet he didn't quite make it home when he expected—and gave us one last bit of political drama.

ONE DAY IN NOVEMBER 2013, as Chuck Johnson and I plotted our daily coverage for the Lee Newspapers State Bureau, he said a neighbor had told him he'd been called by investigators from the U.S. State Department as part of a background check on Baucus.

Right away, I thought it could mean only one thing: Baucus was up for an ambassadorship somewhere (we speculated China or Russia), and if he was appointed by Obama, that would mean his U.S. Senate seat would become vacant. That would allow the governor, Democrat Steve Bullock, to appoint Baucus's successor a year before the successor would have to run for reelection. We started making calls to attempt to break the story but ran into a wall of sources who professed to know nothing. As usual, the story was leaked to the national press a few days later, leaving us with sloppy seconds that Baucus would be appointed as U.S. ambassador to China.

The move to appoint Baucus allowed Governor Steve Bullock to appoint his own lieutenant governor, John Walsh—who was already running to succeed Baucus—as Montana's newest U.S. senator. The appointments were part of an obvious political ploy to put Walsh in a better position to win and keep the seat Democratic, but the plot disastrously failed.

Walsh would quit the campaign six months later, after the *New York Times* reported in July 2014 that he had plagiarized his master's thesis at the U.S. Army War College in 2007. He would be replaced on the November ballot by a little-known high school math teacher, State Representative Amanda Curtis, who would get beaten handily in the general election by Montana's Republican congressman, Steve Daines. Daines became the first Republican to hold the Senate seat in 101 years.

ALL THROUGH THIS FINAL drama, we never talked directly to Baucus. Upon his nomination as U.S. ambassador to China, any contact he had with the media had to be cleared in advance by the State Department. Knowing what an incredible, thankless hassle it was to deal with any aspect of the federal government's press apparatus in Washington, let alone the State Department, we didn't think it was worth even trying to talk to Baucus, and we doubted he would say much of substance to us anyway.

Instead, we put together a lengthy farewell series on his career. It began running in Lee papers just three days after he officially resigned his Senate seat in early February 2014. I drafted the lead story that ran on February 9:

> *As U.S. Sen. Max Baucus departs Congress after 39 years, none would disagree that the senior senator has left an indelible mark on the state and the nation, on everything from health care to highway funds to tax policy.*
>
> *He was chief architect of the controversial Affordable Care Act in 2010—"Obamacare"—and the leading Democrat who said "yes" to the 2001 Bush tax cuts.*
>
> *He led the Democrats' 2005 effort to kill President George W. Bush's plan to partially privatize Social Security, but sided with Bush and Republicans in helping push through the 2003 Medicare prescription drug bill that relied on private insurers.*
>
> *He brought billions of dollars of highway money to Montana and rural America and pushed long and hard for more "free trade" agreements around the globe, often to the chagrin of his organized-labor supporters.*

What emerged from our three-day series was the portrait of a guy who had made a huge impact on the state, the nation and the world. This undeniable fact sometimes got lost in the hundreds of stories we'd written on a political figure who'd never been particularly flashy and whose own monotonous style had lulled us into a belief that he was just another boring guy who advanced merely from hanging around long enough to get promoted. No, it was more than that. He had served power, yes, but he had also cared about using the power of government to help people who needed help and often got it done with the art of compromise, bridging the gap between the political parties to solve a problem and refusing to fall back solely on ideology.

Nothing spelled it out better than the final story I wrote about Baucus, on what he had done for the people of Libby, Montana. Hundreds of residents had been stricken by asbestos-related lung diseases, caused by a long-operating vermiculite mine nearby.

Baucus had placed language in the "Obamacare" bill that said residents of Libby affected by the disease got government-financed health coverage regardless of age. But he'd also worked to establish a special health clinic in Libby, pushed for the town to be declared a "public health emergency" area and supported a $10 million grant to cover screening costs at the clinic. He told the press that after meeting Libby's victims and their advocates in 1999, he made a vow that he "would do whatever it took to help the people of Libby."

"We wouldn't be here where we are today without his support," Tanis Hernandez, director of the clinic, told me for that last story. "He's always been there to hear our latest concerns and struggles, and to try to find a solution."[105]

JON TESTER

Master of the Close Shave

On election night 2006, I crawled into my hotel bed in Great Falls, Montana, sometime after 2:00 a.m., with the race between Republican U.S. Senator Conrad Burns and his Democratic challenger, Jon Tester, still undecided. Control of the U.S. Senate hung in the balance, but I had to get some rest. After two hours of restless sleep, I awoke at 4:15 a.m., threw on some clothes and wandered down the deserted hallways of the Heritage Inn, the site of Tester's election night party.

The ballroom that had been buzzing just hours ago was now virtually empty. When I'd gone to sleep, Tester led by 7,200 votes out of 400,000 cast, but his lead had been shrinking. If he won, Democrats would pick up a half dozen seats in the U.S. Senate, seize majority control after a four-year hiatus and deliver a stinging rebuke to President George W. Bush and the Republican Party.

I made my way to a staging room just off the ballroom floor. As I entered, a solitary person sat hunched on a standard-issue motel chair in the middle of the room. It was Tester.

"What are you doing?" I asked. "What's going on?"

"Somebody's supposed to interview me," he said. "I'm waiting for the *Today Show*." He wore a jacket, tie, slacks and cowboy boots and looked oddly relaxed for having just spent more than a year in one of the most brutal electoral contests in Montana history.

"Did you get any sleep?" I asked him.

"Yeah, a couple of hours, maybe....I literally just climbed out of bed and came down here." I was about to ask him what he knew about the

U.S. Senator Jon Tester drives his tractor on his farm west of Big Sandy, 2018. *Montana Television Network (MTN).*

vote count, but his press guy, Matt McKenna, marched into the room and immediately started prepping Tester for the upcoming interview on national TV. McKenna asked Tester what he would say if NBC asked why the outcome of the vote wasn't known yet.

"Well," said Tester, "I think there were some problems with the vote—"

McKenna cut him off: "We *do* know the outcome. We're ahead in this race. We're going to win this race. We just didn't get to win it Tuesday night."

Within minutes, at 5:05 a.m., *Today Show* interviewers had Tester on the phone, quizzing him about the race, and in short order CNN and the *CBS Early Morning* show talked to him as well.

"I think Montanans wanted change," Tester said, speaking as though he had won. "There are a lot of issues they're concerned about, like health care and foreign policy....Health care is a big issue in this state. We've got a lot of people here who are uninsured, who can't afford to get sick."[106]

Tester's lead in the count, I learned a few minutes later, had shrunk to a mere 1,600 votes, and votes were still being counted in a few counties. If the lead got much smaller, we might be looking at an automatic recount under state law and anything could happen.

But it didn't. The additional votes ended up expanding Tester's margin. By late morning, he was declared the winner, eventually emerging with a 3,562-vote margin over Burns, less than 1 percentage point of difference.

Tester—a fifty-year-old organic farmer with a signature flattop haircut, a potbelly and a lone finger and thumb on the left hand he'd caught in a meat grinder at age nine—had just knocked off Montana's incumbent Republican U.S. senator of eighteen years.

He'd also served up one of the most dramatic, memorable campaigns and election nights I'd covered in twenty-five years of reporting, and six and twelve years later, he would pull off déjà vu experiences, winning bare-knuckled Senate campaigns that would break all records for campaign spending in Montana and not be decided until the next morning, with Tester declaring victory at a Great Falls hotel.

I had covered Tester in many ways on many issues, for he came from Big Sandy, a north-central Montana farming community in the circulation territory of the *Great Falls Tribune*, the paper where I worked as chief political writer for thirteen years. His career as a legislative leader was often front-page news in the *Tribune*, as he rose from unlikely Democratic winner in a rural, conservative district to become state Senate president in red-leaning Montana. I also spent many hours covering his U.S. Senate career, for Montana has only three members of Congress—one U.S. representative, two senators—and that tiny delegation gets plenty of attention from the few newsmen and women who cover politics in Montana.

Yet the essence of covering Tester inevitably came down to his campaigns. He was a central figure in one historic race after another in Montana, from helping Democrats win their only outright majority in Montana's legislature in an almost-thirty-year time span to aiding Barack Obama in winning in 2008 the only meaningful Montana presidential primary had seen in more than a generation to his own epic U.S. Senate battles in 2006, 2012 and 2018.

The paths I traveled with Tester on the campaign trail ran across Montana and to the streets of Washington, D.C., where we walked the halls of the U.S. Capitol complex and sat in a cramped D.C. office while Tester dialed for campaign dollars, methodically going down the list of donors and asking them for money. It also included one of the most difficult stories I ever worked on—a story that all but destroyed the campaign of his 2006 Democratic U.S. primary opponent, Helena attorney John Morrison.

Through it all, I never saw Tester lose an election—even though he often entered as not necessarily the underdog, but a Democrat with a target on his back, in a rural state where Republicans pretty much had a lock on the legislature and presidential campaigns. In 2018, President Donald Trump visited Montana four times in four months to campaign against Tester, in a state that Trump won by twenty points in 2016. A majority of Montana voters still chose Tester.

How did he do it? Hard work, great timing, an inherent political shrewdness and, perhaps most importantly, a down-to-earth quality that was on display just about anywhere.

When I spent a day with Tester in Washington, D.C., as part of my 2012 coverage of that year's Senate campaign, Tester and I climbed into the "senators only" elevator in the Hart Senate Office Building to take us to the basement, where we could grab the tram to the Capitol. About halfway down, the elevator stopped and a pair of middle-aged men—obviously not senators—got on. They weren't sure where they were, and Tester asked them where they intended to go. He gave them directions, telling them which floor to get off and which hallway to take.

"Isn't this the senators-only elevator?" I asked after the two tourists had disembarked.

"Yeah," Tester said matter-of-factly.

"Do non-senators ever get kicked off this elevator?"

"Oh, yeah," Tester replied. "There's a lot of senators who would kick them off." He shrugged. "I don't do that."

Tester started his political career on the local school board in Big Sandy and first ran for partisan office in 1998, when he won an open state Senate seat that had been held by a retiring Republican. He quickly moved into the leadership ranks in the Senate. Upon winning reelection in 2002, he became the Democratic Senate minority leader for the 2003 legislature, chosen by his fellow Senate Democrats.

In an interview for a profile story I did on Tester in November 2002, after his selection as Senate minority leader, he told me he was a Democrat primarily because he believed in a progressive tax system. Those who could most afford to pay the most should, he said, and that money should be used foremost to fund public education and keep the cost of state colleges affordable for students and their families.

"I want my kids to be able to go to college and not be saddled with debt for fifteen years," he said. But Tester also described himself as "an aggie" who wanted to craft policy to help sustain family farms and the rural economy.

The year after he won the Senate minority post, Tester and his fellow Democrats began plotting how they could become the majority at the legislature and break a decade-long stranglehold by Republicans. He led a legislative campaign team in 2004 that recruited candidates and traveled the state, talking up Democrats' plans for education, healthcare reform and other bread-and-butter issues and castigating Republicans for leading the state into a fiscal and economic mire.

Democrats won a 27-23 majority in the Senate that year—the only time since 1992 they've won an outright majority in either house of the Montana legislature—and forged a 50-50 tie in House. Tester was chosen by his Democratic peers as president of the Senate.

At the meeting where Democrats officially elected Tester as Senate leader, he brought his trumpet and blasted out the theme song from the movie *The Magnificent Seven*. The room erupted in raucous applause.

The Democrats and their new governor, Brian Schweitzer, enjoyed many successes during that 2005 legislature, and Tester naturally stood right in the middle of it. He personally sponsored bills to create property tax incentives for wind power projects (that helped jumpstart the wind industry in Montana) and help poor senior citizens buy prescription drugs.

ABOUT HALFWAY THROUGH THE 2005 session, talk began percolating about who would challenge Montana's Republican U.S. senator, Conrad Burns, in 2006.

Burns, seventy, already had said he would run for a fourth term. At that point, he looked like a relatively strong, well-funded incumbent, poised to run as a conservative in a moderate-to-conservative state. Yet seeds of a major scandal that would touch Burns had already started to grow: the D.C. lobbying and influence-peddling of Jack Abramoff, who had billed Native American tribes millions of dollars for some minor lobbying work and used the money to enrich himself and spread favors around Capitol Hill in Washington. As it would be reported later in 2005, Burns had received more money from Abramoff than any other member of Congress.

Not long after the 2005 legislature ended in late April, Tester confirmed in an interview with me that he was seriously considering a run against Burns and that he planned to fly to Washington, D.C., with his wife, Sharla, to talk to the Democratic money boys about whether he might get some help. Another Democrat, State Auditor John Morrison, had already declared his candidacy.

Less than two weeks later, Tester told me he was in and had scheduled a statewide tour to kick off the campaign. Showing a bit of the political savvy that would serve him well, Tester didn't start the campaign at his remote farm or the city (Great Falls) nearest his home but instead headed to Billings, the state's largest city and home to the county that held almost 15 percent of all Montana voters. Tester, clad in jeans, cowboy boots and a white Oxford shirt, drove a sixty-foot-long farm semitrailer truck emblazoned with "Tester for U.S. Senate" and a declaration stenciled on the back that said, "You're behind the right guy!"

It was easy to see why many Democrats thought Tester was the right guy to beat Burns. He was smart, he was funny and he had deep roots in agriculture in an ag-heavy state that could match up with Burns's background as a farm broadcaster and popularity among many in Montana's ag community. And when Tester said, "I'm just a regular guy," as he did, regularly, you knew it was true—and that couldn't hurt in a state populated with more than its share of regular Joes and Janes.

Yet before Tester took on Burns, he first had to beat Morrison, who had outraised Tester two to one in campaign funds by the end of 2005. Morrison also had an impressive political and Democratic pedigree; he was a skilled trial lawyer, son of a former Montana Supreme Court justice and grandson of a former governor of Nebraska. But three months later, Morrison's campaign would be all but dead in the water, cut down by a devastating story that my colleagues and I at the Lee Newspapers State Bureau had been developing for several weeks.

Rumors of Morrison as an unfaithful husband had been around Montana politics for a few years, but I had reason to believe it was more than rumor. Some three years earlier, when I worked as Capitol Bureau chief for the *Great Falls Tribune*, one of the paper's editors called me with very detailed, secondhand information that Morrison had engaged in an extramarital affair with a woman who might have had some connection to Morrison's work as state auditor, which regulated the insurance and investment industries in Montana.

We discussed whether we should look into it but finally agreed it wouldn't rise to the level of a story worth pursuing unless Morrison ran for something big, like the U.S. House, governor…or U.S. Senate.

By 2005, I had left the *Tribune* and joined the Lee Newspapers State Bureau. My new colleagues at Lee, Bureau Chief Chuck Johnson and reporter Jennifer McKee, had heard the same rumor. We sat down in early 2006 to decide whether we would pursue the story. For several reasons, the answer was yes.

For starters, we had word that the Burns camp knew of the Morrison affair and planned to use the information against Morrison should he win the Democratic primary. If the bomb was out there, we thought it should be detonated before the primary election, so voters choosing the Democratic challenger to Burns could have full knowledge of just what they were getting. Second, we heard that the *Missoula Independent*, an alternative weekly paper, was working the story too. We didn't want to get beat.

We also had the name of a woman alleged to have had an affair with Morrison, Suzanne Harding, whose fiancé, David Tacke, had been investigated by Morrison's office from 2001 to 2003 for securities fraud. Tacke, who later married Harding, reached a settlement with Morrison's office that required him to repay investors in his company and have an independent board of directors. However, he later ended up in federal prison, convicted by a jury in Missoula, Montana, in 2005 of fraud and money laundering.

McKee began searching the Internet for any trace of Harding in Montana, found a telephone number and called. She got Harding's mother instead, at a home in Bigfork, a resort town on Flathead Lake about 180 miles northwest of Helena. By the time she was finished talking, Jennifer had extracted an agreement that Harding would talk to us—if the reporter drove up to Bigfork and interviewed her in person.

We thought that Jennifer was the best person for this particular task, but she had already made family plans on the appointed day, so Chuck got in his car and drove to Bigfork on a Saturday in March 2006. When we all got back in the office on Monday and heard Chuck's report on his interview with Harding, we knew we had a story.

Harding spoke to Chuck entirely on the record, meaning we could use whatever she said in a story, with her name attached as attribution. Harding told Chuck that she and Morrison had a brief affair in 1998 and that in 1999, Morrison called her to ask if she had anything against him.

"I said, 'No, why?'" she told Chuck. "He said, 'I'm running for state auditor and I just want to cover my bases.'"[107] Harding said she didn't speak to Morrison again until two years later, when she called him to ask about the investigation against her fiancé. She said state investigators appeared to have a vendetta against Tacke and his companies and asked Morrison if he could find out "what is going on and before any charges are filed or anything happens, call David."

Morrison had to know he was handling political dynamite and did not call her back. But he did hand off the case to an independent investigator to avoid any appearance of conflict of interest. The investigator—Helena attorney Beth Baker, who later became a state Supreme Court justice—decided to settle the case, and a deputy for Morrison signed off on it.

Harding, however, was not happy and told Chuck that she felt Morrison and the office had betrayed her fiancé, because he thought the agreement promised there would be no other investigations. Somehow the FBI had become involved, after talking with state investigators. Harding said that her fiancé never would have signed the agreement had he known state investigators had communicated with the feds.

"Whether [Morrison] pushed too hard or didn't push enough, he was remiss in his duty," she said. "He was out to protect himself, period, without any care for anybody at the company or David or anyone else."[108]

Harding's comments sealed the story, but our work was far from finished. We interviewed perhaps a dozen other people, both on and off the record, about the Tacke investigation and Morrison's relationship with Harding, including former employees of the auditor's office.

Everyone seemed to agree that when it came to the handling of the Tacke case, Morrison did the proper thing: he acknowledged he'd had relationships with people connected to Tacke and the company and didn't try to influence the investigation at all. But these sources, most of them Democrats, made it clear that they didn't think Morrison would be a good Democratic nominee to take on Burns that fall.

Once we had the guts of the story, the only thing left to do was talk to Morrison. We called up his campaign and said we had a big-impact story and asked to speak in person to its top lieutenants. That day in late March 2006, Tylynn Gordon and Karen Powell, two of the campaign's top officials, came to our office. We told them we were preparing a story that said Morrison had an extramarital affair with a woman whose fiancé had been investigated by his office.

Gordon and Powell reacted by insinuating that if we had a story based on secondhand sources, it wouldn't fly. But when we told them our main source was the woman who had the affair, on the record, their demeanor changed. They left the office and said they'd get back to us. By the end of the day, they told us Morrison would talk to us—and that his wife, Catherine Wright, would accompany him to the interview.

We conducted the interview in a tiny, windowless conference room in the basement of our office building. Morrison and his wife sat at the table, facing Chuck, Jennifer, myself and *Helena Independent Record* photographer George Lane. The interview lasted more than an hour. I've rarely felt more uncomfortable in an interview, but no matter how bad it was for us, it had to be many times worse for Morrison and his wife. He gamely defended his actions in the Tacke case, but when it came to the extramarital affair with Harding, he wouldn't talk about it, except to say he and his wife "had problems in our marriage at one time" and that those problems were "far behind us." They'd been married for fifteen years.

"We are deeply committed to each other, to our children, to our faith and to the state of Montana," he told us. "That's all I have to say about it. I'm not going to talk about ancient history."[109]

The interview occurred on Friday, March 31, and we told Morrison that the story probably would run the next week. We considered holding until the following Sunday but thought that was too long. We came into the office on Monday, April 3, and decided that we had to crank out the story as soon as possible. Drawing from the material that all three of us had gathered in interviews, I drafted the story. Chuck and Jennifer suggested some changes, and on Wednesday, April 5, the two-thousand-word piece was published in Lee's Montana papers. It began:

> *State Auditor John Morrison agreed to have an attorney handle a 2003 securities fraud case in part because he earlier had an extra-marital affair with a woman connected to the targeted companies, the Lee Newspapers State Bureau has learned.*
>
> *Morrison, the leading Democrat in Montana's U.S. Senate race, said that hiring an outside attorney is rare but not unprecedented. It was the best thing to do under the circumstances that led to a good result, he said.*
>
> *The companies, operated by David Tacke of Kalispell, were ordered to offer refunds to investors and create an independent board of directors, among other punishments.*
>
> *Tacke eventually ended up in federal prison with an order to repay investors nearly $1 million, Morrison noted, although investors have yet to receive any of that money.*
>
> *"I was not influenced in my decision-making in this case by my acquaintance with anybody in this case," he said in an interview last week. "Importantly, I did not influence this case, except to perhaps suggest that if we could save the* [companies] *while removing any cancer, to do so."*

Further down in the story, we had the damning comments from Harding about Morrison calling her before he ran for office, along with some details of the affair.

The Associated Press picked up the story, distributing it to dozens of other news outlets in the state (and outside the state—the story had some regional and national interest, given the importance of the race). As soon as the local TV stations saw it, they insisted on talking with Morrison as well. With his wife by his side, Morrison did the obligatory TV interviews.

We assumed the story would sink the Morrison campaign, but initially it didn't look that way. Our newspapers paid for a poll in the race in late May that showed Morrison with a 42 percent to 41 percent lead over Tester in the Democratic primary.

At a debate in Helena four weeks later among the Democratic U.S. Senate candidates, Morrison said he was the only candidate who had the finances to take on Burns, who already had more than $4 million in his reelection kitty. Tester, however, had a comeback ready, deftly alluding to the Morrison affair story without mentioning it directly. "I'm the only person on this stage that can go belly to belly with Conrad Burns on the situation of ethics," he said, saying he had no skeletons in his closet.

The third candidate in the race, Paul Richards, looked over at the heavyset Tester and said, "I think Jon Tester can go belly to belly with anyone." Just about everyone in the room broke out laughing, including Tester.[110]

Richards later dropped out of the race and threw his support behind Tester, and as the race wound down to the primary Election Day on June 6, you could sense that Tester had the momentum. As the vote results began to roll in, Tester raced out to a big early lead that just kept getting bigger as the evening proceeded. He beat Morrison 61 percent to 35 percent and bested him in forty-eight of Montana's fifty-six counties, including a nearly three-to-one thrashing in Morrison's home county of Lewis and Clark, which included Helena.

Tester's victory set the stage for what we knew would be a bruising campaign between him and Republican Conrad Burns. It took Burns about fifteen minutes to go on the offensive after Tester won the primary. Burns issued a statement election night calling on Tester to state his positions on constitutional amendments to ban gay marriage and the burning of the U.S. flag and on abolishing the federal estate tax, which Burns dubbed the "death tax."

In an interview with me the day after the election, Tester answered the questions put to him by Burns—he opposed amending the U.S. Constitution to ban gay marriage or flag-burning, and he supported a tax on estates over

$3 million—but said those issues weren't what he heard people talking about. Montanans cared about the cost of healthcare, the influence of multinational corporations, the affordability of their kids' college education, the national debt and the effect of energy, economic and tax policy on working families, he said, as well as ethical behavior in Washington, D.C., such as Burns's relationship with disgraced lobbyist Jack Abramoff.

"Senator Burns hasn't leveled with Montanans about his associations with Jack Abramoff and he's lying about his record on taxes," Tester told me. "Burns has shown he'll do or say anything to keep his job."[111]

Republicans had a 55-45 majority in the U.S. Senate, but with President George W. Bush's popularity in the toilet after his handling of Hurricane Katrina in the fall of 2005, that majority was seen as in jeopardy—and the Burns seat was one Democrats thought they could snag. Most polls either showed the race to be statistically tied, giving Tester a small, single-digit lead within the poll's margin of error, or had it tightening as Election Day drew near. A poll financed by our papers in mid-October showed Tester with a 46 percent to 43 percent lead. But our final poll, conducted less than a week before the election, had the race as a dead heat, with each man at 47 percent and the remainder split between undecideds and the Libertarian in the race, Stan Jones. Burns seemed to be closing the gap, setting up what we thought the race would be all along: damn close and down to the wire.

ON ELECTION NIGHT, THE Tester campaign reserved the ballroom floor of the Heritage Inn in Great Falls, ringing it with huge TVs that broadcast CNN and other national networks that reported election returns from around the country. As the 8:00 p.m. closing time for Montana's polls neared, it looked as though Democrats would pick up U.S. Senate seats in Missouri, Rhode Island, Ohio and Pennsylvania, narrowing the Republicans' majority to 51-49. Two races that could give the Democrats the Senate remained undecided or uncounted: a razor-close battle between Democrat Jim Webb and Republican George Allen in Virginia and, of course, the Montana race.

Early returns in Montana gave Tester the lead, and at one point, he was up by 15,000 votes, which is a good cushion, considering that only 400,000 or so people would vote in this off-year election. But in Montana, the early votes often come from the cities, where Democrats are stronger. When the votes start trickling in from rural areas, where Republicans dominate, they can whittle away at an early Democratic lead until it has disappeared.

The Tester-Burns race was no different in this regard—in fact, the rural areas began coming in even stronger than expected for Burns, and the Tester lead started shrinking as the night wore on and bled into the early morning.

But an unanticipated factor had delayed the vote-counting: Montana's first-ever experience with Election Day voter registration. In the more populous counties, hundreds of people showed up to register at county election offices that day. Under a new law, if they got in line to register by the poll-closing time of 8:00 p.m., they would be allowed to register and vote. In some cities, final votes weren't even cast until hours after the polls had officially closed. Counting of those votes stretched well into Wednesday morning.

When I found Tester sitting alone in a chair in a deserted hotel conference room at 4:40 a.m., getting ready to prep for interviews on the national TV news shows, I was the only reporter within sight. Two hours later, reporters, Tester staffers, TV cameras and hung-over party attendees filled the room, eager to find out where things stood.

Tester's spokesman, Matt McKenna, told reporters that Tester would win. "It's not a question of 'if,'" he said. "It's a question of 'when.' Our goal right now is to make sure that every vote is counted and that every vote counts. We're not declaring victory, but we know we're going to win."[112]

Tester's lead had withered to 1,600 votes, edging the race into recount territory if the margin stayed that small. But 4,000 votes remained uncounted in Butte, one of the most reliable Democratic enclaves in Montana.

With nothing to do but wait, *Missoulian* photographer Tom Bauer and I grabbed some breakfast at a downtown restaurant. Hard as it to believe in today's age of instant news, we had little we could do at 8:00 a.m. as print journalists. Our print deadline was long gone; Twitter, Facebook and smartphones didn't even exist, and our papers rarely updated our newspaper websites during the day, thinking it would be a tipoff to broadcast competitors.

It wasn't until 10:33 a.m. that the Associated Press called the race for Tester, spurred by the counting of the additional Butte ballots that had increased the Tester lead to nearly three thousand votes. Tester's campaign had to vacate the Heritage Inn early that morning and set up a news conference at a tiny room in another hotel about a mile away.

Governor Brian Schweitzer joined the raucous crowd, holding his and Tester's arm aloft in victory. Tester's wife, Sharla, introduced Tester as "my husband, my soul-mate, your U.S. senator, Papa Jon Tester!"[113]

Tester had unseated only the second Republican to ever win a U.S. Senate race in Montana, winning with 49.2 percent of the vote to Burns's 48.3

Jon Tester celebrates his 2006 U.S. Senate victory with Governor Brian Schweitzer. *Robin Loznak*, Great Falls Tribune.

percent. The final margin ended up at 3,562 votes out of 406,505 cast. His victory pushed Democrats to a 50-49 advantage in the U.S. Senate that morning, and Virginia's Jim Webb won his race later that day as well, cementing a 51-49 majority for Senate Democrats.

TESTER'S VICTORY NOT ONLY gave Montana two Democrats in the U.S. Senate—a combination that had endured for most of the past century—but also elevated the state's other senator, Max Baucus, to chair of the powerful Senate Finance Committee, a post Baucus would hold until his retirement in 2014.

Tester quickly set about crafting his own populist, everyman persona in the staid Senate. He called for a withdrawal from the war in Iraq (Baucus did too) and advocated for services for military veterans returning from the wars in the Middle East (he championed a bill that raised, for the first time in thirty-one years, the mileage reimbursement rate for military veterans who travel to get health treatment at VA health centers from 11 cents to 28.5 cents per mile). He voted against the bills that bailed out the banks and the auto industry during the 2008 financial crisis. He authored a bill that would create new wilderness in Montana for the first time in thirty years but also designate areas for logging to help the timber industry and timber workers (a bill that would be pilloried by the hard right and hard left and would not pass).

Yet while Tester did the work of a freshman U.S. senator, in my mind, it all seemed like a prelude to the next election. We knew the Republicans would come after him, big time, thinking that a freshman Democratic senator would be ripe for the picking in a state that leans conservative.

As they eyed the 2012 campaign, Republicans had good reason to think it might be a different story for Tester's election prospects. The political world had once again shifted on its axis, in dramatic, unforeseen ways.

Barack Obama had become president, but in Montana, his popularity had seriously waned, in part because of the passage of the Affordable Care Act. Democrats would get slaughtered in the 2010 midterm elections, nationally and in Montana, where the state House went from a 50-50 tie to a 68-32 majority for Republicans. The change gave the GOP a stage to hammer away on Obama policies, in Congress and the state legislature—and to link Tester to those policies.

The first month of 2010 also saw another event that roiled the political world: the U.S. Supreme Court decision known as *Citizens United*, which declared that corporations could spend directly on "independent expenditures" in campaigns. The 5-4 decision opened the door for corporations, labor unions and, later, individuals, to spend vast, additional sums of money trying to influence elections. The GOP and its allies used the decision to its advantage in the 2010 elections, and one assumed they would do the same in 2012, targeting freshman Democratic U.S. senators who had won close races in 2006, like Tester. But as the Tester reelection battle would show, Democrats and their political friends could read and understand the new rules as well.

As political reporters, we geared up for covering a race sure to be soaked with millions of dollars in campaign cash and populated by Montana's most colorful and seasoned political pros and personalities. It didn't disappoint, right down to its weirdly déjà vu finish, with myself, photographer Tom Bauer and the rest of the Montana media spending another all-nighter at a Great Falls hotel.

WE ALL KNEW WHO Tester's 2012 opponent would be: Denny Rehberg (pronounced "*ree*-burg"), Montana's only U.S. representative, a six-term incumbent and seasoned veteran of Montana politics. Rehberg, fifty-five when the campaign began, already had nearly thirty years in Montana politics under his belt. He had won a state House seat at age twenty-nine, managed the successful 1988 U.S. Senate campaign of Conrad Burns, became lieutenant governor in 1993, challenged Senator Baucus in 1996 and lost a relatively close race and took Montana's sole U.S. House seat in 2000. He'd won reelection five times in contests that weren't close. Rehberg also had remained closely allied with Burns and the Burns machine throughout his political career and no doubt relished the prospect of knocking off the man who had taken down his longtime pal in 2006.

Rehberg goes after Tester

By MATT GOURAS
Associated Press

HELENA — U.S. Rep. Denny Rehberg told Republicans on Saturday that backlash in Montana to "liberal know-it-alls" running the nation was a big reason he has decided to challenge Sen. Jon Tester in 2012.

Rehberg

Tester

Great Falls Tribune headline in February 2011.

Rehberg made his challenge of Tester official on February 5, 2011, telling a packed GOP dinner in Helena that he was in. He made it clear that the campaign would be a hard-punching, partisan affair. "The truth is that Jon Tester has been a reliable 'yes man' for Barack Obama and Harry Reid—and he's voted for the Obama administration 97 percent of the time," he said. "I will vote to cut federal spending, reduce the federal debt and repeal Obamacare.... Government spending is not the right solution."[114]

He also said if elected U.S. senator, he would block any Obama appointments of "liberal" judges to the federal bench in Montana, work to remove wolves from the endangered species list, fight a "secret plan" by the Obama administration to take over millions of acres in Montana by declaring them as national monuments, oppose gay marriage and oppose abortion.

Tester, however, wasn't one to sit pretty and take it. At the state's major Democratic Party dinner in Helena a month later, he unloaded on Rehberg and previewed his campaign strategy as well. Tester said he'd be running on his record—helping veterans, supporting the Obama administration's overhaul of Wall Street regulation, advocating for both logging and wilderness in Montana's forests—but spent most of his speech bashing Rehberg, calling him a do-nothing congressman with a record of opposing just about any proposed solution to any problem.

That same month, our newspapers paid for a wide-ranging telephone poll of Montanans, including questions about Rehberg, Tester and the Senate race. As expected, the contest looked to be razor-close in every way: 46 percent of those polled said they would vote to reelect Tester; 45 percent said they would go for Rehberg. Tester had a 50 percent "approval rating"—the total of people saying he was doing an "excellent" or "pretty good" job—while Rehberg's approval rating clocked in at 48 percent.

By mid-2011, outside groups already had begun turning out their wallets to alternately bash or support the respective candidates. When the contest concluded in November 2012, these outside groups spent in excess of $30 million—on top of the $22 million spent by the two candidates' campaigns—making this single race in Montana an incredible $50 million-plus affair.

The Wesleyan Media Project, a group run by political scientists tracking TV campaign ads nationwide, said that from June to October of that year, the Tester-Rehberg race had seen eighty-nine thousand separate TV ads—more than any other Senate race in the country.

President Trump campaigns against Tester in Bozeman, Montana, November 2018. *Montana Television Network (MTN).*

While we thought 2012 was a record that would stand for a while, it didn't. Six years later, when Tester ran for a third Senate term, forty-some outside groups would spend nearly $38 million on broadcast ads, digital ads, mailers, canvassing and other material, both for and against Tester— and the two candidates that year would spend more than $25 million, making it a $63 million race. And those amounts didn't include the cost of four visits to the state in 2018 by President Donald Trump to stump against Tester—a cost Trump's campaign declined to reveal, ignoring my inquiries about it.

Yet while we spent plenty of time scrutinizing the money in 2012, we suspected that, in the end, it might come down to something as simple as personality. How did the public perceive each candidate, as to what type of man they were and job they did in Washington, D.C.?

That question led my newspapers to send me to Washington, D.C., to spend time with both Rehberg and Tester for a firsthand look at how they did their job in the nation's capital. I flew to Washington in late March 2012— the first time in my twenty-plus years of covering Montana's Congressional delegation that I'd set foot there for a story.

In covering Tester and Rehberg in Washington, D.C., the first thing I noticed is the incredible gulf between the resources of a senator and a House member.

The entryway to Rehberg's office in the Rayburn Building, just south of the U.S. Capitol, looked like the lobby of a cheap hotel, with a tiny counter crammed into a relatively small space. A staffer manned the telephone and acted as receptionist. A door to the left led directly into Rehberg's office, a good-sized room that, in addition to his desk, had a table and chairs where he could meet with people, a black leather couch where he slept (rather than rent an apartment) and a large, flat-screen TV on the wall usually tuned in to Fox News. The only other rooms, off the other side of the entryway, were cramped quarters for staff, who shared the space with copiers, computers and other office equipment.

Tester's digs in the modern Hart Building had an expansive reception area and a maze of hallways and multiple offices and staffers before one finally reached Tester's actual office, a room more than double the size of Rehberg's and filled with fine furniture, artwork, plants and, of course, the requisite TV.

Tester had three people alone working in his office "press room," a sizeable office whose walls were plastered with news clippings, amid several TVs and computers. And if Tester wanted to keep in touch with reporters from the state's smaller newspapers and radio stations (which he did, monthly), he would stop in at the multimillion-dollar Senate media center in the same building, prearranging with control room staff to set up the joint interview, hooked in to a dozen outlets in Montana while Tester sat at a desk with headphones.

As I walked into Tester's office on Wednesday, March 28, at 7:45 a.m., he was at his expansive wood desk.

"Well, Mike Dennison," he said with a grin. "How the hell are ya? And here you are, in Washington, D.C."

This easygoing persona was the common thread that ran through almost all of his interactions with people I saw that day—an ability to converse with them as he welcomed them into his home and his world, while all the while winking about what a crazy world it was here in Washington, D.C., and how they all knew it. That theme led my story as well, three weeks later:

> *"People ask me how things are going," Tester says. "I say, 'Hey, things are going great at the farm, I feel great, the family's great, things are fine everywhere—except here. It's here that it's all screwed up.'"*

"Here" is Washington, D.C., and, more specifically, the halls of Congress, where Tester has spent the past five years working as Montana's junior senator.

Now, the freshman Democrat is locked in a re-election battle against Republican U.S. Rep. Denny Rehberg that's not only close, but also could decide party control of the U.S. Senate.

Tester, the farmer from Big Sandy with his signature flat-top haircut and two-fingered left hand, is comfortable and relaxed as he moves from constituent meetings to interviews to hearings, often stopping to jaw with everyone, from military brass to high school kids from Montana.

Yet an hour rarely passes without Tester expressing frustration with the ways of Washington, and how the politics of the moment seem to prevent Congress from tackling the nation's pressing problems.

I got along well with Rehberg and liked the guy, but he was more of a just-business personality, speaking fairly freely but still seeming to hold me at arm's length. Several times during the day, Rehberg would say to me, "Gotta conduct some business," disappear into his office and close the door, without any further explanation. Each time he'd emerge a few minutes later, and we'd continue whatever we were doing.

I also wasn't allowed to attend his meeting with Defense Secretary Leon Panetta (to talk about military base closings) or his fellow House Appropriations Committee subcommittee chairs (to talk budget targets). Rehberg said the no-press policy was being enforced by the people holding the meetings and not him.

During the day with Tester, only once did he ask for some time without me, explaining that he needed to spend a few minutes with his staff to discuss campaign-related strategy. But when I asked if I could go with him to his tiny campaign office just off Massachusetts Avenue and observe while he made personal fundraising calls, he said OK.

Tester said that almost every day, he penciled time into the schedule for what most politicians in the midst of a big-time campaign called "dialing for dollars"—the obligatory calls to people with money, asking for money, to finance the campaign. That day, for ninety minutes before heading back to the Capitol for votes in the Senate, he worked from a list of previous or prospective donors his campaign staff had provided, calling them to ask if they could attend an upcoming fundraiser in Bozeman. Most of the time no one answered and he left a message.

At one point, Tester paused, telephone in hand, thinking out loud, "I gotta call my daughter. It's her birthday today."

I left Washington, D.C., thinking that if this race rises and falls on personality, advantage Tester. Yet I thought it would hinge on much more and felt the smart money had to be on Rehberg to win, by a whisker.

Some voters, however, looked at Rehberg and Tester and decided they didn't want either candidate—and their third choice, Libertarian Dan Cox, would end up playing a crucial role, with an unusual, last-minute assist from a Tester ally.

Ten days before Election Day, Cox and every other Montanan who watched television would see a dramatic, professionally produced and widely distributed TV commercial promoting his candidacy, but Cox had nothing to do with it and was just as surprised as anyone else.

The ad featured a black-and-white shot of a man and his son on a hunting trip in the woods, recorded by a government surveillance camera perched in a tree. The son looks up, points directly at the camera and speaks to the father, who fetches his rifle and aims at and shoots the camera.

In a foreboding voiceover, the ad's narrator intones, "Congressman Dennis Rehberg would let the Department of Homeland Security monitor and control access on public lands. That may look good in Washington, but in Montana, not by a long shot." The screen then flashed a message in bold red letters: "Vote Cox—the Real Conservative."

The ad had been produced by the Montana Hunters and Anglers Leadership Fund, which was a political action committee formed by one of Tester's biggest supporters, the League of Conservation Voters. With some help from a political consultant I knew, I tracked down and reported that the group had spent $500,000 to produce and distribute the ad—a very large buy in the last week of an election. Rehberg's campaign angrily denounced the ad as a transparent attempt by Tester supporters to drain votes away from Rehberg.

Cox said he'd never heard of the Montana Hunters and Anglers group but loved the ad. "I couldn't have put together a better commercial against Rehberg on my behalf," he told me.[115]

Yet our newspapers' final poll in the race, conducted just as the pro-Cox ad ran on TV statewide, indicated that the Libertarian ploy wasn't working. The poll showed Rehberg leading Tester by 49 percent to 45 percent, with only 1 percent of the voters choosing Cox. Our pollster, Brad Coker, said in a high-profile race like this one, voters aren't likely to "waste their votes" on a candidate they know won't win.

Tester's communications director, Aaron Murphy, called me after the poll story appeared on the Sunday before the election and insisted our poll was wrong, especially when it came to Cox. Two days later, we'd find out how wrong we were.

ELECTION DAY 2012 BEGAN eerily the same as Tester's victory day six years earlier, as a balmy, unseasonably warm Tuesday in November. I stayed at the Great Falls hotel again (this time, the Holiday Inn), and again Tom Bauer of the *Missoulian* was there as the photographer.

Republicans nationwide had entered the 2012 campaign season thinking they would easily retake the U.S. Senate and erase the Democrats' 53-47 majority and likely oust President Barack Obama, building on their stunning 2010 successes and capitalizing on the nation's slower-than-expected recovery from the Great Recession of 2008 and 2009.

Yet several of their Senate candidates self-destructed (à la Missouri Republican Todd Akin, who said that women could not become pregnant if they were the victims of a "legitimate rape"), and Obama had shown himself to be remarkably resilient, entering the final days as a slight favorite to win reelection.

The Tester-Rehberg contest remained a high-profile race on the national stage, as Republicans thought they still had an outside chance to make gains or maybe even pull off a majority-stealing victory.

Yet when the initial returns began rolling in, Tester staked out a narrow yet comfortable lead—a lead he would never relinquish. Those first returns also manifested another trend that would hold throughout the evening: Cox, the Libertarian, garnered much more than our poll's predicted 1 percent. He started out around 5 percent to 6 percent and would hold steady for the entire run of vote-counting, which, like in 2006, stretched into Wednesday morning.

By 9:30 p.m. Mountain Time, Obama had won reelection as president, and with Tester leading (and circulating in the hotel ballroom), the pro-Democratic crowd was in full-on party mode. Democrats had actually picked up a pair of U.S. Senate seats, in Massachusetts and Indiana, and in the early returns, Tester had well over 50 percent of the vote.

He'd rolled up a twenty-thousand-vote lead by 11:30 p.m., when I tweeted that many rural areas had yet to be counted, but they would not be enough to save Rehberg. I made one last tweet at 2:30 a.m. that Tester's lead still sat at sixteen thousand votes, but when I got up some four hours later, his lead had increased by another thousand. When I last checked the ballroom before hitting the sack, I saw Tester, still out there, chatting with friends and supporters.

At around 8:00 a.m., Bauer and I sat down in the hotel restaurant for breakfast. Several tables away, Tester sat with his wife, family and a few key staffers. By the time we had finished our breakfast, the Associated Press had just called the race in Tester's favor, shortly before 9:00 a.m., and I sat down at his table to interview him.

The race "pretty much went true to form—we figured it would be a long night," he said. But Tester said he'd also felt a surge of energy among his supporters in the final days, as he barnstormed the state, and was confident he would win: "That really translated into making me feel good about what was going on."[116]

Tester had done it again—and almost made it look easier, although I know it wasn't. Tester beat Rehberg by eighteen thousand votes but didn't win a majority, capturing 48.6 percent of the vote (Libertarian Cox ended up with a surprisingly strong 6.5 percent). Tester raised and spent some $13 million and had to face down at least $26 million spent by Rehberg and his allies to defeat him.

Tester after winning reelection, November 2012. *Larry Beckner,* Great Falls Tribune.

But Tester also had more than a little help from his friends. The League of Conservation Voters spent $1.45 million on Tester's behalf, including door-to-door canvassers, mailers and phone calls to get out the vote. Organized labor knocked on sixty-eight thousand doors across the state, including five thousand in the final four days of the campaign. Planned Parenthood hit the bricks (and its bank account) for Tester as well. It all led to Tester rolling up a 38,500-vote margin in six of the state's eight most populous counties—a margin that Rehberg simply couldn't overcome in the remaining rural or Republican urban counties.[117]

As I walked out of the hotel lobby late Wednesday morning to head back to Helena, I ran into Barrett Kaiser, a longtime Democratic operative who'd worked for years for Max Baucus and had been a consultant for the Tester campaign.

"Man," I said, "I'm impressed."

"What do you mean?" he asked.

"I thought Rehberg was going to win. I really did."

"Really?" Kaiser said, sounding incredulous. Then he smiled. "Nah. We knew we were going to win."

Democrats would end up padding their U.S. Senate margin that election to 55-45 but would see it all evaporate two years later in the Republican landslide of 2014. Baucus's seat, which he vacated by retiring, was captured by Republican Steve Daines, who was Rehberg's successor as congressman. Daines's open Congressional seat stayed Republican in 2014 as well. Already, pundits had Tester in trouble for 2018.

YET TWO YEARS BEFORE Tester's anticipated reelection run in 2018, an unexpected development would alter it in many ways: the election of Donald Trump as president.

Tester dutifully supported Hillary Clinton during the 2016 presidential election, although she was broadly unpopular and a sure loser in Montana that year. Political prognosticators also said that if Clinton was president, Tester was in big trouble in 2018, when the president's party usually gets punished in midterm elections.

Trump's surprise victory in 2016 turned that prospect on its head, seen as a positive for Tester's reelection prospects. But midway through 2018, the president decided that the conventional wisdom shouldn't apply and made defeating Tester a personal goal.

In late March, Trump fired the current head of the Veterans Affairs Department and nominated the White House physician, Ronny Jackson, to become the new VA secretary. Tester, the highest-ranking Democrat on the Senate Committee on Veterans Affairs, was poised to play a key role on whether Jackson would be confirmed.

One month later, Tester went public with some stunning news: allegations that Jackson had engaged in misconduct at work, excessive prescribing of drugs to White House staff and drinking on the job. Tester also said he had misgivings about whether Jackson had the experience to run a large, troubled organization like the VA Department and health system. Within days, Jackson withdrew his name for consideration.

Trump immediately attacked Tester on Twitter, saying that he should resign and calling him "dishonest and sick." He later told Fox News that Tester would have "a big price to pay in Montana" for his actions and said Tester's actions were "an absolute disgrace."[118]

The president's super PAC, America First Action, began producing and buying TV ads attacking Tester. Trump would visit Montana himself in July, September, October and November to address large campaign rallies, where he excoriated Tester as a "liberal Democrat" who needed to be retired.

At the October 18 rally in Missoula, Trump said Tester "led the Democratic mob in an effort to destroy the reputation" of Jackson. "All lies, all made-up stuff," the president asserted. "They made up a series of lies

The author and KPAX-Missoula anchor Jill Valley covering President Trump's October 2018 campaign rally against Tester in Missoula, Montana. *Montana Television Network (MTN).*

that were horrible. That's really why I'm here….I can never forget what Jon Tester did to a man of the highest quality."

Trump repeated those comments at his final Montana rally on November 3 at Bozeman Yellowstone International Airport, just three days before the election. Tester stood by his comments about Jackson, who had declined to appear before the Senate committee to defend himself.

Just as they did in 2012, multiple Super PACs and other political groups also lined up to spend money to defeat Tester, dropping more than $22 million on the 2018 campaign. They blanketed Montana air waves with commercials casting Tester as someone who had "gone Washington," was in too deep with special-interest lobbyists and who was a handmaiden to Democrats whom conservatives loved to hate, such as then House Minority Leader Nancy Pelosi of California and Senate Minority Leader Chuck Schumer of New York.

Tester's Republican opponent in 2018, State Auditor Matt Rosendale, appeared at all four Montana rallies with the president and declared himself all in on the Trump agenda. He called Tester an "obstructionist" to the president's major initiatives, such as two Supreme Court nominees, the repeal of "Obamacare" and the 2017 GOP tax cut bill.

Tester, however, had plenty of resources to respond, as well as the power of his considerable personality and brand. "We know what they're gonna do," he told me more than a year before the election. "They're going to try

Tester at a Helena campaign rally six days before the November 2018 election. *Montana Television Network (MTN).*

to make me something that I'm not and then run against that person. They tried to do that in 2006, they tried to do that in 2012. We've got a great record to run on; we're going to focus on making that record even better over the next 15 months."[119]

He cosponsored more than a dozen bills that would be signed by the president, including major reforms of the VA health system, and touted this cooperation in a state that Trump had won by 20 percentage points in 2016 and where Trump remained popular. Tester also raised nearly $20 million in campaign funds—four times what his opponent could muster—and built a formidable get-out-the-vote organization.

On election night, November 6, 2018, the words of Yogi Berra would apply precisely: "Déjà vu all over again."

Tester's campaign had reserved the same ballroom at the Great Falls Holiday Inn. Polls, including one sponsored by my employer, the Montana Television Network, had the contest as a dead heat or Tester as a slight favorite.

As I sat in the hotel ballroom, the first returns rolled in about 8:30 p.m. Tester was almost tied in Montana's biggest county, Yellowstone, where Republicans must do well to win statewide, and was up two to one in Lewis and Clark County (home to Helena, the state capital), which Trump had won in 2016.

More than 90 percent of the votes had yet to be counted. But right then, I turned to some fellow reporters and said that Tester would win. We all laughed—and then watched as the race got tighter and tighter as the night wore on.

"Any way you slice it, Tester has to be feeling pretty good at this moment," I said for my segment on MTN's 10:00 p.m. news. "But we still have many votes to count before the evening is over."

Just before 11:00 p.m., Tester came out to address the crowd. Although his lead had shrunk to a few thousand votes, he exuded confidence. "I feel absolutely, unequivocally very good about where we're at right now," he said. "And I will tell you that I look forward to sharing with you tomorrow some very good news....We'll let the [county election] clerks around the state do their job...and tomorrow? What are we gonna do tomorrow? You're damn right we're gonna celebrate!"[120]

But after midnight, Rosendale inched ahead in the vote count. As more and more rural counties' totals came in, his lead continued to increase. I slept for several hours before waking at 4:00 a.m. Wednesday to pen a story for the morning news shows, and Rosendale was still leading, by 2,600 votes. I wondered, "Might Rosendale win? Was Tester wrong last night?"

After I filed the story and took a shower, I headed down the hotel's main floor hallway. The Tester campaign's lead press guy, Chris Meagher, sat by himself in the staff room, staring at his laptop. I asked him what he knew.

"They're telling us at least 70,000 votes are still out there," he said.

Actually, it was more than 100,000 votes—almost one-fifth of the entire amount of votes that would be cast in a record-setting turnout for a midterm election. And the vast majority of those votes would be in Democratic counties, particularly Missoula and Gallatin, home to Montana's two public universities, where hundreds of students had registered to vote on Election Day. Once I determined where most of those uncounted votes were, I knew it was pretty much over—and that the result, once again, would be a Tester victory on Wednesday morning after the election.

I ate breakfast in the same restaurant where I'd interviewed Tester as the winner six years earlier. When I got back to my hotel room, new vote totals had been posted from Bozeman and Missoula. Tester had regained the lead, and it would continue to grow.

By the time all the votes were counted later that week, Tester had beaten Rosendale by nearly eighteen thousand votes and, for the first time in his

Tester gestures at a news conference in Great Falls November 7, 2018, moments after winning a third term. *Montana Television Network (MTN)*.

Senate career, captured more than 50 percent of the vote (50.33 percent, to be precise).

At 11:00 a.m. on November 7, the day after the election, the Associated Press called the race in Tester's favor, as he addressed a raucous room of supporters at the Holiday Inn. Tester came back to one of his favorite themes: screwed-up Washington, D.C., and how it's time to set the differences aside and accomplish something.

"We need to work together and put aside the political pettiness and work to get things done," he said. "And I will tell you why. Because as I traverse this state, north, south, east and west, the people I've talked to, the biggest issue they bring up is, 'Why can't you guys work together?' Well, we can, and we will, and it will happen because the American people are demanding it."[121]

Chapter 8

CODY MARBLE

An Innocent Man

O n a brisk March morning in 2008, I entered the visiting area of the Missoula County Jail, a series of booths with Plexiglas partitions between visitor and inmate. Minutes later, a guard ushered in twenty-three-year-old Cody Marble, who had been convicted six years earlier of raping a fellow juvenile inmate in this same building. His father had insisted to me that his son was wrongly convicted. Evidence I'd seen had convinced me at least to take a look at it. I had not yet spoken to his son.

"So, Cody," I said. "What do you see as the story here? Why is this something I should write about?"

Marble abruptly sat up straight and leaned forward, an incredulous look on his face, as though I'd asked the most obvious question in the world. "Because I'm innocent, because I didn't do it!" he exclaimed without hesitation, looking me straight in the eye. "That's the story."[122]

I had pored over hundreds of pages of documents, trial transcripts and other material on the six-year-old case. I'd talked to his father multiple times and interviewed people involved in proceedings. But Marble's response seemed to bring it all into focus. After almost thirty years of reporting, the bullshit detector in me was second nature—and Cody Marble didn't register. I knew I had a story.

Marble's denial wasn't the only piece of the puzzle of course. In the weeks before I spoke with him that first time, I'd put together a growing list of items that cast doubt on his conviction for raping a thirteen-year-old male juvenile

Cody Marble at the Missoula County Courthouse in December 2010, after filing the petition that led to his exoneration almost eight years later. *Linda Thompson, Missoulian.*

inmate in the Missoula County Juvenile Detention Center in March 2002, when Marble himself was only seventeen.

Two of the sex offender counselors assigned to evaluate or treat Marble said, in writing or on the record or both, that they thought Marble hadn't raped anyone. One of the detention center guards on duty the evening of the alleged rape told me she didn't believe it happened (and was never asked her opinion at the trial). Another guard said she'd like to talk to me, but she couldn't risk losing her job.

The juvenile delinquent who initially told jail officials he'd seen the rape had been sitting in his detention center cell when the rape occurred and couldn't possibly have seen it. He was released from the jail three months later, disappeared and could not be found to testify at the trial.

Another jail guard, who had told fellow guards that he believed Marble's story of being set up by the other inmates, died of a heart attack five months before the trial.

Marble's defense attorney at the November 2002 trial decided that Marble shouldn't testify in his own defense, denying the jury an opportunity to see the same forthright denial that helped convince me Marble might be telling the truth.

I would write my initial story on the case in May 2008, running in two of Lee Newspapers' Montana dailies. But it would be another nine years until Marble was exonerated and a decade until he was entirely free of the Montana correctional system—some sixteen years after he was falsely accused.

It's not easy to beat a justice system determined not to admit it made a mistake, but Marble did it—along with the Montana chapter of the Innocence Project, the perseverance of his father, the dogged pursuit of his last lawyer, a crucial Supreme Court decision and the willingness of one prosecutor to reexamine the evidence.

I KNEW NOTHING OF Marble's case until his father, Jerry Marble, called me in late 2007 at my office. Jerry had read a story I wrote about an accused child rapist in Billings cleared by DNA evidence. He asked whether I might be interested in another case where a rapist had been wrongly convicted: his son.

The first piece of evidence that grabbed my attention was a sworn statement from Missoula psychologist Michael Scolatti, who evaluated Marble before his 2003 sentencing for the rape conviction. Scolatti said Marble didn't seem anything like the sex offenders he had treated or interviewed. In a later interview with me, Scolatti said he'd watched videotapes of the detention center pod the night of the alleged rape and that nothing in the demeanor of the inmates indicated that anything traumatic had happened. He also told me it was the first time in his twenty-eight-year career that he'd gone on record saying he thought one of the accused sex offenders he'd interviewed was innocent.

Scolatti's statement was part of Cody Marble's petition, filed early in 2007, to overturn his conviction, alleging "ineffective [defense] counsel" at his 2002 trial and misconduct by prosecutors. A judge rejected his petition shortly after I started examining the case.

I had some questions about the status of the case and called the assistant attorney general handling it, Carlo Canty, who asked if I'd covered the trial. I said no, and he said before I wrote anything, perhaps I should read the trial transcript, which was on file at his office, a few blocks from mine. I wasn't sure if I wanted to slog through the transcript of a three-and-a-half-day trial but eventually did—and by the time I'd finished, I had no doubt that, at the very least, Marble's defense lawyer had missed some opportunities to undermine the prosecution's case.

The juvenile inmate who had initially reported seeing the rape and then had to admit that he didn't, a transient named Scott Kruse, had disappeared from Missoula and couldn't be found. The judge then required the lead prosecutor to take the stand, to be questioned by Cody's lawyer. His attorney, Kathleen Foley, barely got out a few questions about Kruse's lie and credibility.

When the detention center guards testified, questions about whether and how the crime could have occurred went unasked. And the decision not to have Marble testify to rebut damning testimony by his accusers made no sense to me.

Canty called me later to ask me what I thought.

"It seems like Marble had a pretty weak defense," I said.

"Oh, and this is based on your experience as an attorney?"

"No," I replied. "It's based on my experience as a reporter covering trials and the criminal justice system."

MARBLE'S ACCUSERS—A HALF DOZEN juvenile offenders who'd happened to be in the detention center along with Cody—said Cody and the alleged victim, thirteen-year-old Robert "Bobby" Thomas, had gone into the changing area outside the shower area of the jail "pod" and that Cody had raped Thomas there, as the other teenage inmates sat on the other side of a partition, where they could see the feet of anyone standing in the area and hear whoever might be talking or showering. A drawing of the detention area's floor plan also indicated that the guards on duty might have some ability to see into the shower area.

I wanted to see for myself what the guards could and could not see and what the other inmates could see as well. I called the Missoula County Sheriff's Office, which runs the jail, to ask when I could visit the jail and see the scene of the alleged crime.

The office rejected my request, telling me they don't give "tours" of the jail to the public. I wrote a formal request, but they rejected that as well and said if I wanted to see the jail, I had to get a court order or permission of the county attorney's office—which, of course, wasn't going to help me undermine its conviction. To this day, I've never seen firsthand the layout of Pod C in the juvenile detention center where Marble allegedly raped Thomas in the open shower/changing area.

But I had the names of two of the detention center guards who had worked there the night of the alleged rape. The first one, Susan Latimer, had moved to the Bitterroot Valley, some sixty miles south of Missoula, and no longer worked at the jail. I ran down her number, called and left a message. A day later, she called back.

The Missoula County Juvenile Detention Center, where Marble was falsely accused of raping a fellow teenage inmate. *Mike Dennison.*

Latimer told me the guard's station is no farther than fifteen feet from Pod C. She said while the guards can't see directly into the shower area, they can see people going in and out and that the window for any rape occurring would be perhaps ten minutes, given the frequency of cell checks by the guards. When I asked her if she thought Cody had raped Thomas, Latimer said she did not.

"I was shocked that Cody was accused of rape just before he was due to get out," she told me. "Cody is not a stupid young man. He's a smart young man. The whole thing just…I really felt that if something happened, it would have triggered something for me." She also said Marble was not "assaultive or aggressive" and was not one of the inmates who "picked on people."

Latimer said when Marble's defense attorney, Kathleen Foley, deposed her before the trial, "she treated me like the enemy." "I thought, 'My gosh, I could have been her best friend,'" Latimer said.[123]

She also said when she took the witness stand at the trial, she was shocked when Foley didn't ask questions that would have elicited comments from the guards that they did not believe Marble had raped anyone. "She didn't ask me anything that I can remember that would have supported Cody," Latimer told me. "Kathleen Foley had a great opportunity, and she releases me [as a witness], and I'm thinking, 'My God, this kid is sunk.' [She] had people who believed in Cody's innocence and tried to maintain objectivity and she didn't use it at all."[124]

She went on to say that other guards, including Keith Williamson, believed the accusation was a setup by inmates who wanted to get back at Cody. Williamson, however, died of a heart attack in June 2002, three months after Cody was accused and arrested and five months before the trial.

Later that week, I reached another guard who still worked at the jail. She wanted to talk to me, but said she feared if her name appeared in the story, she might get in trouble at work or even lose her job. It wasn't worth the risk, she said—although she, too, indicated she had doubts about Marble's guilt.

I also interviewed a sex offender counselor, Roger Dowty, who had the largest treatment practice in western Montana for sex offenders. Dowty told me he was one of only three counselors in the state who would consider counseling "deniers"—people who won't admit to their crime, when admitting guilt is a prerequisite for advancing to higher levels of counseling and getting out of prison on parole.

Dowty told me he'd bet "a large amount of money" that Marble was innocent, based on his experience with deniers and guilty sex offenders.[125] He said he'd known convicted sex offenders who were innocent but who agreed to admit to the crime, so they could get through the treatment and get paroled. Cody wouldn't do that, he said. Rather than come up with a lengthy explanation of why he was innocent, "Marble just says, 'I didn't do it,'" Dowty told me.[126]

CODY HAD BEEN IN and out of the criminal justice system since he was thirteen, starting not long before his mentally troubled mother, Toni, committed suicide in July 1999 by locking herself in the garage and turning on the car. His mom had tried to kill herself several times in the previous three years.

After his mother's suicide, Cody had a series of run-ins with the law, mostly related to marijuana use. Marble told me he'd never had any counseling or treatment to help him deal with his mother's death and that his marijuana use was his form of "self-medicating." When he was fifteen, he got sent to the Swan Valley Youth Center Academy, a boot camp–like facility for juvenile offenders in western Montana's Seeley-Swan Valley, where he graduated and earned his general equivalency diploma.

The boot camp education didn't stick, however. Additional drug possession offenses landed him at the Wilderness Treatment Center, a privately run program in northwest Montana for juvenile offenders. He walked away from the center in late 2001 and was hitchhiking back to Missoula when authorities picked him up. The wilderness center declined to take Cody back because he had a "dual diagnosis" of drug dependency and posttraumatic stress syndrome (from his mother's death). That's when authorities sent him to the Missoula County Juvenile Detention Center while prosecutors and the courts decided what to do with him.

On March 10, 2002, after Cody had been at the detention center for five months, his father visited him and told him he would be bailing him out two days later. Cody, now seventeen, told his fellow inmates he'd be gone in a few days. Jerry Marble took his son home on March 12, but four days later, sheriff's deputies came to arrest Cody. Robert "Bobby" Thomas and six other juvenile inmates had reported that Marble raped Thomas in the Pod C shower changing area several days earlier—on the very day Cody's father had earlier told Cody he'd be out on bail in two days.

THE INITIAL REPORT THAT Marble had raped Thomas came from Scott Kruse, a teenager who'd been arrested and charged as an accessory to the murder of a fellow transient under a bridge near the Clark Fork River in Missoula. He'd been in jail with Cody and several others in Pod C. Several days after Cody was discharged, Kruse—still an inmate—told detention center guards that Marble had raped Thomas.

In an interview with Sheriff's Sergeant Brad Giffin on March 16, four days after Cody had been released, Kruse said he saw Bobby bent over in the shower changing area and Cody behind him, moving "like he was fucking him"—although, based on other statements, a partition was between the shower area and the rest of the inmates, so if Kruse saw anything, it would be only a person's feet and lower legs or head. Under questioning from Giffin, Kruse said he "didn't even know it was Bobby" but that he had the skinniest arms of anyone, so he could recognize him.[127]

Videotapes of the cells of Pod C later showed Kruse to be inside his cell the entire time that the alleged rape occurred, so it was impossible for him to see what had occurred. He then changed his story to say that he reported the rape after he had heard about it from other inmates.

Six other juvenile inmates told Giffin and other investigators similar stories, although two of them first said that Thomas had been subjected to oral, not anal sex, with Cody.

Deputy Rob Taylor also interviewed Thomas, who said he had been raped by Cody and that Cody had later told him not to tell anyone what had happened—even though the half dozen other inmates had allegedly witnessed it.

At no time during the interviews of the six other juvenile inmates or Thomas did the investigators drill down on the "why" of the incident or the dubious proposition that Marble, a minor drug offender with no history of violence, would suddenly decide to rape a thirteen-year-old boy in an open shower area, in partial view of six other people and, potentially, the detention center guards, right before he was to be released from the jail. Investigators also didn't formally interview any of the guards on duty at the time.

A doctor examined Thomas that week and reported finding no physical evidence of rape, although he did say it was possible that any injuries might have healed in the week or so since the alleged crime.

The county prosecutor's office filed a rape charge against Marble ten days later. Nine days after the filing, Sergeant Scott Newman, a sheriff's deputy in charge of the jail, wrote a memo to the state Department of Corrections, which had inquired about the incident in its role of licenser of jail facilities in Montana. Newman said:

> *I have checked the log for activity during the time frame in question (approximately 22:00, Sunday, March 10) as well as the officers that were on duty at the time. And the window of opportunity to commit the crime for all intents and purposes appears to be virtually non-existent, as there were five officers on at that time. And the fact that there were cell checks, pencil passes and general activity by officers going on at that time.*

Nonetheless, the trial went forward, beginning in mid-November 2002, after Cody refused a plea bargain that would have required him to plead guilty to rape in exchange for a deferred sentence and no prison time. Marble had been assigned an experienced public defender as his attorney, William Boggs, but the case was handled primarily by Boggs's associate, Kathleen Foley.

Neither the defense nor the prosecutors asked Newman about his opinion that the rape probably could not have occurred.

At the trial, Foley also never asked the two guards who testified—Bigelow and Latimer—if they thought a rape had occurred or could occur. When I asked Boggs about this omission regarding Latimer, he pointed to Latimer's pretrial deposition (conducted by Foley), noting that Latimer said then she didn't know if Cody was guilty or innocent. Boggs said she had essentially "made the state's case" by suggesting there was a window of opportunity for Cody to rape Thomas in the shower area.

"If she's saying now that she thinks he's innocent, then she was perjuring herself in her deposition," Boggs told me. "She was evasive and slippery and uncooperative during the entire deposition. You see a witness like that, and you keep your distance like you would from a coiled snake."[128]

Foley deposed Latimer almost two months before the trial. While Latimer said several times during the deposition that she couldn't know for certain whether Cody was guilty or innocent, she also said that she liked Cody Marble, that "from the depths of her heart," she wanted him to be innocent and that she would "like to believe" that he didn't commit any rape. Foley never came out and asked Latimer directly whether she thought Marble had raped Thomas or could have raped Thomas.[129]

Thomas and four of the six inmates who leveled the charges testified at the trial, recounting their initial accusations. Kruse did not, for he had been released from jail in August after his accessory to murder charge had been pleaded down to misdemeanor assault and trespassing. He then promptly disappeared from Missoula. He could not be asked about how he had lied initially when reporting that he'd seen Marble rape Thomas.

Marble also never took the witness stand on his own behalf to explain that he believed his fellow inmates had simply made the whole thing up, as a twisted form of jailhouse retribution, because they didn't like him or thought it might enable them to get a better deal with prosecutors in their own respective cases.

Marble told me in a telephone interview in early 2008 that he wanted to testify at the trial but that Foley told him he shouldn't because the prosecution would drag out his criminal history to make him look bad.

"I really didn't take the whole thing that seriously," he said. "Why would I? I didn't commit a crime. I trusted the system and was pretty naïve.…I thought it would be dismissed, that the truth would come out, and that I would be vindicated.…I'd been charged before with crimes that I didn't do and they had been dismissed. I had no reason to think that the system would fail me."[130]

When I asked Marble why a half dozen juvenile delinquents would concoct such an elaborate scheme to get him for some perceived slight and take it all the way through an investigation and trial, he said one of his accusers,

Nicholas Melton-Roberts, had approached him earlier about a similar scheme. Another inmate had assaulted Melton-Roberts and stolen things from him, Cody told me, and Melton-Roberts asked Cody to corroborate a trumped-up charge that the inmate had raped Melton-Roberts.

"I told him, 'Absolutely not,'" Cody said. "I said if you're going to tell the guards a story, don't just make one up." He also told me he believed Thomas might have been pressured to go along with the scheme to set up Cody and that Thomas was "scared to death" of Kruse, whom Cody called "a scary guy."[131]

In my interview with Cody in 2008, he also described to me the shower area (and site of the alleged rape) that jail authorities had refused to let me see. Showers were allowed in the morning, after which it was an "unauthorized area" where people likely couldn't get into without the guards knowing about it, he said. If you were spotted in the shower area during any but the morning shower time, "it would be a big deal, it would be a write-up," he said.

"You'd be locked down as a punishment, they'd be yelling over the speaker," he told me. "I've never seen anybody caught in the shower area. Nobody does it. It's a known fact that you'd be caught."

After a three-and-a-half-day trial, the jury deliberated for two and a half hours before finding Marble guilty of sexual intercourse without consent, the legal term in Montana for rape. He never had the chance to tell the jury any of the things he had told me more than five years later.

Once I had interviewed Cody, I had only three other interviews to conduct: his defense lawyers, the prosecutor and the man Cody allegedly raped, Bobby Thomas.

His two defense lawyers, Boggs and Foley, said they'd talk to me only if I submitted my questions in writing, which I did. They then agreed to meet at their Missoula office eight days later, but only to discuss the case on background. Boggs and Foley vigorously argued that they had done the best job possible defending Marble and questioned why I was even doing a story.

Foley refused to talk on the record for the story and called my boss, Chuck Johnson, at least once, trying to convince him to pull the plug on the story. Chuck told her he trusted me to be fair and to know what was or wasn't a story and wouldn't overrule me unless the circumstances were extraordinary. He also suggested she talk directly to me, but she would not. Boggs spoke to me on the record only once, about Latimer's deposition.

The lead prosecutor, Missoula County deputy attorney Dori Brownlow, told me she had no doubt the jury rightfully convicted Marble. She said the way the rape had been reported, days after it occurred, was not unusual and actually added to the credibility of the report.

She said Thomas, the accuser, had been afraid of what might happen to him if he reported the rape while his assailant was still in jail with him, so waiting until Marble was released made sense (although Thomas had not been the person who first told authorities about the alleged crime).

As for Thomas himself, I would never speak with him. He was in prison for statutory rape (he'd had sex with an underage girl at a party and later violated his parole and got sent to prison) and ignored messages I sent him via prison authorities.

MY INITIAL STORY ON the Marble case, nearly 2,500 words long, ran on May 11, 2008. Only two of the five papers I worked for carried it: Marble's hometown paper, the *Missoulian*, and the *Helena Independent Record*. It was a tough story to write, relying more on an accumulation of evidence rather than a clear, single action. I led with the evidence and then zeroed in on Marble himself:

> *Indeed, Marble is hardly a sympathetic figure, having been in and out of jails, juvenile programs and prison since age 14, repeatedly violating probation or parole by using marijuana and methamphetamine.*
>
> *He also ignored defense counsel's advice to accept a deal on the rape charge, to plead guilty in exchange for a three-year deferred sentence, avoiding prison. Instead, he insisted on a trial, was convicted and received a 20-year sentence.*
>
> *There's also no black-and-white evidence, such as DNA, that could exonerate him. In fact, there was no physical evidence at all of the rape....*
>
> *"There's no one thing that I can say that will make you say, 'I believe you,'" Marble said in a recent interview from the Missoula County Detention Center. "You have to listen to the [counselors] who evaluated me. Look at my criminal past. Come talk to me, look at me."*

The story generated almost zero media buzz statewide. But it did provoke a response from one of the prosecutors in the case, Missoula County deputy attorney Andrew Paul.

Less than three weeks after the story ran, Paul was questioning potential jurors in a separate case in Missoula. One of the prospective jurors had been a juror at Marble's trial, and Paul, not knowing that fact, asked him if any prior jury experience had made him not want to sit on another jury. The juror then referred directly to my article about the Marble case and said it made him wonder if that jury had made the right decision.

According to a transcript I saw later, Paul teed off on my article. "That article was, in my opinion, grossly misleading," he told the court and the juror from Marble's case. "You had a lot more evidence that was presented to you at that trial than the writer of that story…who has never seen the videotapes, who has never seen the testimony.…I want you to be aware that the people who wrote that article did not see even a quarter of what you saw as a juror, when you were sitting on that case."[132]

Actually, I had seen some of the videotapes (of the juvenile inmates the day of the alleged crime) and had read the entire trial transcript and seen and heard quite a bit more than the jury did. Paul, who had never spoken to me, had stated in court that he knew what I had seen or not seen. I wrote him a letter asking him why he would make these false comments in a court of law.

In his reply, Paul said "as one who heard and saw the witnesses testify on the stand and was present for the entire trial, I reasonably concluded that you were not privy to the same quality of information presented to [the jury]."

Marble in 2017, several months after he was released from prison. *Montana Innocence Project.*

Then, in another incredible turn of presumption, Paul said the "most misleading aspect of the story" was using sex offender counselor Roger Dowty's statement that he would bet a large sum of money that Cody was not guilty. Paul said Dowty had been referring to a different case when he made that statement and that I had opened my interview with Dowty by saying "there wasn't any way Cody could have been guilty." Paul claimed he had spoken to Dowty and that Dowty said I had misinterpreted his statements.[133]

I had Dowty's interview on tape; I had neither misinterpreted what he said nor opened the interview by declaring Cody to be innocent. I tried unsuccessfully to reach Dowty in the weeks to come but didn't see him again until twenty months later, at a parole hearing for Cody.

Dowty told me then he considered me a "hero of journalism" for writing about the case and that without my reporting, its flaws wouldn't have come to light. At that February 2010 parole hearing, Dowty testified in favor of Marble's parole request. He told the parole board that most people who knew anything about the case had concluded that Marble was innocent.

While my coverage of Marble's case seemed to generate little public interest, it did get the attention of a group just getting under way in Montana: the Innocence Project.

Its first executive director, Jessie McQuillan, called me not long after the first story ran, to pick my brain about the case and see if I knew anything else that might point to or prove Cody's innocence. I told her what she probably already knew—that the only way Cody might be cleared or get a new trial would be convincing Thomas or any of the other witnesses to admit they had lied.

Over the next year or so, Innocence Project staffers began doing just what McQuillan and I had discussed. They began contacting witnesses and also contacted Thomas, who was still in prison. Cody had told them he'd heard Thomas was telling other inmates that the 2002 rape never occurred.

Innocence Project attorney Larry Mansch later said in court records that he first spoke to Thomas at a privately run state prison in Shelby, Montana, and that Thomas said he had not been raped by Marble in 2002 and that "he never thought it would go this far." A few months later, on April 1, 2010, Mansch and McQuillan returned to Shelby to speak again with Thomas. They said Thomas adamantly said the rape didn't happen and that he had agreed with the older juvenile inmates to set up Cody for a rape charge. But when McQuillan asked him to sign a statement to that effect, Thomas balked. He told them he wanted the truth to be known, but not if it meant bringing harm or consequences to himself.

Prison authorities later transferred Thomas back to the Montana State Prison at Deer Lodge, where McQuillan and Mansch went unannounced on July 10 and asked to visit Thomas. He agreed to see them. Thomas again said the rape did not occur and had been a setup. This time, Thomas agreed to sign a statement and did so ten days later, saying three other inmates told him they wanted to frame Marble and that Thomas would pretend to be the victim.

COPY

8 or so years ago when I was 13 at Missoula County Juvenile Detention Facility I was sitting at a table in the dayroom. There were three other people at the table. They told me to say that Cody Marble raped me. But this did not happen. And now today I want to come out and let it be known. I'm coming forward now because I'm in prison o. a sex crime and know what it is like. So I don't want him to be charged with one when innocent. When I was in jail, I was the youngest + smallest and I was pressured into going along with it.

7·15·10 Robert Thomas

Robert Thomas's 2010 statement recanting his 2002 rape accusation against Marble. *Courtesy Jerry Marble.*

"They told me that they would be released from jail, or receive lighter sentences, if they framed Marble and then cooperated with law enforcement," he wrote. "Because I was younger than the others, and because I was often teased and bullied by them, I decided to go along with the plan. The story was not true. I was never raped by Cody Marble in the detention facility."[134]

His statement also said he testified falsely at the trial because he thought the story "had gone too far and I could not go back," that he never thought Marble would be convicted, and now wanted to "set the record straight."

Armed with Thomas's statement and other information, Innocence Project lawyers and pro bono counsel Colin Stephens filed a petition in state court in Missoula in December 2010, asking the judge who'd presided over Cody's trial to either vacate his conviction or order a new trial.

On the day of the filing, I met Cody and his father, Jerry, at the office of the *Missoulian* for an interview. Marble, then twenty-six and out on parole, told me, "I just want my life back. I want my life back from parole, from sex-offender registration, from this accusation….When you have to write down that you're a registered sex offender [on job applications], I think they just throw it in the trash. It's kind of like prison outside of prison."

I left a message for Thomas at the prison but heard nothing. I also called the Missoula County attorney, Fred Van Valkenburg, who made it clear he would fight the petition. "It's just one more thing that Cody Marble is trying to do to avoid responsibility for his case," he said. "We're just going to have to deal with it."[135]

District Judge Douglas Harkin, who had presided over the trial, set a hearing and granted Thomas immunity from prosecution for any statements he might make at the hearing. Marble's attorney said the immunity ruling would give Thomas the chance to "tell the truth without having to get charged with perjury."

But more than a year later, in early 2012, Marble's slow-moving petition suffered a major setback, courtesy of Van Valkenburg, the county attorney. On January 26 of that year, Van Valkenburg deposed Thomas, under oath. He started by essentially telling Thomas that if he changed his trial testimony or said he lied under oath at the trial, Van Valkenburg would do whatever he could to prosecute him for perjury.

Not long after Van Valkenburg's statement, Thomas backtracked on the entire statement that he gave the Montana Innocence Project and said its officials had "badgered" him into signing it. "I just told them what they wanted to hear," he said. "They just kept coming to me until they heard what they wanted to hear."[136]

Van Valkenburg then filed a request to dismiss Marble's request for a new trial, citing Thomas's recantation of his recantation. Harkin, however, went ahead with the hearing, in October 2012.

Thomas, still serving time for the statutory rape offense, appeared in court clad in orange jail coveralls, handcuffs and leg chains, with closely cropped dark hair and a sullen, emotionless expression on his face. Thomas had grown into a tall, lean young man, more than ten years after he'd said he'd been raped as a thirteen-year-old in the county juvenile jail.

Mansch and McQuillan from the Innocence Project testified in detail how they had spoken with Thomas in prison three separate times—and each time, he said the rape did not occur. But the star witness of the hearing was Thomas. When he took the stand, he reiterated his claim made in his January deposition, as reported in my story:

> *When asked by Missoula County Attorney Fred Van Valkenburg whether he would testify again at trial that he was raped,* [Thomas] *said "I would tell the truth."*
>
> *"And what is the truth?" Van Valkenburg asked.*

"That it happened," replied [Thomas], *who appeared in orange jail coveralls, leg chains and handcuffs.*[137]

It took Harkin more than a year to rule, but he rejected Marble's request for a new trial. He cited a recent state Supreme Court decision that said in order to get a new trial, a convict had to "affirmatively and unquestionably establish his innocence" based on "reliable new evidence." Harkin said the new evidence—Thomas's initial recantation—had been reduced to "minimal value," given that Thomas had taken it back.[138]

Cody's lawyer said he would appeal the ruling. But several months later, Marble's father called me with some startling news: Bobby Thomas was dead.

Thomas, out on parole after nearly six years in prison for statutory rape, had been living in Cut Bank, a town near the Canadian border, when he failed to report to his parole officer in January 2014. Four months later, on the night of April 6, police in Havre, Montana—about 125 miles east of Cut Bank—pulled Thomas over for a traffic violation in the middle of town. He got out of the car and ran. When police finally cornered him near a bank, he pulled out a pistol. The police in Havre showed remarkable restraint, talking to Thomas for twenty-one hours without attempting to shoot him. But Thomas decided to end it. He turned the pistol on himself, fatally shooting himself in the abdomen. He was twenty-five years old.

Police said Thomas kept saying he didn't want to go back to jail. They told him he probably wouldn't go to jail for anything he'd done that night, but they couldn't know that he had violated his parole. He'd given a fake name.

With Thomas in the grave, his last words on record about the Marble case were that he'd been raped by Marble. Marble's lead lawyer, Colin Stephens, told me that Thomas's death certainly wasn't a positive development, as far as Marble was concerned.

I wrote a column about Thomas's death, closing with a few poignant words from Jerry:

> *Marble's father, Jerry, said last week that Thomas' death is just the latest tragic turn in a case that never should have happened.*
>
> *"It's very sad," he said. "Three of those kids* [who accused Cody] *are dead now.... The ones that aren't dead, except for one, have all gone to prison. I just think it's very sad that it would come to this....*
>
> *"I do know that* [Thomas] *tried to come clean—when you read those Innocence Project reports, those letters that he wrote to them. He tried to come clean."*

At this point, I thought Cody's quest to clear his name was over. But more than a year later, a pair of unconnected developments would change everything.

In August 2015, the Montana Supreme Court overturned Harkin's rejection of Marble's request for a new trial, saying the judge used the wrong standard. The court's 5-2 decision sent it back to Harkin for another analysis, leaving Marble to ponder how long it would take to plumb yet another ruling based on a new standard that said he might get relief if new evidence "proved, and viewed in light of the evidence as a whole, would establish that the [convict] did not engage in the criminal conduct for which the petitioner was convicted."

Yet Missoula County had a new county attorney. Van Valkenburg had retired, and one of his deputies, Kirsten Pabst, had won election to succeed him in 2014.

Marble's lawyer, Colin Stephens, thought the Supreme Court decision gave the prosecutor the option to take a new look at the case, and he also knew that Pabst had long harbored doubts about Marble's conviction. He contacted her, and Pabst agreed that her office would reexamine the evidence before having another hearing and analysis based on the Supreme Court's newly defined standards.

Eight months later, on April 19, 2016—fourteen years after Marble had faced the initial charge that started his nightmare odyssey through the justice system—Pabst filed a petition in state District Court in Missoula to dismiss that charge and free Marble from prison.

By now, I was working as a reporter for the Montana Television Network in Helena. I drove to Missoula to cover the news conference where Pabst, Larry Mansch and other supporters of Cody gathered in a small conference room at the Missoula County Justice Center. There, Pabst told us her office had reviewed "thousands of pages of documents spanning 14 years" and determined that the evidence couldn't support the 2002 conviction.

"That's what prosecutors do," she said. "We convict the guilty, we exonerate the innocent and, in some cases, reunite a man with his family, because it's never too late to the do the right thing."[139]

Stephens had given me a draft of the petition earlier that day, and I had written and posted an initial story when the document was filed, adding Pabst's comments later. It was a story I had thought, many times, I might never write. Jerry, who had spoken that morning with Cody by telephone at the prison in Shelby, said they were both "walking on air."

Missoula county attorney Kirsten Pabst announcing she had filed to dismiss Marble's rape charge, April 2016. *Montana Television Network (MTN)*.

Two days later, Cody would walk out of the Shelby prison, freed by a court order from the judge considering Pabst's petition. Jerry picked up his son, who spoke with one of MTN's reporters. Cody said while he was looking forward to a new life, he couldn't believe it took fourteen years to clear his name. "I just thought they'd figure it out sooner," he said. "I thought they'd figure out right quick what didn't happen, but here we are, 14 years later."[140]

And yet, even then, it wasn't entirely over. Van Valkenburg asked the new presiding judge, Ed McLean, to let him to intervene in the case as a private citizen. The judge allowed it, and Van Valkenburg proceeded to fight Pabst's effort to dismiss the case. He said the 2002 conviction should stand and that there was no new evidence to present to the court.

Yet Van Valkenburg's one last attempt to keep Marble in prison would fail. McLean held a hearing in December 2016, giving all sides the chance to present evidence in the case, and then vacated Marble's conviction. Technically, the ruling set the stage for a new trial, but Pabst had already decided not to try Marble again and the charge was dismissed. Marble was a free man, although he still had to spend more than a year on probation, for a drug possession charge from when he was out on parole in 2013.

Those final months on probation led to one last run-in with the correctional system—and convinced Marble he'd be better off somewhere other than Montana. In May 2017, while living in his father's hometown of Conrad, Montana, he was accosted in a parking lot by a woman who called him a rapist. The exchange escalated when her boyfriend and another man showed up and blocked Marble's car. A scuffle ensued and was reported to police. When Marble spoke with his probation officer, he was told to report to jail, but Marble decided otherwise and fled the state, driving hundreds of miles

Marble outside the state's private prison near Shelby, where he was released in 2016 after prosecutors filed to erase his fourteen-year-old rape conviction. *Montana Television Network (MTN).*

away and traveling through the Midwest and South for several weeks. He decided three months later to turn himself in and was arrested in Spearfish, South Dakota, on his way back to Montana. Cody's father told me that both he and his son felt like the state should have no claim on him at all, since he'd spent more than a decade in prison for a crime he didn't commit.

"It's disgusting; it's deplorable," Jerry Marble said in August after Cody was ordered by a Montana judge to spend another 254 days on probation. "But it is what it is. It's just wrong....It's almost like that 15 years of wrongful imprisonment doesn't mean anything."[141]

It wasn't until June 2018, more than sixteen years after the rape charge was filed, that Marble would be entirely free of the criminal justice system. He celebrated by leaving Montana to travel the country and eventually ended up in the South, two thousand miles from Montana, where he joined a childhood friend in a business venture.

"It was really a matter of just how far away I needed to go," he told me in an interview in late October 2018. "I just feel like those people in Montana are just careless and they ruined my life. I'm scared to death of that up there....I've been cooped up my whole life and never was able to travel. I like being anonymous down here."[142]

Chapter 9

RIOT AT MAX

Montana's Deadly, Costly Prison Riot

The call came in on a lazy, sun-baked September afternoon in 1991 as I worked a solo shift at the Associated Press office in Helena, Montana—a Sunday, when news almost never happened, and the person on the "desk" spends the shift rewriting stories from the morning papers to send out on the wire for the AP's member newspapers, radio and TV stations.

"Yeah," said the voice on the other end of the telephone, "something's going on at the prison, in Deer Lodge. I think it's a riot. I heard something about inmates taking over some cells."

"What?" I said, perking up. "Heard where? How did you hear?"

"On the police scanner. I heard our cops talking about it."

The caller was a radio jock from KSEN in Shelby, Montana, an oil and farming town 180 miles north of Helena and a good 250 miles from Deer Lodge, site of Montana State Prison, the only state prison facility at the time.

Radio announcers often called the AP with news stories and tips, but this one sounded too weird to be true. A guy from Shelby, calling me on a Sunday, about a prison riot 250 miles away?

"Tell me more," I said. "What did you hear again?"

He told me again, this time in more detail, and insisted it was no joke: a riot was under way at the state prison. I started calling people—the prison, the governor's press secretary, the Corrections Department, the sheriff's office in Deer Lodge. Just about everyone's line was busy (no cellphones, no ubiquitous voicemail in those days), and the cops in Deer Lodge wouldn't tell

The Montana State Prison's maximum-security unit today, site of the prison's deadliest riot in history, in September 1991. *Mike Dennison.*

me a thing. I called my boss, AP Bureau chief John Kuglin, who then called in AP capitol reporter Bob Anez on his day off to chase the story firsthand.

What we didn't know until hours later was that a group of inmates in the state prison's maximum-security unit—a barren, round mass of concrete and steel filled with the scariest guys in the prison system—had somehow taken control of the unit, barricaded five guards in a shower and went on a four-hour rampage.

Five inmates were dead—brutally stabbed, strangled and beaten to death by their fellow prisoners, who knew their victims as "snitches" held in protective custody (which, on that fateful day, turned out to be not very protective). Eight other inmates had been injured. By the time Anez arrived at the prison—flying down there from Helena with Governor Stan Stephens, state corrections director Curt Chisholm and the governor's press secretary, Victor Bjornberg—a SWAT team had stormed the unit and taken control. They rescued the five guards, uninjured, from the shower room; rounded up the sixty-some inmates who'd been freed from their cells; marched them outside; and ordered them to strip naked and lie in the scrub of the prison

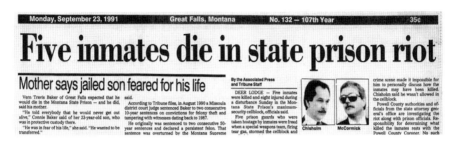

Monday, September 23, 1991   Great Falls, Montana   No. 132 — 107th Year   35¢

Five inmates die in state prison riot

Mother says jailed son feared for his life

Vern Travis Baker of Great Falls expected that he would die in the Montana State Prison — and he did, said his mother.

"He told everybody that he would never get out alive," Connie Baker said of her 33-year-old son, who was in protective custody there.

"He was in fear of his life," she said. "He wanted to be transferred."

According to Tribune files, in August 1990 a Missoula district court judge sentenced Baker to two consecutive 10-year sentences on convictions for felony theft and tampering with witnesses dating back to 1987.

He originally was sentenced to two consecutive 50-year sentences and declared a persistent felon. That sentence was overturned by the Montana Supreme

By the Associated Press and Tribune Staff

DEER LODGE — Five inmates were killed and eight injured during a disturbance Sunday in the Montana State Prison's maximum-security cellblock, officials said.

Five prison guards who were taken hostage by inmates were freed when a special weapons team, firing tear gas, stormed the cellblock and

Chisholm   *McCormick*

crime scene made it impossible for him to personally discuss how the inmates may have been killed. Chisholm said he wasn't allowed in the cellblock.

Powell County authorities and officials from the state attorney general's office are investigating the riot along with prison officials. Responsibility for determining what killed the inmates rests with the Powell County Coroner. No such

Great Falls Tribune headline the day after the September 22, 1991 riot. *From the* Great Falls Tribune.

yard, under armed guard, while prison officials surveyed the damage in the maximum-security unit.[143]

The 1991 "Riot at Max" is the deadliest incident in the history of Montana's prison system, a jagged scar that cut a swath of expensive, messy consequences through many tiers of Montana government, the criminal justice system and the legal community. It led to several full-scale investigations of the riot itself and the prison administration, spurred charges by the American Civil Liberties Union of prisoner mistreatment, exposed the underbelly of the cruelest of prison conditions in Montana and unleashed a years-long string of prosecutions, trials and civil cases that would end up costing the state millions of dollars.

It also would spawn a steady, prolific stream of news coverage over many years, the likes of which you rarely see in Montana journalism now. Today, basically no reporters cover the prison system as a beat, let alone with the doggedness and intensity that the riot and its aftermath deserved and, for the most part, received.

The *Montana Standard*, the daily newspaper whose circulation area included the prison, had a full-time, aggressive reporter in Anaconda, Duncan Adams, who broke and wrote many great stories on the riot and its aftermath. AP reporter Bob Anez, the only reporter who accompanied the governor and prison officials into the prison grounds the day of the riot, churned out his usual well-written and consistent coverage over the years. I also wrote extensively about the costs racked up by the state in defending multiple lawsuits, including $2.5 million paid to private attorneys. At least a half dozen other reporters also made their own contributions to an impressive body of work that gave Montana readers an in-depth and extensive view of this bloody day and its costly trail.

Although I took the initial call for the AP, I didn't see the scene of the riot until four days later, when I joined a couple dozen other reporters for the first press tour of the damaged maximum-security unit. We walked among the melted and smashed Plexiglas cages that had protected the electronic controls of the four cellblocks. The cages were opened by riot leaders as they spread throughout the unit to pursue and murder their inmate targets. It was a rare glimpse into a peculiar hell, where, for a few harrowing hours, the law of the jungle had ruled and the prey had nowhere to run.

ON THE DAY OF the riot—September 22, 1991—Anez had tried calling the same people I called and got nowhere. He initially got in his car and prepared to drive the sixty miles to Deer Lodge. But before he left, he decided to drop by the Corrections Department's old main administrative building, a few blocks from the capitol. It was a Sunday afternoon. He walked into the unlocked building through the back door and right into the department director's office, where he found Governor Stan Stephens, Director Chisholm and Bjornberg, the governor's press secretary. Staffer Mike Ferriter, who would become the department's director fourteen years later, manned a telephone with a direct link to a captain at the prison.

Sometime before, unbeknownst to Anez, Warden Jack McCormick had recommended that the SWAT (Special Weapons and Tactical) team storm the building, as staffers had been able to look inside and see inmates being beaten. Chisholm had already OK'ed the assault, which began shortly after 2:00 p.m. and lasted about fifteen minutes. The governor had been notified that the building was secured and the riot over. Stephens, Chisholm, Bjornberg and the governor's security chief, Fritz Behr, prepared to take the governor's plane to Deer Lodge. Anez asked if he could tag along. Sure, they said, and the fivesome took the minutes-long flight over the Continental Divide to Deer Lodge. Anez still had only a limited knowledge of what had happened and didn't know the bloody details.

Once the plane landed, Anez got into a van with the governor's entourage and zipped past the prison's entry checkpoint on the incoming road, where other reporters had gathered, unable to get into the locked-down prison or its grounds. The Montana State Prison, built in the 1970s, is a sprawling complex set on open prairie several miles west of Deer Lodge, connected to town by a lone paved road.

"I remember thinking, hey, I'm in the right place at the right time," Anez said some years later. But he really wasn't. As the governor and Chisholm were taken inside the grounds to view the riot scene, Anez was left isolated in a prison administrative building, unable to see what had happened and

The south end of the Montana State Prison yard, near Deer Lodge. The maximum-security unit is the concrete building to the left. *Mike Dennison.*

able to call out only on a pay phone. It was 1991—no one had a cellphone. Without reams of coins in his pocket, the only call he could make was the toll-free line to the AP office in Helena, but he had little to tell us.

"I was really frustrated, because for the longest time, every minute that passes like that, and you don't have any information to call in, it drives you nuts, because you don't know what you're missing," he said. "I was left there incommunicado, really."[144]

Almost two hours passed before Anez finally got the word about the casualties and how the unit was damaged to the point that inmates couldn't be returned there for days. Prison officials never let Anez see the site of the riot or the prison yard that day.

Anez said Chisholm, the corrections director, later told him that not allowing in the media sooner had been a crucial mistake, for the state spent years fending off lawsuits from the ACLU on behalf of inmates who claimed they'd been mistreated by guards after the riot, made to lie naked in the sun for hours, some of them beaten—charges that the prison denied. Chisholm told Anez that an independent set of eyes at the scene, such as the media, could have rebutted what he felt were false charges made by inmates.

It would be five days before authorities let reporters see the ransacked maximum-security unit, although details of the carnage leaked out, both through official and non-official sources.

The riot began at about ten o'clock that morning, when a group of nine inmates somehow broke out of the chain link fence–enclosed exercise area in the middle of the unit. They got through a security door and into the open area of the west half of Max, which contained two of the four cellblocks. Five unarmed guards locked themselves in the west-end shower, and two escaped through a ceiling hatch. Not long after, rioting inmates gained access to the east cellblocks, where the "protective custody" inmates were housed—and where riot leaders assaulted, tortured and killed some of these inmates.

One day after the riot, Duncan Adams reported that one of the inmates who had been murdered—Edmund Davison, a convicted rapist from Kalispell—had been scheduled to testify at the upcoming trial of two maximum-security inmates who'd been charged with murdering another inmate in the prison yard a year earlier with a baseball bat. These two inmates, Douglas Turner and William Gollehon, were thought to be among the riot leaders.[145]

ON THE THURSDAY AFTER the riot, prison authorities finally let the media see firsthand the aftermath of the carnage at "Max." Two dozen reporters, photographers and TV camera men and women, including me, met the warden that morning at the prison headquarters and took the three-hundred-yard walk through the barren yard to the maximum-security unit, set far apart from the main prison buildings. My report for the next day's papers began:

> DEER LODGE, Mont.—On the concrete bed in slain inmate Ernest Holliday's cell, a tell-tale sign of violence remains five days after he was murdered during a prison riot: The unmistakable red of stained blood.
>
> Blood stains also dotted the cell next to Holliday's, in cellblock D, where prison authorities found the bodies of the five Montana State Prison inmates killed during Sunday's four-hour rampage in the maximum-security unit.
>
> Blood stains weren't the only evidence still visible Thursday, when prison authorities provided reporters their first interior view of the damaged cellblock.
>
> Concrete floors were littered with ash and broken glass, walls were blackened by fire, the sting of tear gas was still in the air.

Shattered safety glass still lay on the floor near the unit's two control "cages," circular offices encased in glass, metal and Plexiglass.

The window of the doorway to the east cage was the only one completely knocked out—melted by inmates, authorities said. Blackened walls and ceilings near the cages offered evidence of fires set, possibly to melt the glass.[146]

I'd visited the prison before but never seen the interior of the maximum-security unit, and I doubt any of my colleagues in the press corps had either. Anyone who ever thought prison inmates were coddled had never seen this unit. Some housing units at the state prison resemble college dormitory buildings or apartment complexes. Not this one.

The cells, a few feet wide and maybe a dozen feet long, have nothing more than a concrete bed, sink and toilet. The only view of the outside world is through a window several inches high, that runs the length of the cell's outside wall. Inmates had, at most, only two hours a day outside these tiny, barren cells. Their meals were brought through a slot in the door. They would get one hour a day in the unit's exercise "yard," which then was nothing but a series of cages with concrete floors and outer walls, locked doors and chain link fence partitioning the area. It sat in the middle of the oval-shaped unit, with cellblock wings on each side. The only open air was straight up: a view of the sky, through the cage's chain link "ceiling."

It was from this caged area that the riot began. Somehow, perhaps over a series of weeks or months, the core of the rioters had weakened parts of the chain link fence separating the cages, and on September 22, they got out of the cages together and then charged through the security doors that led to the main cellblocks. Guards who had been escorting other inmates out of the exercise yard had failed to close the security doors, and the riot was on.

One guard each manned each of the unit's two Plexiglas-enclosed electronic control centers, from which anyone could lock and unlock the cell doors and other security doors. These guards, upon seeing inmates running free through the unit and banging on the Plexiglas cage, panicked and fled through hatches in the ceiling. They also neglected to turn off the power to the console and left behind the keys—a fatal lapse in security.

Another security lapse involved a door that separated the west cellblock, which housed death row inmates and some of the prison's most hardened criminals, and the east cellblock, where the protective-custody inmates were held. For some reason, that door was not closed at the time of the riot, and prison officials wouldn't tell us whether it should have been closed. Rioters passed freely down a hallway that led to the east cellblock and, like they did in the west cellblock, began lighting fires to melt the Plexiglas case so they could gain access to the security console.

As I stood next to that melted cage and surveyed Cellblock D and the rest of the battered east wing, I shuddered at the horror that must have been felt by those protective-custody inmates as they saw some of the unit's most dangerous inhabitants break into the control center and start opening their cell doors.

SIX WEEKS AFTER THE riot, the Montana branch of the ACLU released a report that alleged prison guards and personnel had meted out their own brand of vigilante justice in the wake of the riot.

It said after SWAT team members took control of the damaged unit, they stripped and handcuffed the inmates and escorted them outside, where a gauntlet of prison officers waited. Inmates were forced to run through the gauntlet, naked, as officers struck them with nightsticks, belly-chains and kicks. "This was mass punishment," ACLU legal director Jeff Renz told reporters at a news conference in Billings. "And I'm absolutely convinced that this all occurred. We've received confirmation from a number of sources."[147]

Renz called for the dismissal of Warden McCormick. Scott Crichton, executive director of the ACLU in Montana, said the group decided to release the report because state officials refused to release details of alleged civil rights violations after the riot. It also outlined other mistreatment of the maximum-security inmates in the riot's aftermath, such as not allowing them to shower or shave for fifteen days, beating those who wouldn't talk to investigators and handcuffing and hogtying for twenty-four hours some inmates who threatened another rebellion.

Yellowstone County sheriff Mike Schafer, who was leading an in-state team investigating the riot, said he couldn't deny the ACLU's report but that he wanted to wait for his team's report before talking. State corrections director Curt Chisholm had announced a day earlier that the FBI and the U.S. Department of Justice also were investigating possible civil rights abuses in the wake of the riot.

Schafer's team released its report on New Year's Eve 1991, more than three months after the riot. It painted a devastating portrait of a poorly run prison, saying staffers ignored repeated warnings of a possible riot, staged a cover-up of inmate beatings and abuses after the riot and committed frequent violations

The southwest watchtower at Montana State Prison, which overlooks the maximum-security unit and its yard. *Montana Television Network (MTN).*

of security procedures in the hours, day and months leading up to the riot. It agreed with many of the allegations in the ACLU's report.[148]

On February 3, 1992, state and local prosecutors filed seventy charges of deliberate homicide against fourteen inmates involved in the riot. The accused included Turner and Gollehon, the inmates scheduled to go on trial for the murder of Gerald Pileggi, the inmate killed in the prison yard.

Most of the inmates charged in connection with the riot pleaded guilty to charges of burglary and murder; the trials of Gollehon, Turner and two or three other rioters proceeded with grim efficiency that summer of 1992, resulting in convictions.

WHILE THE STATE'S PROSECUTION of criminal trials stemming from the riot began winding down that summer, a second wave of legal action was just getting started: civil lawsuits filed by the families of inmates murdered during the riot and a class-action lawsuit from the ACLU on behalf of the inmates who said they were abused by prison guards and staff during the aftermath of the riot. The ACLU filed its suit in October 1992, even though the U.S. Justice Department concluded that treatment of inmates after the riot violated no federal civil rights laws and declined to file any charges.

By early the next year, more than a dozen lawsuits also had been filed on behalf of inmates killed or injured during the riot, seeking at least $2.5 million in damages.[149]

The state had its own attorneys working on its defense but hired private lawyers to help with the load. Two firms got most of the business: Browning, Kaleczyc, Berry and Hoven, a politically well-connected law firm in Helena, and Boone, Karlberg and Haddon in Missoula, another prominent defense firm not without its own friends in the political world.

In early 1995, the state decided to settle one of the lawsuits, paying $150,000 to Rosa Myhre, whose son, Gary Evans, was one of the five inmates murdered during the riot.[150]

But while the state had agreed to that payment, it already had shelled out nearly $711,000 in fees and costs to the private attorneys defending the state against the multiple riot-related lawsuits. The Browning firm in Helena had collected $461,000 from the state for its work over two years, and the Boone-Haddon firm in Missoula had taken home $102,000 for its work over six months.[151]

John Maynard, the lead attorney on the case for the Browning firm, wouldn't say why the state decided to settle the suit filed by Ms. Myhre. He said settlement talks were happening in the fifteen remaining death-and-injury cases filed in state court but that the state had no intention of settling the civil right lawsuits filed in federal court.

The story wasn't on my radar until later that summer, when someone gave me a tip that the Browning & Kaleczyc firm had continued to rack up big bills for defending the lawsuits filed by the families of the murdered inmates, while not really attempting to settle them. By now, I was working for the *Great Falls Tribune* as its Capitol Bureau reporter. I asked for the latest tally on the firm's tab and found it had now reached $750,000. I spoke with the governor's office, Maynard and the state's attorneys about the story, but it wasn't until I spoke with one of the murdered inmates' lawyers that the story got a sharper edge.

The attorney was Bill Boggs, a longtime Missoula lawyer who specialized in criminal defense work. I called him on a hot Friday afternoon in August 1995. I told him how the governor's press secretary had said the state saw no reason to settle because it had done nothing wrong and that the state felt it was wrong to reward those who file "frivolous lawsuits by agreeing to settlements just because it may be cheaper in the short run."

Boggs angrily replied that the state could have settled the entire case six months ago for $600,000 but refused and suggested the private attorneys representing the case were dragging out the case to make more money off it.

"They've made almost a million bucks defending the indefensible," he said, practically shouting. "A responsible insurance [company] counsel

> "They're ripping off the taxpayers ... and screwing families whose relatives have been murdered horribly."
>
> — Bill Boggs,
> plaintiffs' attorney

Bill Boggs, attorney for relatives of murdered inmates, on the state attorneys defending against the inmates' lawsuits. *From the* Great Falls Tribune.

would have settled this case long ago.... If these guys worked for anybody but the state, they would have been fired a long time ago. They're ripping off the taxpayers, with the governor's approval, and screwing families whose relatives have been murdered horribly."[152]

My story ran on the front page of the August 27, 1995 *Tribune*, with an outtake of Boggs's quote about how the attorneys were "screwing families whose relatives have been murdered horribly."

Boggs also told me what the state had offered at a settlement conference in March: $50,000 each for the four inmates who had been murdered, some attorney fees and nothing for those who'd been assaulted or injured. He said the plaintiffs' attorneys had countered with an offer of $600,000 to settle the whole case, but lawyers for the state refused.

My story also mentioned that one of the partners in Browning & Kaleczyc—Steve Browning—was married to Governor Marc Racicot's chief of staff, Judy Browning. The governor's press secretary, Andrew Malcolm, said Judy Browning had nothing to do with decisions on the prison cases. Also, the firm had been hired about a month before Racicot became governor in January 1993 (although Ms. Browning did work for Attorney General Racicot at that time). Maynard, the lawyer in charge of the case for the Browning firm, was a former chief of the state Risk Management and Tort Defense Division—the state division overseeing the state's defense.

Three days after my Sunday story that featured Boggs unloading, the state, at my request, provided updated figures on how much money it had spent on private lawyers defending the prison riot lawsuits. The Browning & Kaleczyc amount wasn't $750,000—it was more, at $877,000. And the Boone, Karlberg firm in Missoula had been paid $282,000. The total bill, for all private attorneys working on the suits, had now reached $1.16 million.[153]

Two days later, the private lawyers for the state added some more billable hours to the tab when they asked the judge presiding over the death and injury lawsuits to dismiss all of the complaints because Boggs had violated a court order by telling me about the contents of the confidential settlement talks in March. Marcia Davenport, a lawyer for the Browning & Kaleczyc firm, said disclosure of the settlement offers "had caused impermissible, irreversible prejudice to the [state]" and that the only appropriate sanction was to dismiss the cases. State District Judge Ted Mizner of Deer Lodge declined to impose such a penalty on Boggs or his colleagues.[154]

IN NOVEMBER 1995, MIZNER ruled that the state's negligence contributed to the deaths of those murdered during the riot. Seven months later, he expanded on his ruling, calling the evidence "overwhelming" that the state had failed in its duty to safely operate the maximum-security unit and that failure had "directly contributed" to the riot and the damage it caused. "Reasonable minds can only come to this conclusion," he wrote.[155]

Yet Mizner did not rule on the issue or scope of the state's liability for the deaths and injuries and said the cases should go to a jury to decide damages. He also said a jury might be able to decide whether the rioting inmates shared in the liability for the deaths and injuries of fellow inmates, potentially letting the state off the hook. He scheduled a trial for June 1997 one year later.

The lawsuits alleging that prison officials had abused inmates after the riot finally went to trial in 1998, more than six years after the riot. The federal court jury decided that some civil rights violations had occurred but awarded damages of only $5,100. A related lawsuit was settled two weeks later, for $5,570. The inmates' lawyers did much better, splitting court-awarded fees of $327,000 among four attorneys.[156]

But the inmates who'd actually been injured during the riot, and the families of whose who'd been brutally murdered on that September Sunday in 1991, had to wait a bit longer to see their cases resolved.

Four months later, in mid-1998, seven years after the riot, the Racicot administration finally decided to settle the remaining cases, agreeing to pay a total of $600,000 to eight inmates who had been injured during the riot and the families of two of the inmates who had been murdered—the same amount the state had rejected three and a half years earlier to settle all of the death-and-injury cases. Only $370,000 went directly to the families and inmates; the rest went to the lawyers who had worked on the cases. The state also had settled lawsuits filed by the families of two other inmates killed during the riot for an additional $180,000.

In total, the state ended up paying $930,000 to the eight protective-custody inmates who'd been attacked by rioting inmates, the families of the inmates who'd been murdered and their lawyers. And under a new 1997 state law, any money paid to the injured inmates now would be used first to pay outstanding restitution that the inmate owed to their crime victims.[157]

The state claimed that only a portion of the $1.8 million (at least) it had paid to private lawyers for defending the prison riot lawsuits had gone to defend against these particular lawsuits, but I never got a final, definitive amount on what ended up in the pockets of private attorneys for what attorney Bill Boggs described as "defending the indefensible."

NOTES

Chapter 1

1. Dennison, "Energy Consumers," *Great Falls Tribune*.
2. Billings, "Utility's Gannon, Haffey Promoted," *Montana Standard*.
3. Dennison, "Utility Reform '97 Session's 800-lb. Gorilla," *Great Falls Tribune*.
4. Ibid.
5. Dennison, "Who's Representing Consumers?," *Great Falls Tribune*.
6. Dennison, "Your Power Bill," *Great Falls Tribune*.
7. Dennison, "Experts Say MPC Plan," *Great Falls Tribune*.
8. Larcombe and Burchard, "MPC to Sell Dams," *Great Falls Tribune*.
9. Dennison, "MPC Sets Sights," *Great Falls Tribune*.
10. Dennison, "Socialism at MPC?," *Great Falls Tribune*.
11. Dennison, "Touch America Success Story," *Great Falls Tribune*.
12. Anez, "Board Decides," *Great Falls Tribune*.
13. Dennison, "MPC Sells Rest of Operation," *Great Falls Tribune*.
14. Dennison, "Energy Costs Hit Hard," *Great Falls Tribune*.
15. Gross, "Creative Destruction," *New York Times*.
16. Richards, "For Montana Power, a Broadband Dream," *Wall Street Journal*.
17. Dennison, "MPC Shareholders OK Transformation," *Great Falls Tribune*.
18. Dennison, "MPC Reports $27 Million Loss," *Great Falls Tribune*.
19. Falstad, "Touch America Execs," *Billings Gazette*.
20. Kemmick, "Gannon's Letter," *Billings Gazette*.
21. Dennison, "Touch America—Winners & Losers," *Great Falls Tribune*.

Chapter 2

22. Anez, "Racicot Enters GOP Race," *Helena Independent Record*.
23. Dennison, "Racicot Stumps for Sales Tax," *Great Falls Tribune*.
24. Letter from Andrew Malcolm, January 4, 1995.
25. Johnson, "Racicot: Let's Keep 'Civility,'" *Great Falls Tribune*.
26. Letter from Racicot to *Great Falls Tribune* executive editor Jim Strauss, December 21, 1995.
27. Johnson, "Racicot Helps Bush," *Helena Independent Record*.
28. Dennison, "Racicot Has Close-Up View," *Great Falls Tribune*.
29. Associated Press, "Racicot Leads Assault on Recount," *Great Falls Tribune*.
30. Hosler, "Racicot Steps into the Spotlight," *Great Falls Tribune*.
31. Anez, "Racicot Says No to AG Job," *Great Falls Tribune*.
32. Dennison, "Racicot Lobbying on Behalf of Enron," *Great Falls Tribune*.
33. Vertuno, "Racicot Hopes to Buoy GOP," *Great Falls Tribune*.

Chapter 3

34. Dennison, "Martz Relishes Campaigning," *Great Falls Tribune*.
35. Anez, "Martz Says She Will Bow to Industry," *Great Falls Tribune*.
36. Billings, "Martz's 'Lap Dog' Remark," *Helena Independent Record*.
37. Johnson, "Talks Get Testy on Energy Bills," *Helena Independent Record*.
38. Dennison, "Hedges Avoids Prison Sentence," *Great Falls Tribune*.
39. Anez, "Top Martz Aide Hedges Resigns," *Great Falls Tribune*.
40. Anez, "Martz Washed Clothes," *Great Falls Tribune*.
41. Dennison, "More Questions in Sliter Fatality," *Great Falls Tribune*.
42. McLaughlin, "Hedges Heads Up PAC," *Helena Independent Record*.
43. McLaughlin, "Demos Assail 'Stealth PAC,'" *Helena Independent Record*.
44. McLaughlin, "Martz Says News Reports Hampering," *Helena Independent Record*.
45. Associated Press, "Settlement Reached," *Helena Independent Record*.
46. Associated Press, "Martz Tells Group," *Great Falls Tribune*.
47. Interview with Bob Anez, 2014.

Chapter 4

48. Interview with Cass Chinske, 2014.
49. Dennison, "Man of This Land," *Billings Gazette*.
50. Florio, "Abramoff Says He Got 'Every Appropriation We Wanted,'" *Great Falls Tribune*.
51. Dennison, "Both Sides Agree," *Helena Independent Record*.
52. Dennison, "Burns Takes Melcher Senate Seat," *Great Falls Tribune*.
53. Dennison, "Burns: Senate to Be 'No Real Difference,'" *Great Falls Tribune*.
54. Associated Press, "'Racist Remarks 'Not My Words,'" *Great Falls Tribune*.
55. Interview with Dan Burkhart, 2014.
56. Interview with Gail Schontzler, 2014.
57. *Washington Post*, "Racial Crack Betrays Burns."
58. Schontzler, "Lawyer Says Burns Told Racist Joke," *Bozeman Daily Chronicle*.
59. Dennison, "New Charges Add Heat," *Great Falls Tribune*.
60. Gransbery, "Burns Apologizes for Calling Arabs 'Ragheads,'" *Billings Gazette*.
61. Johnson, "Burns' Criticism Cut from Report," *Missoulian*.
62. Schmidt, "Burns' Role in Tribal Grant Under Question," *Washington Post*.
63. Dennison, "Lobbyist, Tribes Contributed to Montana Delegation," *Great Falls Tribune*.
64. Lee State Bureau, "Lobbyist Probe Widens," *Helena Independent Record*.
65. McKee, "Burns Flipped Vote After Donation," *Helena Independent Record*.
66. McKee, "Burns: Abramoff 'a Bad Guy,'" *Helena Independent Record*.
67. McKee, "Burns: Dems Behind Abramoff Story," *Helena Independent Record*.
68. Dennison, "Man of This Land," *Billings Gazette*.
69. Associated Press, "Burns Says Media Dishonest," *Billings Gazette*.
70. Interview with DEA agent, 1991.
71. Interview with Cass Chinske, 2014.
72. Dennison, "Former Sen. Burns Delights GOP Crowd," *Billings Gazette*.

Chapter 5

73. Dennison, "Schweitzer Dogged, Determined," *Great Falls Tribune*.
74. Dennison, "Canada Drug Run Racks Up Political Mileage," *Great Falls Tribune*.
75. Dennison, "Schweitzer Rallies Party's Faithful," *Great Falls Tribune*.

76. Dennison, "Schweitzer Dogged, Determined," *Great Falls Tribune*.
77. Interview with Brian Schweitzer, December 2018.
78. Dennison, "Bills Win Razor-Thin Victories," *Great Falls Tribune*.
79. Farrell, "GOP: Schweitzer Tactics Out of Line," *Helena Independent Record*.
80. Johnson, "GOP Steams After Meeting with Governor," *Helena Independent Record*.
81. Anez, "Keenan Accuses Schweitzer," *Great Falls Tribune*.
82. Dennison and McKee, "Brothers in Arms," *Billings Gazette*.
83. Dennison and Johnson, "Angry Lange Lashes Out," *Billings Gazette*.
84. Dennison, "Legislators OK Budget, End Session," *Helena Independent Record*.
85. Dennison, "Schweitzer: Showman," *Billings Gazette*.
86. Dennison, "Schweitzer Likely to Try for U.S. Senate," *Helena Independent Record*.
87. Cogan, "Gonzo Option," *National Journal*.
88. Dennison, "Schweitzer Ignites Media Firestorm," *Billings Gazette*.

Chapter 6

89. Dennison, "Baucus Denounces as 'Personal Smear,'" *Billings Gazette*.
90. Dennison, "Baucus Tireless in Pursuit of Fourth Term," *Great Falls Tribune*.
91. Ibid.
92. Ibid.
93. Dennison, "Anonymous Mailing Contains Divorce Records," *Great Falls Tribune*.
94. Anez, "Fired Aide Says Baucus Harassed Her," *Great Falls Tribune*.
95. Anez, "Republicans Take a Wait-and-See Attitude," *Great Falls Tribune*.
96. Interview with Jim Messina, September 7, 1999.
97. Dennison, "Not Firing Aide Earlier Was Only Mistake," *Great Falls Tribune*.
98. Dennison, "Taylor Quits Senate Race," *Great Falls Tribune*.
99. Dennison, "Baucus Says Health Reform Will Pass," *Billings Gazette*.
100. Dennison, "Senators Hail Health Bill's Passage," *Helena Independent Record*.
101. Dennison, "Baucus Watches Supreme Court," *Billings Gazette*.
102. Dennison, "Baucus Says Public Will 'Take Another Look' at Health-Care Bill," *Missoulian*.

103. Associated Press, "Sen. Baucus Sees 'Train Wreck," *Helena Independent Record*.

104. Johnson, "U.S. Sen. Baucus Won't Seek Re-Election," *Helena Independent Record*.

105. Dennison, "Baucus Took 'Vow' to Help Libby," *Missoulian*.

Chapter 7

106. Dennison, "Victory Caps Long Night's Wait for Tester," *Billings Gazette*.

107. Dennison and Johnson, "Morrison: Personal Conflicts Didn't Alter Investigation," *Billings Gazette*.

108. Ibid.

109. Ibid.

110. McKee, "Democratic Senate Candidates Spar Over Ethics," *Billings Gazette*.

111. Dennison, "Early Action Sets Up 'Bare-Knuckles' Campaign," *Billings Gazette*.

112. Dennison, "Victory Caps Long Night's Wait for Tester," *Billings Gazette*.

113. Dennison and Johnson, "Tester Wins Tight Senate Race," *Billings Gazette*.

114. Johnson, "Crowd Cheers," *Billings Gazette*.

115. Dennison, "Tester Supporters Buy Ad Urging Vote for Libertarian," *Missoulian*.

116. Dennison, "Tester Defeats Rehberg," *Billings Gazette*.

117. Dennison, "News Analysis," *Missoulian*.

118. Stewart, "Trump Calls for Jon Tester to Resign," *Vox*.

119. Interview with Jon Tester, August 2017.

120. Montana Television Network, November 6, 2018.

121. Dennison, "Tester Ekes Out Another Close Victory," Montana Television Network.

Chapter 8

122. Interview with Cody Marble, March 2008.

123. Interview with Susan Latimer, April 2008.

124. Dennison, "Questions Raised Over Rape Conviction," *Missoulian*.

125. Ibid.

126. Interview with Roger Dowty, April 2008.
127. Kruse witness statement, 2002.
128. Dennison, "Questions Raised Over Rape Conviction," *Missoulian*.
129. Interview with Susan Latimer, April 2008.
130. Dennison, "Questions Raised Over Rape Conviction," *Missoulian*.
131. Interview with Cody Marble, March 2008.
132. Transcript, *State of Montana v. Thomas Eugene Scheffer*, May 28, 2008.
133. Letter from Andrew Paul, July 8, 2008.
134. Thomas written statement, 2010.
135. Dennison, "Missoula Man Seeks to Have Rape Conviction Overturned," *Missoulian*.
136. Dennison, "Witness Recants Evidence," *Missoulian*.
137. Dennison, "Missoula Man Convicted," *Missoulian*.
138. Dennison, "Missoula Man Loses Bid for New Trial," *Missoulian*.
139. Dennison, "Missoula Man Exonerated," Montana Television Network.
140. Dennison, "Marble Released from Prison," Montana Television Network.
141. Interview with Jerry Marble, August 2017.
142. Interview with Cody Marble, October 2018.

Chapter 9

143. Associated Press, "Five Inmates Die," *Great Falls Tribune*.
144. Interview with Bob Anez, 2014.
145. Adams, "Slain Inmate Was to Testify," *Montana Standard*.
146. Dennison, "Signs of Rage Linger," *Missoulian*.
147. Ehli, "ACLU: Guards Beat Inmates," *Billings Gazette*.
148. Anez, "Prison-Riot Probe," *Missoulian*.
149. Anez, "Inmate Claims Following Riot," *Helena Independent Record*.
150. Anez, "First Prison Riot Suit Settled," *Great Falls Tribune*.
151. Anez, "State's Bill So Far," *Great Falls Tribune*.
152. Dennison, "Legal Costs Pile Up," *Great Falls Tribune*.
153. Dennison, "State Revises Prison-Suit Costs," *Great Falls Tribune*.
154. Dennison, "State Wants All Riot Suits Dismissed," *Great Falls Tribune*.
155. Dennison, "Judge Rules State Negligent," *Great Falls Tribune*.
156. Anez, "Prison Liable in Riot," *Great Falls Tribune*.
157. Dennison, "State Settles Inmates' Riot Suits," *Great Falls Tribune*.

BIBLIOGRAPHY

Chapter 1

Anez, Bob. "Board Decides to Get Out of Energy Business." *Great Falls Tribune*, March 29, 2000.

Billings, Erin. "Utility's Gannon, Haffey Promoted." *Montana Standard*, January 24, 1996.

Dennison, Mike. "Energy Consumers Could Choose Supplier in the Future." *Great Falls Tribune*, December 12, 1995.

———. "Energy Costs Hit Hard, for Some." *Great Falls Tribune*, July 9, 2000.

———. "Experts Say MPC Plan Won't Help Consumers." *Great Falls Tribune*, November 30, 1997.

———. "MPC Reports $27 Million Loss." *Great Falls Tribune*, November 16, 2001.

———. "MPC Sells Rest of Operation." *Great Falls Tribune*, October 3, 2000.

———. "MPC Sets Sights on Change at Annual Meeting." *Great Falls Tribune*, May 12, 1998.

———. "MPC Shareholders OK Transformation." *Great Falls Tribune*, September 22, 2001.

———. "Socialism at MPC? Well, Sort of...." *Great Falls Tribune*, May 17, 1998.

———. "Touch America Success Story." *Great Falls Tribune*, May 30, 1999.

————. "Touch America—Winners & Losers." *Great Falls Tribune*, October 12, 2003.

————. "Utility Reform '97 Session's 800-lb. Gorilla." *Great Falls Tribune*, January 13, 1997.

————. "Who's Representing Consumers in Utility Restructuring?" *Great Falls Tribune*, March 21, 1997.

————. "Your Power Bill Hinges on Complex Issue." *Great Falls Tribune*, July 25, 1997.

Falstad, Jan. "Touch America Exec Collect Millions." *Billings Gazette*, August 17, 2002.

Gross, Daniel. "Creative Destruction and the Web." *New York Times*, June 20, 2001.

Kemmick, Ed. "Gannon's Letter Lacks that 'Touch.'" *Billings Gazette*, June 22, 2003.

Larcombe, James, and Jacquie Burchard. "MPC to Sell Dams, Coal Plants." *Great Falls Tribune*, December 10, 1997.

Richards, Bill. "For Montana Power, a Broadband Dream May Turn Out to Be More of a Nightmare." *Wall Street Journal*, August 22, 2001.

Chapter 2

Anez, Bob. "Racicot Enters GOP Race." *Helena Independent Record*, February 7, 1992.

————. "Racicot Says No to AG Job." *Great Falls Tribune*, December 21, 2000.

Associated Press. "Racicot Leads Assault on Recount." *Great Falls Tribune*, November 19, 2000.

Dennison, Mike. "Governor's Personal Style Worth a Look." *Great Falls Tribune*, December 17, 2000.

————. "Is Racicot Setting Himself Up for National Cabinet Job?" *Great Falls Tribune*, August 29, 1999.

————. "Racicot Has Close-Up View of History in the Making—the Presidential Election." *Great Falls Tribune*, November 16, 2000.

————. "Racicot Lobbying on Behalf of Enron in Deregulation Debate." *Great Falls Tribune*, May 19, 2001.

————. "Racicot Revisionist History on Utility Regulation." *Helena Independent Record*, January 8, 2006.

———. "Racicot Stumps for Sales Tax." *Great Falls Tribune*, May 30, 1993.

———. "Racicot Taking His Lumps from National Press." *Great Falls Tribune*, January 11, 2002.

———. "War of Words." *Great Falls Tribune*, December 3, 1995.

———. "What Makes Marc Racicot So Darned Popular?" *Great Falls Tribune*, January 2, 1995.

Fenner, David. "The Saint Comes Marching In." *Great Falls Tribune*, May 23, 1992.

Hosler, Karen, of the *Baltimore Sun*. "Racicot Steps into the Spotlight." *Great Falls Tribune*, November 21, 2000.

Johnson, Charles S. "Racicot Helps Bush on Campaign Trail." *Helena Independent Record*, June 8, 1999.

Johnson, Peter. "Racicot: Let's Keep 'Civility' in Campaign." *Great Falls Tribune*, October 6, 1995.

Vertuno, Jim. "Racicot Hopes to Buoy GOP." *Great Falls Tribune*, January 19, 2002.

Chapter 3

Anez, Bob. "Martz Says She Will Bow to Industry." *Great Falls Tribune*, December 7, 2000.

———. "Martz Washed Clothes Worn by Aide in Fatal Crash." *Great Falls Tribune*, January 5, 2002.

———. "Top Martz Aide Hedges Resigns." *Great Falls Tribune*, September 1, 2001.

Associated Press. "Martz Tells Group She Won't Meet with Some Reporters." *Great Falls Tribune*, May 21, 2002.

———. "Settlement Reached in Decade-Long Legal Saga over Yellowstone Club Bankruptcy." *Helena Independent Record*, September 12, 2018.

Billings, Erin. "Martz's 'Lap Dog' Remake Gets Mixed Response." *Helena Independent Record*, December 26, 2000.

Dennison, Mike. "Hedges Avoids Prison Sentence." *Great Falls Tribune*, October 12, 2001.

———. "House Majority Leader Killed in Rollover." *Great Falls Tribune*, August 17, 2001.

———. "Martz Relishes Campaigning." *Great Falls Tribune*, October 9, 2000.

———. "More Questions in Sliter Fatality." *Great Falls Tribune*, February 14, 2002.

Johnson, Charles S. "Talks Get Testy on Energy Bills." *Helena Independent Record*, April 20, 2001.

Kemmick, Ed. "Were Martz, Aides Being Criminal or Misguided?" *Billings Gazette*, February 17, 2002.

McLaughlin, Kathleen. "Demos Assail 'Stealth PAC' Headed by Martz." *Helena Independent Record*, February 26, 2002.

———. "Hedges Heads Up PAC." *Helena Independent Record*, February 23, 2002.

———. "Martz Says News Reports Hampering Economic Development." *Helena Independent Record*, April 4, 2002.

Chapter 4

Associated Press. "Burns Says Media Dishonest to Him." *Billings Gazette*, November 14, 2006.

———. "Racist Remarks 'Not My Words.'" *Great Falls Tribune*, October 21, 1994.

Dennison, Mike. "Both Sides Agree: Burns Closing in on Melcher." *Helena Independent Record*, November 6, 1988.

———. "Burns: Senate to Be 'No Real Difference.'" *Great Falls Tribune*, November 10, 1988.

———. "Burns Takes Melcher Senate Seat." *Great Falls Tribune*, November 9, 1988.

———. "Former Sen. Burns and Friends Delight GOP Crowd at Warm Tribute." *Billings Gazette*, June 18, 2010.

———. "Innovative Communication." *Great Falls Tribune*, January 1, 1992.

———. "Lobbyist, Tribes Contributed to Montana Delegation." *Great Falls Tribune*, May 16, 2005.

———. "'Man of This Land' Wants to Fight for Rural America." *Billings Gazette*, May 6, 2006.

———. "New Charges Add Heat to Bitter Senate Race." *Great Falls Tribune*, November 6, 1994.

Florio, Gwen. "Abramoff Says He Got 'Every Appropriation We Wanted.'" *Great Falls Tribune*, March 9, 2006.

Gransbery, Jim. "Burns Apologizes for Calling Arabs 'Ragheads' in Speech." *Billings Gazette*, March 1999.

Johnson, Charles S. "Burns' Criticism Cut from Report." *Missoulian*, July 28, 2006.

Lee State Bureau. "Lobbyist Probe Widens." *Helena Independent Record*, November 26, 2005.

McKee, Jennifer. "Burns: Abramoff 'a Bad Guy.'" *Helena Independent Record*, December 9, 2005.

————. "Burns: Dems Behind Abramoff Story." *Helena Independent Record*, January 10, 2006.

————. "Burns Flipped Vote After Donation." *Helena Independent Record*, December 3, 2005.

Schmidt, Susan. "Burns' Role in Tribal Grant Under Question." *Washington Post*, March 1, 2005.

Schontzler, Gail. "Lawyer Says Burns Told Racist Joke on Airplane to Chicago." *Bozeman Daily Chronicle*, November 6, 1994.

Washington Post. "Racial Crack Betrays Burns." October 25, 1994.

Chapter 5

Anez, Bob. "Keenan Accuses Schweitzer of Violating Ethical Standards." *Great Falls Tribune*, February 16, 2005.

Cogan, Marin. "The Gonzo Option." *National Journal*, June 18, 2014.

Dennison, Mike. "Bills Win Razor-Thin Victories." *Great Falls Tribune*, April 16, 2005.

————. "Canada Drug Run Racks Up a Lot of Political Mileage." *Great Falls Tribune*, November 26, 1999.

————. "Legislators OK Budget, End Session." *Helena Independent Record*, May 16, 2007.

————. "Schweitzer Dogged, Determined." *Great Falls Tribune*, October 10, 2004.

————. "Schweitzer Ignites Media Firestorm Over Comments on 'Gaydar,' Sen. Feinstein." *Billings Gazette*, June 19, 2014.

————. "Schweitzer Likely to Try for U.S. Senate Seat." *Helena Independent Record*, June 16, 2013.

————. "Schweitzer Rallies Party's Faithful." *Great Falls Tribune*, October 7, 2001.

———. "Schweitzer: Showman, 'Iron Hand' Budget Hawk, Education and Energy Booster." *Billings Gazette*, November 25, 2012.

Dennison, Mike, and Charles S. Johnson. "Angry Lange Lashes Out at Schweitzer." *Billings Gazette*, April 25, 2007.

———. "Special Session Looms After Budget Not Passed." *Helena Independent Record*, April 27, 2007.

Dennison, Mike, and Jennifer McKee. "Brothers in Arms." *Billings Gazette*, December 10, 2006.

Farrell, Allison. "GOP: Schweitzer Tactics Out of Line." *Helena Independent Record*, March 8, 2005.

Johnson, Charles S. "GOP Steams After Meeting with Governor." *Helena Independent Record*, March 10, 2005.

Chapter 6

Anez, Bob. "Fired Aide Says Baucus Harassed Her." *Great Falls Tribune*, September 4, 1999.

———. "Republicans Take a Wait-and-See Attitude." *Great Falls Tribune*, September 9, 1999.

Associated Press. "Sen. Baucus Sees 'Train Wreck' for Health Law Rollout." *Helena Independent Record*, April 17, 2013.

Dennison, Mike. "Anonymous Mailing Contains Baucus Divorce Records." *Great Falls Tribune*, October 9, 1996.

———. "Baucus Denounces as 'Personal Smear' Video that Suggests He Was Drunk on Senate Floor." *Billings Gazette*, December 28, 2009.

———. "Baucus Says Health Reform Will Pass Senate Next Week; Some Montanan Interests Cautiously Sound Off." *Billings Gazette*, December 18, 2009.

———. "Baucus Says Public Will 'Take Another Look' at Health-Care Bill; Rehberg Vows Repeal." *Missoulian*, June 28, 2012.

———. "Baucus Tireless in Pursuit of Fourth Term." *Great Falls Tribune*, October 13, 1996.

———. "Baucus Took 'Vow' to Help Libby Residents Harmed by Asbestos." *Missoulian*, February 10, 2014.

———. "Baucus Watches Supreme Court, Says Case Will Hinge on Constitution's Commerce Clause." *Billings Gazette*, March 27, 2012.

———. "How Does Health Reform Affect My Family? Not Much." *Helena Independent Record*, November 14, 2009.

———. "Not Firing Aide Earlier Was Only Mistake, Baucus Says." *Great Falls Tribune*, September 11, 1999.

———. "Senators Hail Health Bill's Passage." *Helena Independent Record*, March 23, 2010.

———. "Taylor Quits Senate Race." *Great Falls Tribune*, October 10, 2002.

Dennison, Mike, and Charles S. Johnson. "Controversy Aside, It's Been a Long Run for Baucus." *Billings Gazette*, February 9, 2014.

Johnson, Charles S. "U.S. Sen. Baucus Won't Seek Re-Election, Ending 40-Year Career in Congress." *Helena Independent Record*, April 23, 2013.

Chapter 7

Dennison, Mike. "After Five Years in Office, Tester Still Frustrated that D.C. Is 'All Screwed Up.'" *Billings Gazette*, April 22, 2012.

———. "Democrat Tester Ekes Out Another Close Victory in Montana's Big-Bucks U.S Senate Race." Montana Television Network, November 7, 2018.

———. "Early Action Sets Up 'Bare-Knuckles' Campaign." *Billings Gazette*, June 7, 2006.

———. "News Analysis: How Tester Won Montana's U.S. Senate Race." *Missoulian*, November 11, 2012.

———. "Tester Defeats Rehberg in Hard-Fought Senate Battle." *Billings Gazette*, November 7, 2012.

———. "Tester Supporters Buy Ad Urging Conservatives to Vote for Libertarian." *Missoulian*, October 27, 2012.

———. "Victory Caps Long Night's Wait for Tester." *Billings Gazette*, November 8, 2006.

Dennison, Mike, and Charles S. Johnson. "Morrison: Personal Conflicts Didn't Alter Investigation." *Billings Gazette*, April 5, 2006.

———. "Tester Wins Tight Senate Race." *Billings Gazette*, November 7, 2006.

Johnson, Charles S. "Crowd Cheers as Rehberg Says He'll Take on Tester." *Billings Gazette*, February 5, 2011.

McKee, Jennifer. "Democratic Senate Candidates Spar Over Ethics, Electability." *Billings Gazette*, May 4, 2006.

Stewart, Emily. "Trump Calls for Jon Tester to Resign Over Ronny Jackson Saga on Twitter." *Vox*, April 28, 2018.

Chapter 8

Dennison, Mike. "Marble Released from Prison; Rape Conviction Dismissal Not Yet Final." Montana Television Network, April 21, 2016.

———. "Missoula Man Convicted of Jailhouse Rape Seeks New Trial; Victim Denies Recantation." *Missoulian*, October 24, 2012.

———. "Missoula Man Exonerated 14 Years After Rape Charge." Montana Television Network, April 19, 2016.

———. "Missoula Man Loses Bid for New Trial for Juvenile Detention Rape." *Missoulian*, November 5, 2013.

———. "Missoula Man Seeks to Have Rape Conviction Overturned After Alleged Victim Recants Testimony." *Missoulian*, December 14, 2010.

———. "Questions Raised Over Rape Conviction." *Missoulian*, May 11, 2008.

———. "Witness Recants Evidence that Would Exonerate Missoula Man of Rape." *Missoulian*, February 2, 2012.

Chapter 9

Adams, Duncan. "Slain Inmate Was to Testify at Prisoner's Trial." *Montana Standard*, September 24, 1991.

Anez, Bob. "First Prison Riot Suit Settled." *Great Falls Tribune*, January 14, 1995.

———. "Inmate Claims Following Riot Seek $2.5 Million." *Helena Independent Record*, November 3, 1992.

———. "Prison Liable in Riot, but Damages Small." *Great Falls Tribune*, April 3, 1998.

———. "Prison-Riot Probe Finds 'Cover-Up.'" *Missoulian*, January 1, 1992.

Associated Press. "Five Inmates Die in State Prison Riot." *Great Falls Tribune*, September 23, 1991.

———. "State's Bill So Far for Lawyers: $710,627." *Great Falls Tribune*, January 14, 1995.

Dennison, Mike. "Judge Rules State Negligent in Prison Deaths." *Great Falls Tribune*, November 15, 1995.

———. "Legal Costs Pile Up in Riot Suits." *Great Falls Tribune*, August 27, 1995.

———. "Signs of Rage Linger at Prison." *Missoulian*, September 27, 1991.

————. "State Revises Prison-Suit Legal Costs." *Great Falls Tribune*, August 31, 1995.

————. "State Settles Inmates' Riot Suits." *Great Falls Tribune*, August 1, 1998.

————. "State Wants All Riot Suits Dismissed." *Great Falls Tribune*, September 2, 1995.

Ehli, Nick. "ACLU: Guards Beat Inmates." *Billings Gazette*, November 2, 1991.

INDEX

ABOUT THE AUTHOR

Mike Dennison has been a journalist for thirty-eight years, almost entirely in Montana. Since 1992, he has worked full time as an investigative and beat reporter covering Montana politics and state government, for newspapers and television. Since 2015, he's been chief political reporter for the Montana Television Network, which operates nine television stations across the state. Before joining MTN, he worked as a political reporter for Lee Newspapers in Montana and the *Great Falls (MT) Tribune*. He also has worked as a reporter for the Associated Press in Helena, Montana, and Grand Junction, Colorado, and for United Press International in Seattle. He grew up in Seattle, attended the University of Washington and later earned bachelor's degrees in journalism and English at the University of Montana in Missoula. He and his wife, Sue O'Connell, live in Helena.